FROM IRONCLADS TO ADMIRAL

From IRONCLADS TO ADMIRAL

JOHN LORIMER WORDEN AND NAVAL LEADERSHIP

John Lorimer Worden

JOHN V. QUARSTEIN AND ROBERT L. WORDEN

Naval Institute Press
Annapolis, Maryland

Naval Institute Press
291 Wood Road
Annapolis, MD 21402

© 2025 by the U.S. Naval Institute
All rights reserved. No part of this book may be reproduced or utilized in any form or by any means, electronic or mechanical, including photocopying and recording, or by any information storage and retrieval system, without permission in writing from the publisher.

Library of Congress Cataloging-in-Publication Data

Names: Quarstein, John V., author. | Worden, Robert L., author.
Title: From Ironclads to admiral: John Lorimer Worden and naval leadership / John V. Quarstein and Robert L. Worden.
Other titles: John Lorimer Worden and naval leadership
Description: Annapolis, Maryland: Naval Institute Press, [2025] | Includes bibliographical references and index.
Identifiers: LCCN 2024055899 (print) | LCCN 2024055900 (ebook) | ISBN 9781682474440 (hardback) | ISBN 9781682474884 (paperback) | ISBN 9781682477977 (ebook)
Subjects: LCSH: Worden, John Lorimer, 1818-1897. | Worden, John Lorimer, 1818-1897—Military leadership. | United States. Navy—Officers—Biography. | Monitor (Ironclad)—Biography. | Admirals—United States—Biography. | United States—History—Civil War, 1861-1865—Naval operations.
Classification: LCC E467.1.W88 Q37 2025 (print) | LCC E467.1.W88 (ebook) | DDC 359.00973092 [B]—dc23/eng/20250203
LC record available at https://lccn.loc.gov/2024055899
LC ebook record available at https://lccn.loc.gov/2024055900

♾ Print editions meet the requirements of ANSI/NISO z39.48–1992 (Permanence of Paper).
Printed in the United States of America.

33 32 31 30 29 28 27 26 25   9 8 7 6 5 4 3 2 1
First printing

Maps created by Chris Robinson.
Title Page: John Lorimer Worden's signature from a ship's log in 1848. NARA RG24

CONTENTS

List of Maps	vii
List of Illustrations	ix
Foreword	xi
Acknowledgments	xiii
Introduction	1
1 Early Life	6
2 Beginning a Naval Career	12
3 Science Is the Key	30
4 From Storeship to Warship	39
5 Between the Wars	52
6 On the Edge of War	67
7 To Prove *Monitor* a Success	79
8 Recovery and Recognition	96
9 Meeting *Rattlesnake*	104
10 Into the Ring of Fire	121
11 The Expert	135
12 Training the Navy's Future Leaders	154
13 Commanding the European Squadron	173
14 Service in Washington and Retirement Years	189
Epilogue: A Hero for All Times	203
Appendix A. Chronology	209
Appendix B. Associated U.S. Navy Ships	215
Appendix C. Medical Conditions	227
Essay on Sources	231
Notes	235
Index	267

MAPS

1 Mexico and the Californias, 1842–49   46
2 Battle of Hampton Roads, 9 March 1862   92
3 Fort McAllister and Ogeechee River, January–February 1863   111
4 Ironclad Attack on Charleston, South Carolina, 7 April 1863   124

ILLUSTRATIONS

1.1	Worden's letter to Secretary of the Navy Levi Woodbury, 6 February 1834	10
2.1	Sloop of War *Erie* at Rio de Janeiro, 1837	14
2.2	Sloop of War *Cyane*	21
3.1	U.S. Naval Observatory, circa 1845	32
4.1	Worden's former ship *Dale*, 1847	50
5.1	Frigate *Cumberland* lithograph	60
6.1	Fort Pickens, Pensacola Harbor, Florida	70
6.2	Jack Worden in Montgomery City Jail	75
7.1	Painting of battle between *Virginia* and *Monitor*	90
7.2	Deck and turret of *Monitor* with shot damage, 1862	94
7.3	Lieutenant Worden, 1862	95
8.1	Lieutenant Worden at the Naval Observatory, 1862	98
8.2	Presentation sword given to Lt. John L. Worden by the New York Assembly, 1862	101
9.1	Worden stands on the deck of *Montauk* with Fort McAllister in the background	116
9.2	*Rattlesnake* [*Nashville*] burning after being shelled by *Montauk*	119
10.1	*Grand Attack of the Ironclads on Charleston*, 7 April 1863	127
11.1	*Pensacola* at an unidentified anchorage, 1861–65	142
11.2	*Idaho* in its original steam screw configuration, 1866	143
11.3	Captain Worden on the deck of *Pensacola*, 8 May 1867	148
11.4	Portrait of Commodore Worden at Dresden, 1869	152
12.1	Board of Visitors at the U.S. Naval Academy, 1873	156
12.2	Family of Commodore Worden in front of the superintendent's residence, U.S. Naval Academy, 1873	169
13.1	*Franklin*, flagship of the European Squadron, circa 1874–76	175
14.1	Rear Admiral Worden in civilian clothes, 1881	190
14.2	Worden's grave, Pawling Cemetery, Pawling, New York	201
15.1	Bronze bas relief plaque of Worden	205

FOREWORD

Retired and active-duty U.S. Navy officers with whom I work love to give me, a former Army officer commissioned as an infantryman out of West Point, a ton of grief. "What business does an Army grunt have serving as president and CEO of The Mariners' Museum?" The good-natured ribbing motivated me early on to expand my leadership studies of Army leaders to include those of the Navy—Nimitz, Halsey, King, Leahy, Spruance, John Paul Jones, and even Nelson. Since The Mariners' Museum and Park is home to the largest conservation project of its type in the world—the conservation of more than two hundred tons of artifacts recovered from the shipwreck of the USS *Monitor*—I have also read everything that I can on *Monitor*, including John V. Quarstein's *The Monitor Boys: The Crew of the Union's First Ironclad*, *The Battle of the Ironclads*, and *The History of Ironclads*. My seven years of study exposed a gap. There exists no definitive biography on arguably one of the most influential naval leaders in U.S. history, as measured by his record of command, his contributions to science, and his influence on a generation of U.S. Naval Academy graduates.

Until now. It is difficult to imagine two authors better qualified to write *From Ironclads to Admiral* than John V. Quarstein and Robert L. Worden. I have had the honor of working for nearly the past decade with John Quarstein, first when he was the director of the USS *Monitor* Center here at The Mariners' Museum, and subsequently through the many blogs, lectures, and tours that he develops under the umbrella of our Mariners' *Monitor* Legacy Program. The book evidences John's mastery of every detail of Worden's career and his dynamic and engaging storytelling. My relationship with Robert L. Worden, a collateral descendant of Rear Admiral Worden, spans the entirety of my tenure at The Mariners' Museum. Robert's relentless commitment to rigorous research, born of a lengthy career in service to the Library of

Congress, ensures that this book will be the quintessential authority on the life and service of Rear Adm. John Lorimer Worden.

The study of leadership that follows—the study of John Worden—is one of the great examples of the courage, perseverance, decision-making, and tactical and technical proficiency that we associate with combat leadership paired with the total commitment to empowering and developing a generation of naval officers that we associate with servant leadership. The measure of John Worden is not so much in his inspirational performance in particular moments—although those moments are legendary—but in his long and sustained commitment, through the U.S. Naval Academy, the founding of the U.S. Naval Institute, and many other examples, to the leadership development of others. He avoided the spotlight and the credit, although he could have claimed it, and elected instead to drive the U.S. Navy through the revolution in military affairs represented by the ironclad. In doing so, Worden became one of our nation's most consequential naval leaders. I suspect that I will return to John Worden and *From Ironclads to Admiral* again and again, if only to steel my own resolve to follow the Worden example.

—HOWARD H. HOEGE III
President and CEO
The Mariners' Museum and Park
Newport News, Virginia

ACKNOWLEDGMENTS

The authors wish to extend their gratitude to the many individuals and institutions that provided essential support for this book. Foremost, we want to thank Howard H. Hoege III, president and chief executive officer of The Mariners' Museum and Park, Newport News, Virginia, for encouraging and supporting the production of this book, writing the foreword, and providing underwriting for part of the book. Also, thanks are due to Julie Murphy, former editor for The Mariners' Museum and now president of Circle C Communications Ltd., for editing the original manuscript and preparing the index. Illustrating the book are four excellent maps designed and prepared by Christopher Robinson of Crusoe Graphics.

Invaluable support to our research was provided by the reference and curatorial staff at the Manuscript Division and the Humanities and Social Science Division of the Library of Congress, Washington, DC, and the staff at the National Archives in Washington, DC, and Philadelphia, Pennsylvania. We also grateful for the ongoing support given by Jennifer Bryan, head of Special Collections and Archives, and her staff at Nimitz Library; Tracie Logan, senior curator; and James Cheevers, former associate director and senior curator of the Naval Academy Museum, at the United States Naval Academy, Annapolis, Maryland. Timely assistance also was provided by Michael Lynch, director of the Abraham Lincoln Library and Museum, and Lawrence Mott and Michelle Ganz, archivists and librarians, Abraham Lincoln Memorial University, in Harrogate, Tennessee.

Many other institutions also provided materials used in the book, including the Maryland State Archives, and the United States Naval Institute Archives, both in Annapolis, Maryland, as well as The Mariners' Museum library in Newport News, Huntington Library in San Marino, California, New-York Historical Society in New York City, and the Westchester County Archives in White Plains, New York.

The authors want to give a special thanks to Angela M. Riotto, at the time assistant professor of history at the U.S. Army Command and General Staff College, Fort Leavenworth, Kansas; and Laura Davis, assistant professor of history at Columbus State University, Columbus, Georgia. They read the preliminary draft and made many insightful and useful comments on improving the content and structure of the book.

The final publication of this book would not have been possible without the hard work done by Padraic (Pat) Carlin, senior acquisitions editor; Mindy Conner, copy editor; Ashley Baird, production editor; Adam Kane, director; and the entire team at the Naval Institute Press.

Robert Worden is grateful to fellow historian Robert Bailey for insights and leads to the Worden letters at the Huntington Library, and to Timothy Caldwell of Fort Worden State Park for sharing his research on the fort's namesake. He also thanks his cousins Howard B. Lowell, a direct descendant of Rear Admiral Worden, and Leone M. Stangle, a collateral descendant, for sharing rare family materials relating to Rear Admiral Worden. Finally, several oceans worth of gratitude are due to his wife, Norma Chue Worden, for accompanying him on visits to out-of-town research institutions, deciphering difficult nineteenth-century handwriting, discussing and reading draft chapters, and always patiently supporting the preparation of this book; and thanks to his extended family for listening to endless Admiral Worden stories. Finally, he thanks John Quarstein for inviting him to join this voyage into the history of Rear Admiral Worden.

John Quarstein drafted his chapters using a Pelikan 440 fountain pen. The manuscript was transcribed and typed by Rebecca Suerderick, Rebecca Parsons, and Hannah Byler. Emily Clause assisted with identifying many of the images. Also, John thanks Brock Switzer, chief photographer at The Mariners' Museum and Park, for his assistance in securing additional images from the museum's collection. The Mariners' Museum was a fabulous partner in this book venture. The Museum was designated by the National Oceanic and Atmospheric Administration (NOAA), on behalf of the federal government, as the repository for artifacts from USS *Monitor*. Working jointly with NOAA and the U.S. Navy, the Museum has received more than 1,200 artifacts from *Monitor*, including the steam engine, propeller, two XI-inch Dahlgren shell guns with their gun tools, and the iconic revolving gun turret, all now permanently housed in the state-of-the-art USS *Monitor* Center. *From Ironclads to Admiral* is a tribute to Rear Adm. John Lorimer Worden, who made *Monitor* on 9 March 1862 into the "little ship that saved the nation."

John also must extend his sincerest thanks to his friends Anna Gibson Holloway, supervisory historian, History and Heritage Program, Maritime Administration, U.S. Department of Transportation; the late William N. Still, former professor at East Carolina University; and the late Joseph Gutierrez, former museum director for the Jamestown-Yorktown Foundation, who encouraged John to pursue writing this volume. He is pleased he was able to devote three years to prepare this story about a naval officer whom he genuinely considers to be a hero for all times. Of course, working with Robert Worden to co-write this much-needed biography of our hero, Rear Adm. John Lorimer Worden, was a great privilege and pleasure.

INTRODUCTION

This book is long overdue. The heroics of John Lorimer Worden as captain of the ironclad *Monitor*—"the little ship that saved the nation"—have been analyzed and debated in newspapers, congressional documents, scholarly and popular articles, nineteenth- and twentieth-century encyclopedias, museum displays, and blogs. There is even a Wikipedia entry describing Worden's exploits at the Battle of Hampton Roads. Several master's theses on the subject exist, one from 1965 and another from 2007.[1] Only a few of these sources mention Worden's equally heroic actions as captain of another ironclad, *Montauk*.

But what of the rest of his fifty-two-year career? What led a Hudson Valley farmer's son to become a "scientific officer" in command of experimental vessels of war? Worden went to sea at age sixteen, deployed on sailing ships in the Atlantic and Pacific Oceans and the Mediterranean and Caribbean Seas. He was in California and Mexico several years before the Mexican-American War and returned there during that conflict. In the first instance he was preparing to face a potential British foe; in the second, he was on the war front against the actual enemy. He had three tours at the U.S. Naval Observatory in Washington and three at the Brooklyn Navy Yard (officially known as the New York Navy Yard). He was midshipman, sailing master, lieutenant, and executive officer in pre–Civil War vessels and, after the Civil War, the captain of ships other than *Monitor* and *Montauk*. He supervised the construction of wartime ironclads, superintended the U.S. Naval Academy, helped found the U.S. Naval Institute, and was commander in chief of the U.S. naval forces in Europe. This book seeks to fill the enormous gap in the biography of a historically significant naval officer.

A major inspiration for this book was found in the motto of the fourth USS *Worden*, a *Leahy*-class guided missile frigate (DGL 18/CG 18): *id fi at Wordensi*, which translates as "Let Worden Do It." The 1963 commissioning program for USS *Worden* explains that the motto "is indicative of the spirit in which *Worden* will undertake all tasks." It also exemplifies the Navy Department's penchant for giving John Lorimer Worden assignments he might not have sought or wanted but felt bound to carry out to the best of his capabilities. From acting midshipman to rear admiral, from sailing supply ship officer to commander of a steam-powered experimental iron vessel that forever changed the course of naval warfare, Worden never lost his overriding sense of duty and determination. He was not physically formidable: a slight six-footer, some even said "effeminate," and was frequently in poor health. His widow's pension application attests that he suffered from "stomach and liver trouble, mumps, orchitis, ulcerated stomach, intermittent fever, jaundice, catarrh, bilious colic, contusion of the right foot, constipation, nephralgia, malarial cachexia, and la grippe."[2] Worden also suffered permanent damage to his eyes resulting from wounds received during the 9 March 1862 Battle of Hampton Roads. He died of pneumonia incurred "in line of duty . . . and exposure incident thereto."

Unlike many military leaders, the reticent Worden left no personal memoir and declined more than once to write one. He sought no public praise and made no effort to promote himself as a hero. Although he gained nationwide fame during his Civil War assignments, he made no effort to capitalize on it for his own benefit. His focus was to preserve the Union and nothing more. Worden was a true servant leader who asked only that others follow his example and serve without fear.

Although he was newsworthy, especially after 9 March 1862, Worden was a reluctant public speaker and granted few interviews; perhaps he was guilty of too much humility. The authorship of a twenty-two-page essay in *The Monitor and the Merrimac: Both Sides of the Story* is attributed jointly to

Worden and his executive officer, Lt. Samuel Dana Greene. Ashton Ramsey, chief engineer of CSS *Virginia*, the third author listed, published the work years after both men had died, so the attribution to Worden remains dubious. However, two premier collections of Worden's personal papers survive. Both had been in the possession of his daughter, Olivia Steele Worden Busbee Hammond. One collection is now at Abraham Lincoln Memorial University in Harrogate, Tennessee, and the other is at The Mariners' Museum and Park in Newport News, Virginia. These documents include Worden's personal accounts of some of his Civil War exploits and events from his long Navy career. These papers also provide evidence of a family man who pined for his wife and children when he was at sea and when he endured six months as the Civil War's first prisoner of war. The Library of Congress has a small Worden Papers collection; other personal letters are in various collections in American libraries.

On the bonus side for researchers, Worden wrote thousands of pages of official letters, orders, and reports during his fifty-two-year career. These documents reveal his character, his strong sense of duty and responsibility, and his loyalty to his nation and its leaders. They show a tough-minded commander who had empathy for his fellow sailors. He was bold enough as a junior officer to sue the U.S. government over what he considered an injustice in his pay. As a senior officer, he did not hesitate to argue against what he considered ill-conceived Navy Department directives. The National Archives in Washington, DC, is the richest repository of such documentation.

Worden was celebrated in poetry, art, and photography following his rise to fame at Hampton Roads. Within days of *Monitor*'s famous 9 March 1862 battle, no less a writer than Herman Melville invoked Worden's name in his poem "In the Turret." The opening stanza begins:

> Your honest heart of duty, Worden,
> So helped you that in fame you dwell;
> You bore the first iron battle's burden
> Sealed as in a diving-bell.[3]

The rhyming scheme shows that Melville knew the correct pronunciation of Worden's name, which was originally spelled Werden in England and colonial America. The poem continues with a description of the demeanor of our man:

> What poet shall uplift his charm,
> Bold Sailor, to your height of daring,
> And interblend therewith the calm,
> And build a goodly style upon your bearing.

In the summer of 1862, industrious Manhattan engraver and publisher John C. Buttre obtained an antebellum studio photograph of Worden in civilian clothes. He tidied up Worden's scraggly beard, superimposed his head on a uniformed Navy lieutenant's upper body, and added Worden's signature and name, "Lieut. John L. Worden." Originals of this carte de visite image still show up at auctions.

When the secessionist crisis struck the United States, John Worden was a veteran Navy lieutenant with twenty-seven years of service behind him. His loyalty to the Union and trustworthiness made him the perfect choice for a secret mission to save Fort Pickens, which guarded Pensacola, Florida. Had the Confederates been able to occupy the fort, the Warrington Navy Yard at Pensacola would have become a major naval base for the South. Worden delivered the message from Secretary of the Navy Gideon Welles that ordered the landing of Union soldiers to secure the fort. As he was returning from this dangerous mission, Worden was captured and became the Civil War's first prisoner of war. His imprisonment in the Montgomery, Alabama, city jail drew national attention, and he was eventually exchanged after spending six months incarcerated.

Before 1861 few would have considered Worden a daring officer. Fellow shipmates knew him to be somewhat sickly although always ready to perform his duties. His successful mission to Fort Pickens brought him to the attention of his superiors, and in January 1862 he was given charge of the Navy's newest experimental warship—the ironclad *Monitor*. Flag Officer Joseph Smith considered Worden the "right sort of officer" to command this strange new vessel. Worden's victory in *Monitor* came at a time when the nation desperately needed a success. Yet despite being feted as a great hero and receiving fabulous gifts and public accolades, Worden remained unaffected. He had simply been following orders and doing his assigned duty.

This book will shine a light on Rear Adm. John Lorimer Worden's complete career, showing how each of his assignments added to his character, composure, and conduct. Each skill he learned was a stepping stone for his next duty. During his command of *Monitor* Worden developed a new style of naval combat. The knowledge he later gained commanding ships such as *Montauk* and *Pensacola* made him aware that new types of ships and ordnance would soon rule the waves. He also came to understand that many of the tools of war in the nation's arsenal were flawed and needed to be either upgraded or abandoned. A realist, he sought to make things work for the betterment of the Navy and thus of the nation. Worden's actions helped prepare future naval leaders to recognize how to integrate technology with tradition to make the U.S. Navy the cornerstone of national defense.

On the day of Worden's death—18 October 1897—the Board of Directors of the Metropolitan Club of Washington, of which he had been vice president for many years and briefly president, passed a resolution. Hyperbole aside, it is an apt description of the man:

> John L. Worden was cast in the simple heroic mold of our early patriots.
> ... It fell to his lot to render perhaps the most conspicuous and illustrious and single act of service to the Union cause, of any man who took part in the War of Rebellion. His victory revolutionized naval warfare, changed the course of history, and wrote the name of Worden with those of John Paul Jones, Perry, and Farragut on the scroll of imperishable renown.[4]

Despite his "imperishable renown," Worden has never been the subject of a full-length published biography. This book seeks to remedy that shortfall.

CHAPTER 1

EARLY LIFE

John Lorimer Worden was born into a family of stalwart Americans. His DNA included a healthy dose of optimism, confidence, dedication, determination, and wanderlust. Worden's immigrant paternal ancestor, Peter Werden (later styled Worden), a widower merchant from Lancashire, England, migrated to Cape Cod, Plymouth Colony, in 1636/37. John Lorimer's grandfather, George Worden, was a Revolutionary War veteran who in the 1790s owned two farms in Westchester County, New York. One of them was in a Hudson River rural township called Mount Pleasant, where John Lorimer was born.[1]

In John Lorimer's maternal line, the Rev. John Graham was born in County Armagh, northern Ireland, and migrated to Boston in 1718. He served there as a preacher in the Congregational Church and later carried on his ministry in New Hampshire.[2] Reverend Graham's son Andrew was a surgeon for Connecticut troops in the Continental Army during the American Revolution. Andrew's son, Isaac Gilbert, also served in the Continental Army, as a surgeon for Massachusetts soldiers. After the war, Isaac—John Lorimer's grandfather—moved to Mount Pleasant, established his postwar medical practice, operated a farm, and raised his family. Isaac and his wife, Auley Bancker, of Dutch colonial heritage, were the parents of Harriet Graham, John Lorimer's mother, who was born in Mount Pleasant in 1793.[3]

John Lorimer's father, Ananias Worden, was born in the Town of Bedford in eastern Westchester County, New York, in 1790 and moved with his parents to Mount Pleasant in 1794. In 1813 he married Harriet Graham in Mount Pleasant. Ananias and Harriet had twelve children. John Lorimer, their third child and eldest son, was born on Thursday, 12 March 1818, on the family farm in Mount Pleasant. The Worden homestead was at Scarborough Corners, a crossroads just southeast of the unincorporated hamlet of Sparta. A New York State Department of Education historical marker erected in 1949 on U.S. Route 9, the old Albany Post Road, marks Worden's birth site: "Birthplace of John L. Worden 1818–1897, Rear Admiral U.S. Navy, Commanded 'Monitor' against 'Merrimac' Hampton Roads, Virginia, March 9, 1862."[4]

The house where Worden was born is long gone. It was probably demolished before 1840 when Rosemont, a Greek revival mansion, was erected on or near the site. Rosemont was razed in 1990, and the property, now part of the village of Briarcliff Manor, features five upscale homes on acre-plus-size lots with addresses on Admiral Wordens Lane.

John Lorimer spent his early years near his uncles, aunts, and cousins in rural Mount Pleasant. In 1827 Ananias and Harriet relocated with eleven of their children north to Swartoutville, Town of Fishkill, in Dutchess County, New York. John Lorimer Worden may have received his early education in Westchester and Dutchess Counties, but sometime after the family moved to Dutchess County his parents decided that their oldest son should have the benefit of an urban education. They sent him south to Manhattan to live with the family of his mother's first cousin, his namesake John Lorimer Graham.[5]

Early Education
The well-to-do Grahams opened young John's eyes to a much wider world. John Lorimer Graham's father, John Andrew Graham, had traveled twice to England, the first time in 1794–95 as a special envoy of the Episcopal Church of Vermont, and the second time in pursuit of British investments in a Vermont precious metal–mining and smelting venture and a canal-building project to connect Lake Champlain to the St. Lawrence River. John Andrew's younger brother, Nathan Burr Graham, also spent time in London, where he ran a company that exported British-made goods to America.

During this time, John Andrew lodged with a well-to-do Scottish couple, James and Susannah Lorimer, and fell in love with their nineteen-year-old daughter, Margaret. They were married in 1796 with Rev. Samuel Peters, the bishop-elect of Vermont, presiding. Their son, John Lorimer Graham, was born in London ten months later. Nathan Burr Graham married Margaret's younger sister, Jean, in 1797 and returned the next year to Vermont with his new bride. John Andrew, Margaret, and little John Lorimer Graham followed in 1800. By 1803 the two brothers had moved from Vermont to New York City, where they practiced law together. John's court cases and law publications attracted notice in national political circles, and the family prospered.[6]

John Lorimer Graham followed his father into the practice of law in 1818 and quickly drew the attention of Governor DeWitt Clinton, who appointed him as a military aide with the rank of colonel in 1819. He was admitted to the New York bar in 1821 and joined his father's Broadway law firm. The same year he married Emily Matilda Clason, with whom he would have eight children between 1822 and 1836. It was with the Grahams' two older children—John Lorimer Graham Jr. and DeWitt Clinton Graham—that John Lorimer Worden most likely studied. At the time, the John Lorimer Graham Sr. family lived in a sumptuous Fulton Street home, which undoubtedly included an extensive library. Thus young Worden would have heard stories of life abroad and observed firsthand the day-to-day activities of the bustling port city. John Lorimer Graham is said to have been "a man of commanding figure" who "liberally patronized various literary and scientific institutions." He and his cousin, James Lorimer Graham (son of Nathan Burr Graham and Jean Lorimer), practiced mercantile law together and became a force in the development of the Williamsburg section of Brooklyn, just east of the Brooklyn Navy Yard. Two parallel Brooklyn streets were named after these two cousins in 1836: Lorimer Street and Graham Avenue. In 1840 President Martin Van Buren—said to have been "a frequent visitor" at Grahams' home—appointed John L. Graham postmaster of New York City, a position he held until 1845, further establishing his prominence in New York society. After John Andrew's death in 1841, Graham lost much of his fortune and the family was forced to assume a humbler existence.[7]

Inspired to Go to Sea

The Graham family must have stimulated young John Worden's imagination with their stories of early America. There were numerous Revolutionary War veterans in the extended Graham family. One of John's great-grandmothers lived in Sleepy Hollow, in the Town of Mount Pleasant, and was named Katrina Van Tassel, the same as the eighteen-year-old woman of Washington Irving's "Legend of Sleepy Hollow," which was popular reading when Worden was a boy. His mother's cousin Sylvester Graham, a vegetarian and temperance advocate, inspired the invention of the Graham cracker.

Worden doubtless benefitted greatly from the Graham family's largesse and learned much of the family lore from them. A hefty volume of Byron's verse that John Worden later took to sea with him has annotations that provide clues to his interests not only in poetry but in classical history, geography, and geopolitics.[8]

His Graham family connections are believed to have inspired Worden's subsequent naval career. Another of his mother's first cousins—John Hodges Graham—was a career officer in the U.S. Navy. At the onset of the War of 1812, Midshipman Graham lost a leg during an attack across the Niagara River into Canada. He was fitted with a prosthetic limb and went on to serve in *Saratoga*, a vessel of the American squadron that defeated the British naval fleet at the Battle of Lake Champlain on 11 September 1814. The victory strengthened America's position in the peace negotiations in Ghent, Belgium. When young John Worden arrived in New York around 1827, Lt. John Hodges Graham was assigned to the Brooklyn Navy Yard across the East River from Manhattan. Graham would one day rise to the rank of commodore.[9]

Several other family connections also likely contributed to young Worden's decision to join the Navy. Early in the War of 1812, John Hodges Graham's first superior officer was John Worden's third cousin, Commo. Isaac Chauncey, commander of American naval forces on the Great Lakes. Chauncey was commandant of the Brooklyn Navy Yard from 1825 to 1832, and Worden might have met him at his Brooklyn office. Isaac Chauncey's younger brother, Wolcott, was also a career Navy officer. Worden may not have met his cousin Wolcott face to face, but he had likely heard about him. Wolcott was involved in a notorious affair in the late 1820s when he supervised the construction of two frigates for the Greek navy that resulted in charges of mismanagement and enormous cost overruns. Wolcott later died on active duty as commandant of the Pensacola Navy Yard. Two of Isaac Chauncey's sons were career Navy officers. The older, Charles Wolcott Chauncey, who had been appointed a midshipman in 1822 and a lieutenant in 1828, was in command of the gunboat *Spitfire* at Veracruz in 1847 when he died from yellow fever. Charles' younger brother, John St. Clair Chauncey, was appointed a midshipman in 1812 and was promoted to lieutenant in 1825. At that time, he commanded sloop of war *Ontario* of the Mediterranean Squadron. He retired in 1861 with the rank of commodore. With five active-duty Navy officers in the extended family, young Jack (a nickname used by friends) Worden likely heard the call to national service.[10]

Little else is known about Worden's early life. By the time he sought his Navy appointment, he was living once again with his parents in Fishkill. He was nominated by Dutchess County congressman Abraham Bockee, a Jacksonian Democrat and lawyer, and received his appointment as acting midshipman effective 10 January 1834. He was excited about the appointment and quickly replied to Secretary of the Navy Levi Woodbury, "I should be glad to be emploid [sic] immediately if it accord with your wishes." Woodbury's response was also quick and to the point: "I have to inform you that your application for orders is entered, and as soon as your services are needed you will be notified."[11]

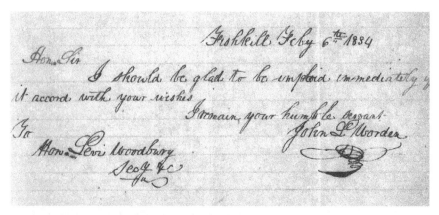

Photo 1.1 John L. Worden's letter to Secretary of the Navy Levi Woodbury accepting his appointment as acting midshipman, 6 February 1834 *NARA M148, RG 45*

Two months later, on 5 May, Worden and other acting midshipmen received orders to proceed to Boston by 20 June, there to report to the commandant of the Charlestown Navy Yard for duty. Sixteen-year-old John Worden was about to embark on an exceptional fifty-two-year Navy career (see appendix A).[12]

CHAPTER 2

BEGINNING A NAVAL CAREER

On 22 August 1834, following two months of training at the Charlestown Navy Yard, Acting Midn. John Lorimer Worden was off to sea in the sloop of war *Erie* to join the Brazil Squadron, whose mission was to protect American interests and collect intelligence in Argentina, Brazil, and Uruguay. Worden had an able captain for his inaugural cruise: Cdr. John "Mad Jack" Percival.[1]

Training in *Erie*

Percival ran a tight ship. He frequently mustered all hands and read out the rules and regulations governing the behavior of the armed forces, probably concentrating on the sections dealing with infractions and punishments. Hardly a day passed in *Erie* without enlisted men receiving lashes with the colt or the cat-o'-nine-tails. Additional punishment included forcing offenders to drink saltwater, confinement in double irons, and reduced rank. Although the midshipmen did not suffer corporal punishment, this was a sobering introduction for Worden to the brutality of life at sea.[2]

Among Worden's six fellow midshipmen were Reed Werden, a distant cousin, and Henry Augustus Wise, who became a lifelong friend. The midshipmen learned shipboard routines, starting with rigging and provisioning the ship before leaving port, and, once at sea, how to sail the vessel, exercise at battle stations and operate the great guns, and fight with cutlasses and muskets.[3]

Worden saw his first naval action just eleven days after leaving Boston when an unidentified brig was sighted ahead. The vessel abruptly changed course, and *Erie* ran up the colors, turned to pursue, and fired a gun to signal the brig to haul up. When the brig did not respond, a second shot was fired and the chase was on. *Erie* began firing live shots at the fleeing brig, which, according to the log, "she did not notice." Percival ordered the crew beat to quarters, and the guns were run in and housed so all hands could assist with sailing the ship. The brig escaped during the night but was spotted again the next morning. After more hours of pursuit, it finally hove to and was identified as a Spanish ship bound for Cuba. Its captain explained that he had fled because he thought *Erie* might have been carrying anti–Spanish government rebels.[4]

While on station, Worden observed numerous interactions with other U.S. Navy ships and American commercial vessels. When a slave uprising occurred in Bahia, Percival made *Erie* available as a refuge for American and foreign consuls and their families and offered protection to American and other nations' commercial ships in port. In addition to protecting American interests, *Erie* was also performing the Navy's mission to suppress the international slave trade, an effort begun in 1820 when the Navy began deploying ships to the coast of West Africa. A slave uprising in Brazil was thus of concern, especially in an area where the slave trade was rife.[5]

Erie sailed in rotation from Rio de Janeiro to Montevideo and Buenos Aires. When squadron commander Commo. James Renshaw moved his pennant from *Natchez* to *Erie* in August 1835, Percival "reacted with choler" at having to give up his stateroom and move into cramped quarters on his own ship. Renshaw was already angry with Percival for having usurped his authority by making an unauthorized inspection of the Navy's Rio storehouse. He became even more irate when he discovered that Percival had gone around the chain of command and written directly to the Navy Department asking permission for *Erie* to pursue pirates who had attacked an American merchant ship off the Brazilian coast and fled with their booty to West Africa. The department agreed to Percival's request and added that he should evaluate the conditions of American Black settlers in Liberia before returning to

Brazil. Chasing pirates would have thrilled the midshipmen, but it was not to be. Renshaw relieved Percival of command for his perceived insubordination and ordered him home.[6]

Worden's cruise journal has not survived, but one kept by his shipmate Henry Wise exists and reflects the midshipmen's training regimen. The journal includes detailed instructions on seamanship and the functions of each crewmember, from the boatswains to the ship's cook, from gun captains to powder boys. Unfortunately, the ship's log covers only the first four months of Worden's time on *Erie*, which ended on 20 September 1837. The last entry was made in December 1835, and the next surviving volume begins with February 1838. By then Worden had passed his first test. President Andrew Jackson signed his midshipman's warrant on 1 June 1835, retroactive to 10 January 1834 (see appendix B for a list of all the ships on which Worden served).[7]

Photo 2.1 Sloop of War *Erie* at Rio de Janeiro, 1837, drawing by Midn. Henry A. Wise in his private journal *Journals of Henry A. Wise, Appendix M-60, NARA, entry 608, RG 45*

With Percival in *Cyane*

When his post-cruise leave expired in December 1837, Worden asked the Navy Department for a two-month extension to deal with "family affairs of some importance that require my attention." What these important affairs were is not known. They may have involved his father's desire to move the family to Michigan, although the family did not actually move there until 1844. The department granted his request but reminded him that he was in "awaiting orders" status. A midshipman's pay while on leave or awaiting orders was 25 percent less than when at sea, so it was financially advantageous for Worden to seek a new assignment. On 29 March 1838 he requested orders for Charlestown. His request was granted, and on 3 May he was ordered to report for duty in the new twenty-gun sloop *Cyane*.[8]

Cyane's commander, again John Percival, supported Worden's request with a letter to the Secretary of the Navy:

> I would most respectfully request that midshipman John L. Worden may receive orders to the *Cyane*. He is the son of an industrious farmer on the Banks of the Hudson. He says he has no friends to aid him but the Department, and has solicited me to represent his dependent situation to the same, and request, if there is no particular objection, he may be permitted to have orders to the *Cyane*, as he commenced his profession with me in the U.S.S. *Erie*. I should feel honored if a compliance with his wish could be accorded him.[9]

The department had already issued Worden's orders by the time Percival's letter arrived. All parties were satisfied, and Worden had a berth in *Cyane*. Three of *Cyane*'s fifteen midshipmen had been Worden's *Erie* shipmates: George Wells, Reed Werden, and Henry Wise. A new comrade on board was Gustavus Vasa Fox. In his journal, Wise noted the presence of his old *Erie* messmates and wrote that *Cyane* was "the finest sloop of war in the Navy" with "an upright competent Captain—agreeable Officers & totally good crew." During the seventeen days *Cyane* was anchored in Boston Harbor, Wells, Werden, and Worden served as watch officers for the first time. The ship's lieutenants took over that duty just before going to sea, and the young reefers renewed their studies in earnest. When the ship left Boston, Wise noted that they were bound to the Mediterranean, "the pleasantest cruising ground in the universe—what more can a midshipman require?"[10]

Eleven days out of Boston, *Cyane* encountered the British merchant brig *Isabella*, out of Australia and bound for London. Its captain, William Ryan, explained that a day earlier his ship had been boarded "by a Spanish Brig, robbed of sundry articles after which the Spanish Brig stood towards Gibraltar." Because *Isabella* was in "want of Cabin necessities," Percival supplied Ryan with water, whiskey, bread, sugar, tea, tobacco, and cocoa and then "immediately hauled up to the South Eastward in pursuit of the pirate." The *Boston Courier* later reported more vividly that *Isabella* had been "boarded by a Spanish piratical brig of 8 guns, and full of armed men, who took from them their spare sails, cordage, canvas and twine; also robbed the passengers and crew of all their clothing, and everything that seemed to answer their purpose."[11]

Henry Wise added details in his private journal that the newspaper omitted: the pirates had "ill used" the three women on board the *Isabella*. Wise described *Cyane*'s chase and subsequent confrontation with the pirates in colorful fashion. The pirates were "dark, bushy whiskered desperadoes" with daggers and pistols "stuck all over them" and sailed on a dark, low, black ship named *Clara*. In addition to his fantasies about how he would spend his share of the prize money for capturing the pirates, Wise wrote a fictionalized version of the affair, first in his private journal in 1845, and then published in 1855 as *Tales for the Marines*. Writing as "Harry Gringo," Wise conflated *Cyane*'s 1838 episode with *Erie*'s pursuit of a suspicious ship in 1834. In Gringo's telling, the pirate ship was captured after a fifty-mile chase with guns blazing. Worden apparently appeared in this account as Gringo's "sweet-tempered friend Jack Gracieux" (Jack Graceful), "as noble and handsome a fellow as ever lived," and a man with whom Gringo "sailed many a year together." Wise called John Worden "Jack" throughout their long friendship. Gracieux played an important role in the action-packed pursuit of the pirates.[12]

In fact, *Cyane* encountered a new suspicious ship, a Portuguese vessel headed for Cuba. The pirate ship was found at Tenerife. Its crew was taken into custody by *Cyane*'s officers and remanded to the Spanish authorities. This episode was important for Worden, Wise's sensationalized version aside, because he was involved in an action that U.S. Navy ships performed in international waters: the interdiction of pirates.[13]

Cyane's log did not mention the midshipmen until 2 September, when Percival ordered a letter inscribed in it. The letter, addressed to Executive Officer Lt. Samuel Lockwood, concerned a disciplinary action.

> The following Midshipmen, who have been attached to this ship by the order of their Government, having manifested by a non-compliance with the orders of the same of not writing up and sending in their Journals &c. on the first of each month to be examined by their Commander, a disposition to continue to set at defiance my legal and proper authority it not being the first offense, you are hereby as 1st Lieutenant of this ship, not to grant permission to either [*sic*] of them to visit the shore or any strange ship except on special duty days, and after that only with consulting me: Henry A. Wise, John L. Worden, Reed Werden, F. W. Colby, John Downes, J. Edward Allen, Edward F. Tatnall, C. H. B. Caldwell. You will have this order instated in the rough and fine log as one of the occurrences of this ship.[14]

Not only were Worden and the others in "non-compliance" with official orders, it was not their first offense. Percival was not a man to be trifled with, and "defiance" was a risky business for midshipmen. Percival reported that he focused on "the education, reformation, and well being of his midshipmen" and "constantly stressed to them the importance of their schoolwork."[15]

Before 1835, shipboard and Navy Yard education of midshipmen had been ad hoc and uneven. That year, however, Congress authorized the position of professor of mathematics and an improved pay scale to attract qualified instructors and improve the young men's instruction.[16] *Cyane* was fortunate to have one of the few professors available, James Major, who reported to Percival the "names of the young gentlemen . . . in the order of merit, commencing with the attentive and studious and ending with the careless and indifferent." Worden's name was twelfth on the list of fourteen midshipmen. Major noted that "Mr. John L. Worden attends the school very irregularly and consequently has not gained much mathematical knowledge. He learns plane trigonometry and algebra."[17]

Worden was likely more attentive to lessons on how to sail a ship; and to be fair, his classroom education faced a "thousand interruptions and impediments." As one pundit put it, training was "made to bend to the man-of-war . . . reefing of a topsail, the crossing of a yard, or the cleaning of a cutlass." When Worden and Major later served together at the Naval Observatory, Worden's math skills obviously had improved.[18]

A midshipman's life was not all work and study. When *Cyane* reached Naples in October 1838, Worden, Wise, Reed Werden, the captain's clerk, and the purser's steward went ashore before dawn to climb Mount Vesuvius. According to Wise, they wore "stout boots & old clothes" and carried thick staves and rope to make their way up "the almost perpendicular cone of the volcano." They walked out on lava so hot that it burnt the tips of their staves and finally peered down into the "roaring, flaming volcano." They were a few minutes too late to see the sunrise but remained for an hour and a half to enjoy the view of Naples and its scenic bay. After descending they visited the ruins at Pompeii and Herculaneum and the Neapolitan royal palace at Portici. On subsequent days, and dressed in civilian clothes, Worden and Wise toured a museum, dined at a fancy hotel, and attended a ballet and an opera. They also exchanged shipboard visits with midshipmen from HMS *Hastings*, which was carrying the dowager Queen Adelaide, the widow of King George IV, who had died the year before. Worden and the other midshipmen gave tours of their ship to visiting Neapolitan dignitaries and oversaw the loading of supplies during the three-week stay at Naples. *Cyane* also stopped in Genoa, Leghorn, Civitavecchia—Rome's seaport—Messina and Palermo in Sicily, Port Mahón on Menorca, Marseille, and various port cities in Spain, Portugal, Morocco, and Greece. The Hudson Valley farmer's son who had once seen the world only in books and lithographs now observed the European littoral firsthand.[19]

On 1 January 1839 Worden, Werden, and Wise wrote to the Secretary of the Navy requesting orders to leave *Cyane* on or after 1 September to prepare for their examination. They were ready for the next stage: attendance at the new Naval School in Philadelphia.[20]

While still at sea, they were given limited authority over the enlisted crew as they stepped up training with muskets and going aloft to reef sails. During this time *Cyane* cruised the western Mediterranean. The midshipmen toured the Spanish naval arsenal at Cartagena in May 1839, and what Worden saw there may have inspired his later request to be sent to the Navy's Depot of Charts and Instruments in Washington. Wise reported in his journal that "we saw innumerable chronometers, quadrants & all kinds of models of blocks" and toured Spain's naval academy and its observatory.[21]

Around this time, Wise recorded an incident that exemplifies Worden's character. It began when another midshipman and his friends got into an angry exchange of insults with the ship's assistant surgeon in the steerage mess. To preserve his offended honor, the midshipman decided to challenge the doctor to a duel. Wise later intimated that it might have been a "muzzle to muzzle" affair, as was the custom in those days. The aggrieved midshipman asked Worden to carry the challenge note; Wise was to be his second. Wary of being involved in the affair, Worden demurred. Perhaps he believed, as other officers of his day did, that it was better to fight for the honor of his country than to avenge perceived personal insults. He went on sick call later that day, whether because of the stress of the situation or due to some lingering illness is not known. When Percival got wind of the proposed duel, Wise wrote, "there [was] hell to pay & pitch hot too." The would-be challenger and three of his companions were put under arrest, and other midshipmen were subject to "long audiences" with their furious captain. Later in the year, Wise himself got into a dispute with an aggrieved middy and "was on the point of knocking him down," but "John Worden advised me by no means to treat him with so much importance."[22]

Although some eighty-two duels involving officers of the "Old Navy" were documented between 1798 and 1848, dueling between officers—most often hotheaded midshipmen—had largely gone by the wayside by the time of the *Cyane* affair. Duels were considered disruptive and dishonored the Navy's reputation. Commanding officers were expected to act vigorously to prevent such fights, which is exactly what Percival did on *Cyane*. In 1845 the Secretary of the Navy banned dueling by his officers. One of the perpetrators of the 1839 proposed duel, Midn. Robert A. Knapp, was severely wounded in an 1842 duel while attending the Naval School at Philadelphia. Three years later he was cashiered from the Navy, thus validating Worden's decision to stay away from such belligerent young men.[23]

When *Cyane* reached Piraeus in August, Worden, Werden, and Wise learned that their requests for Naval School orders had been approved by the squadron commander, Commo. Isaac Hull. The young men planned to leave from Smyrna, but on arriving there they discovered that the only ship that could take them home was not due to depart for a month. They continued on to Malta, where Worden and Werden embarked on the American brig *Dove* bound for Boston. Percival asked Wise to travel home with him via Paris. Upon docking at Boston on 2 December 1839, Worden and Werden reported their arrival for the purpose of "preparing for the next examination of Midshipmen." Worden also requested twenty days' leave of absence, "as affairs of a private nature require my attention." He remained in Boston until receiving orders on 12 December. Then he went home to Fishkill to await his new assignment.[24]

Philadelphia Naval School

Despite apparent deficiencies in his studies on *Cyane*, Worden was ready to proceed to Philadelphia in January 1840 to prepare for the examinations that would make or break his naval career. Worden, along with twenty-three other midshipmen, was in the first full class to attend the new Naval School. Classes were held in the basement of the Naval Asylum, and the faculty consisted of a professor of mathematics and navigation and a French-language teacher.[25]

The examinations covering seamanship, gunnery, and mathematics—which the Secretary of the Navy directed "will be rigid"—were held on 6 July 1840. On *Cyane* in 1838, Worden had been ranked twelfth of fourteen students in those subjects. On 16 July 1840 the Examining Board ranked him fourth out of the twenty-one who passed the exams. His warrant as a passed midshipman was effective 20 July 1840, and in accordance with protocol, he now ranked fourth among the newly commissioned junior officers. Anxious to spend time with his family after seven months in Philadelphia, Worden requested a leave of absence. He was informed that the services of officers of his grade were "much in demand" and was granted only a month's leave. He reported to the department on 28 August that his leave had expired and he was ready for orders, but the orders were not issued until 9 October, so he gained an extra five weeks with his family. It would be a long time before he saw them again.[26]

With the Pacific Squadron

Worden's orders told him to "proceed without delay" to New York for duty in the storeship *Relief*. It must have been a disappointment. Other top graduates

Photo 2.2 Sloop of War *Cyane* by Gunner William H. Myers, USN *Naval History and Heritage Command NH 603*

had been assigned to Navy combatants, but *Relief* was not a career-enhancing assignment. Although it was a relatively new ship, *Relief* was a slow sailer, more of a merchantman, really, than a warship. And although constructed to accommodate sixteen small guns, the supplies it carried took up a great deal of space, so it usually carried only four to six guns. *Relief* had extensive prior service in the Pacific, followed by a major overhaul at the Brooklyn Navy Yard.[27]

Worden's feelings about his assignment are not known, but he was likely pleased when *Relief*'s commander, Lt. John Nicholas, informed him that he would be the acting master. As master, he supervised the stowing of water, ballast, provisions, "and all other articles in the hold or spirit room," to which he held the keys. When not performing his duties belowdecks, he was responsible for preparing for anchoring, mooring, unmooring, and getting under way, ensuring that rigging and sails were always in good order. He kept track of fuel and water expenditures, and when the ship was approaching land, he monitored soundings and possible dangers to the vessel. Worden had charge of nautical books, instruments, charts, national flags, and telegraphic signals and had to ascertain the ship's location at noon each day. He also had charge of the log and was directed to "see that all required particulars" were duly entered.[28]

Relief reached Rio de Janeiro in January 1841 and joined the sloops of war *Dale* and *Yorktown*, also bound for the Pacific Squadron. By May, *Relief* was on the Pacific coast and began a pattern it continued for much of its Pacific deployment, sailing between Valparaíso and Callao, delivering supplies to the squadron and then refilling its hold with new stores. The log coinciding with Worden's service as master of *Relief* has not survived, so the exact day he arrived on board is unknown. Since he was ordered on 9 October to "proceed without delay," he likely embarked within several days of receiving the Secretary's letter. According to a later court document, Worden's time as acting master of *Relief* commenced on 1 December 1840 and ended on 30 May 1842.[29]

The first extant *Relief* log begins on 30 May 1842, the day a change of command took place in Callao. Lt. Isaac Sterrett replaced Nicholas, and Worden was replaced as acting master by Passed Midn. William L. Blanton, a man junior to Worden in the order of merit of passed midshipmen. Worden remained on *Relief*, stood watch most days, and may have continued overseeing squadron supply distributions, but his duties would soon change substantially.[30]

That change came on 6 September when Worden became the acting master of *Dale*. Worden had spent most of his time with the Pacific Squadron overseeing supply acquisitions and deliveries in ports and on local coastal runs. Being a supply ship master in peaceful waters was quite different from serving as master of a sixteen-gun warship on the high seas navigating toward potential danger.[31]

The early 1840s were a period of unrest in the Americas. In 1838 the French blockaded Veracruz, demanding overdue payment of debts. Bolivia defeated Peru in a war in 1841, and civil war broke out in Peru in 1842. Mexico invaded the breakaway Republic of Texas in March that year, and fighting continued into the summer as tensions rose between Mexico and the United States, which had its eye on California.

The tempo increased in August 1842 when Commo. Thomas ap Catesby Jones' Pacific Squadron—the flagship *United States* plus *Cyane, Dale, Relief, Shark,* and *Yorktown*—was at Callao. A French squadron sailed "under sealed orders" from Callao for an unknown purpose that turned out to be the military occupation of the Marquesa Islands in the South Pacific, an area of American whaling and commercial interest. Relations with Britain were already tense because of the Aroostoock War of 1838–39, which pitted armed residents of Maine and New Brunswick against each other over disputed territory. The Webster-Ashburton Treaty of 9 August 1842 had settled this and other differences between the United States and Britain. But now newspapers were publishing rumors that Mexico had secretly agreed to sell Alta and Baja California to Britain for $7 million. U.S.-Mexican relations further deteriorated in May 1842 when Mexico's foreign minister issued a formal complaint to Washington concerning the U.S. position on the war between Texas and Mexico.[32]

In August 1842 Commodore Jones received a dispatch from John Parrott, the U.S. consul at Mazatlán, Mexico. Parrott enclosed a newspaper article that included the text of the Mexican foreign minister's complaint to the secretary of state that convinced Jones that Mexico had issued a "conditional declaration of war" against the United States.[33]

Mexico and the United States had clashed repeatedly during the 1830s over U.S. expansionism. The Texas revolution of 1836–37 exacerbated the situation, resulting in U.S. Navy interventions along the Gulf Coast. Discontent among Mexican and Anglo American residents of Texas with Mexico's central authorities created new tensions. There were rumors that America and Britain were conspiring to annex Alta California and overthrow its Mexican governor. In 1840 the governor imprisoned the American and British conspirators. They were released after the sloop of war *St. Louis* arrived at Monterey, the capital of Alta California, carrying demands for an explanation.[34]

Mexico was angry over the loss of Texas, and talk of war abounded on both sides. Now the U.S. Pacific Squadron watched the British squadron arrive at Callao only to make a "very sudden and unexpected departure." HMS *Carysfort* and *Champion* left Callao on 28 August, followed by *Dublin* on 5 September. According to an unidentified *Dale* officer, they "sailed thence on *secret service*!" Based on Parrott's information, Jones believed the British squadron was headed to Panama to load troops from the West Indies and then proceed on to occupy Alta California. Delayed only "by want of wind," *United States, Cyane, Dale*, and *Shark* left Callao on 7 September in pursuit of the British squadron, despite—as Jones later admitted to authorities in Washington—having no specific orders to do so. The four ships sailed all night, although *Shark* returned to Callao at daybreak. Jones called the captains of the other vessels—Capt. James Armstrong of *United States*, Cdr. Cornelius Kincheloe Stribling of *Cyane*, and Cdr. Thomas Aloysius Dornin of *Dale*—to join him on board the flagship on 8 September.[35]

When the three captains had joined him on the flagship, Jones told them that it was "quite probable" that the United States was in a state of war with Mexico, which might already have ceded or sold the Californias to Britain. All present agreed on the need to pursue the British squadron and find out. Jones ordered Dornin to proceed directly to the Isthmus of Panama. When he arrived there, Dornin was to obtain the latest news from Washington and learn anything he could about the British squadron's movements if it was not there. He was also to land Lt. William Green, who was carrying dispatches from James Pickett, the U.S. chargé d'affaires at Lima, to the State Department, and a letter from Jones to the Secretary of the Navy explaining his decision to sail to California. Then *Dale* was to meet *United States* and *Cyane* on the California coast. Because Jones believed the British squadron would be at Panama, and the United States might already be at war with Britain and Mexico, he cautioned Dornin to avoid any risk of capture. After Dornin returned to *Dale*, he told his officers, including Worden, of Jones' warning: Should a state of war exist, "you will do the enemy all the harm you can, without seriously deviating from the most certain route to your ultimate destination."[36]

Dornin received additional instructions on 11 September, and the three ships parted on 14 September. *United States* and *Cyane* headed out to sea, and *Dale* set a course for Panama. En route, *Dale*'s crew trained daily at the guns and small arms "as if in action." On 22 September *Dale* entered the Gulf of Panama, again exercising the crew at small arms and on the great guns while keeping a close watch for British warships.[37]

Worden cautiously maneuvered *Dale* up the gulf and anchored off Panama City on 25 September. U.S. consul William Nelson came on board to confer with Dornin, and Green landed the next day as planned. Two days later, with Worden as officer of the deck, *Dale* moved back out into the bay. The only warship spotted was a New Grenada schooner of war. The Pacific Squadron learned much later that *Dublin* and *Carysfort*, rather than going north to California, had instead headed west to the Sandwich Islands, hoping to gain them for Britain. *Champion* was seen at Mazatlán six months later, after the war rumor had been quashed. After being detained by "violent winds & squally weather" for several days, *Dale* upped anchor and departed Panama on 1 October. The crew would not touch land again for seventy-three days.[38]

Having loaded fresh provisions and plotted a northerly course—and still wary of the British—*Dale* approached the open sea on 4 October. The crew was beat to quarters, and the guns were run out for more gun and small arms practice. *Dale* proceeded first in a southerly direction, then tacked to a northerly course toward California. Severe weather drove the ship south to Ecuador instead. Worden reported *Dale* had nearly 13,000 gallons of water on board when it left Panama, but as a precaution the crew collected another 2,500 gallons of rainwater from the ship's awnings. The sailmakers could not repair the weather-damaged sails until they dried out, but the rain was "incessant." Dornin wrote in his journal, "We were thus harassed & worried with a succession of squalls, some very violent, constant deluges of rain night and day, so that our crew are necessarily broke down." An inaccurate chronometer further complicated navigation.[39]

On 23 October, after three weeks at sea, Worden discovered that a critical supply was running low: "Broke out the spirit room and examined all the casks to ascertain the amount whiskey on hand; found but a small quantity remaining at the bottom of each cask, the whole amount of which I judged to be sufficient for but three days servings. John L. Worden Acting Master."[40]

It is unclear whether Worden or someone else crossed out the word "Acting." Perhaps he crossed it out because he anticipated that he might request commensurate pay from the Navy for duties performed above his rank (see chapter 3, "Marriage and Searching for Equity"). Or it may have been done by Dornin, who saw that Worden was fully in charge of his position. Regardless, the whiskey ration had run out.

Dornin had the option of sailing to Oahu or back to Peru or Chile for additional supplies. He decided on Oahu, and on 11 November Worden set a westerly course toward the Sandwich Islands. Other supplies were seriously low as well, and the ship's water was down by 50 percent. Wood fuel had diminished from 7,120 sticks of firewood on hand at Panama to 1,540 sticks. *Dale* was about 900 miles southwest of the Galápagos Islands and still 4,100 miles from Oahu on 16 November when it encountered the American whaler *Narragansett,* whose captain provided an emergency supply of beef, pork, flour, bread, and oil. No longer in dire need of supplies, Dornin decided to continue to 125 degrees west longitude—about midway between Ecuador and Oahu—and then cross the equator to catch trade winds that would take *Dale* northeasterly to Alta California. These courses finally brought them into San Francisco Bay on 13 December 1842. The ship had traveled nearly 9,000 miles since leaving Panama in early October. Despite the long and difficult voyage, the crew remained healthy, with only two or three men on sick call each day.[41]

All hands increased their vigilance as *Dale* approached the California coast. The crew was exercised at general quarters, and as the ship entered the mouth of San Francisco Bay, Worden ordered blank cartridges fired to scale the guns. As the ship entered the bay during the next watch, the guns were loaded. It must have been a relief when lookouts spotted *Cyane* early the next morning. Signals were exchanged, and *Cyane* immediately sent boats with fresh provisions. Most important, the log reported, "Rec[d] on board from the *Cyane* 134 Gallons Whiskey." Marines and sailors, Worden included, were soon given liberty to go ashore. The next two weeks were spent loading fresh provisions, water, and fuel. Meanwhile, Jones had moved his pennant to *Cyane* and sent *United States* to the Sandwich Island for supplies.[42]

Dale's officers and crew were eager for news when they reached San Francisco. After *Dale* had parted from *United States* and *Cyane* on 14 September, Jones' ship had also run into "obstinate head winds" that took his vessel nearly as far west as the Sandwich Islands without ever sighting any British warships. When *United States* rejoined *Cyane,* the two ships sailed into Monterey Bay on 19 October. Still convinced that war had begun with Mexico and still concerned about a possible British intervention, Jones proclaimed the "time for *action* had now arrived."[43]

The two warships trained their guns on Monterey, and Jones demanded the city's surrender. The local authorities insisted that they knew of no state of war between the two nations, but after due consideration they capitulated. The U.S. flag was raised over the fort on 20 October as the Americans celebrated their "victory" with gunfire. It was lowered two days later when local residents produced recent newspapers that said nothing about war between Mexico and the United States. Jones also learned that a six-hundred-man

Mexican force was approaching the city and a Mexican ship with military stores was expected.[44]

The incident at Monterey ended peacefully, but the Mexican federal government was furious over the violation of its sovereignty. The Tyler administration was forced to suspend negotiations for the purchase of Alta California and agreed to pay any claims for reparations that arose. The American press later characterized Jones' action at Monterey as an "unlucky and ill-timed *faux pas*." Jones was recalled by the Navy Department, which deemed that he had acted imprudently but took no further action against him. Indeed, rather than censure or punishment, he was given a new ship and restored to command of the Pacific Squadron. Historians consider Jones' seizure of Monterey an important precedent in accord with the manifest destiny concept implied in the Monroe Doctrine of 1823. What Worden knew of all this is unknown. But Jones and his officers recognized the importance of California to America's plan of westward expansion to the Pacific and made it their business to learn all they could about California and its inhabitants.[45]

Intelligence Gathering

Having now landed on the California coast, Worden and *Dale*'s other officers went to work gathering information that would benefit the American forces when real war broke out in 1846. *Dale* sailed south to Monterey and spent nearly two months there. Beginning on the morning of 20 February 1843, a party went ashore to survey the harbor. The log did not identify the survey party, but it had to have included Lt. Thomas Brasher, Lt. William Ball, Lt. Dominick Lynch, and Master John Worden, none of whom stood watch between 20 February and 6 March, along with a detachment of sailors. Midshipmen took the lieutenants' place while the surveyors gathered intelligence for future naval operations. The U.S. Coast Survey published the results of the survey as a map that would have been critical to Pacific Squadron ships when they sailed in to capture Monterey on 7 July 1846. Two years later the survey was incorporated as an inset on an American company's map of the west coast of North and Central America.[46]

Dornin's private journal reveals his keen interest in the natural world, and he may have influenced Worden's own pursuits in that regard. For example, Worden's interest in astronomy manifested itself while *Dale* was anchored at

Monterey. On 7 March, Lieutenant Lynch noted that "a bright streak made its appearance in the heavens." Two nights later, while on watch, Worden wrote in a log addendum, "At 6.30 saw the light streak in the heavens mentioned on the 7th inst." He wrote about it again on 17 March. If other watch officers saw the streak they failed to record it. But Worden added it to his watch comments again on 20 and 25 March, when he noted, "The comet visible, its tail being about 35' long." On 31 March it was only "dimly visible." The streak was what later astronomers named the Great March Comet (1843 D1), a bright, sun-grazing comet of just under −3 magnitude. It was visible for the last time on 1 April, after *Dale* had left Monterey.[47]

In April and May *Dale* entered Baja California waters and cruised in the Gulf of California for five weeks continuing to gather intelligence. *Dale*'s purser wrote later that they kept "a vigilant eye on American commerce and American interests, affording protection to the weak, an asylum to the wanderer, and aid and assistance to the distressed of our countrymen, who, by their misfortunes or wayward propensities, may have been cast 'adrift' on inhospitable shores."[48] But more important for future tactical purposes, *Dale*'s officers observed port conditions at Mazatlán and Guaymas and mapped the shorelines on both the mainland and Baja sides of the gulf. His activities there would prove useful to Worden when he returned to the gulf during the Mexican-American War.

Around this time, Worden assumed responsibility for recording temperatures. The officer previously responsible had done this once a day or less. Worden recorded temperatures during all of his watches, and by the end of the voyage he saw to it that hourly temperatures and the distance covered each day were recorded in the log, as required by the 1841 *Regulations for the Navy*.[49]

During Worden's time in the Pacific he witnessed several burials at sea. A Marine, Michael Johnson, died during Worden's evening watch on 9 September 1842. The following morning, again during Worden's watch, *Dale* hove to, the colors were hoisted to half-mast, and Johnson's remains, sewn inside a weighted canvas shroud, were "committed to the deep." It was the first of many such burials at sea that Worden would witness. Two months later, captain's clerk John M. Williams died. According to Navy custom, all hands were assembled on deck the next morning, the burial service was read, and Williams' body was likewise committed to the deep. Had Williams been a warrant or commissioned officer, the colors would have been hoisted to half-mast and three musket volleys fired. A ship's commander who died at sea would have been honored with the firing of guns at one-minute intervals according to his rank. If death had occurred in or near port, following the requisite honors the remains would have been taken on shore for burial. All told, Worden witnessed twenty-six burials during his time at sea, either at sea or at graveyards on shore.[50]

Home at Last

Dale navigated through snow squalls and rain rounding Cape Horn on the way home, testing Worden's sailing skills, and then headed directly north to the Philadelphia Navy Yard. The ship arrived on 20 October 1843, having completed an 11,000-nautical-mile voyage nonstop from Valparaíso with John Worden as master. His duties in *Dale* continued for several more days. The bottom of the last page of *Dale*'s log is signed, "Respectfully &c., John L. Worden, Acting Master."

Worden's scientific activities on *Dale* prepared him for his next assignment, at the Depot of Charts and Instruments in Washington, DC. Before he began that, he took leave in Fishkill. It was one of his last visits there, because his parents and siblings, except for a married sister, moved the next year to western Michigan.[51]

CHAPTER 3

SCIENCE IS THE KEY

John Worden was introduced to the public as a "scientific officer" after the 9 March 1862 Battle of Hampton Roads, but this status was achieved during sea service assignments and three tours at the Naval Observatory well before the Civil War. The postings to the Observatory put him securely on the scientific officer career track. The Navy had been showing significant interest in scientific expeditions since the 1830s and was eager to enhance the status of the Naval Observatory. Although he was not assigned to exploring expeditions, Worden was a keen observer of scientific data while at sea and was at the Naval Observatory during its transition from the Depot of Charts and Instruments to an internationally recognized institution.

Becoming a Scientific Officer

The Depot of Charts and Instruments, the Naval Observatory's predecessor, was an underfunded and itinerant organization established in 1830 to maintain nautical instruments, books, and charts for use in Navy ships. According to historian Steven Dick, the Depot "began to blossom into something beyond its humble beginnings" during the tenure of Lt. James Gilliss, coinciding with Congress' 1842 authorization for a permanent facility on government-owned property in Washington, DC. As construction was beginning under Gilliss' direction, the Navy appointed Lt. Matthew Fontaine Maury as the Depot's new officer in charge.[1]

Although Maury lacked astronomical credentials, he had published a textbook on navigation—*A New Theoretical and Practical Treatise on Navigation*—in 1836 and was widely known for his work on hydrography, winds, and currents. In 1844 the department elevated Maury's title to superintendent, and in 1845 the Depot was renamed the Naval Observatory. Maury worked diligently to increase the Observatory's stature and promoted the use of scientific data for the Navy and commercial mariners. He envisioned creating a national observatory as a world-class scientific organization on a par with those in Europe. In line with this thinking, he developed a new publication, *Astronomical Observations*; the first volume appeared in 1846.[2]

The Observatory came into being during the age of the grand naval expeditions in the Pacific Ocean. The ocean's wind and current charts were frequently updated and widely disseminated to naval and merchant vessels. Under Maury's direction, the Observatory also became the first stop for new instruments, which were given "careful trial & proof" before being assigned to Navy ships.[3]

Twenty-six-year-old Passed Midshipman Worden was one of the first officers assigned to the Depot at its new Foggy Bottom location. He arrived on either 7 April or 9 April 1844 and remained for twenty-five and a half months, a typical assignment for a passed midshipman learning scientific techniques.[4]

There were three lieutenants assigned to the Depot: one rated chronometers and compiled charts, another collected and collated hydrographic materials, and the third recorded astronomical observations. The first commissioned professors of mathematics arrived in 1845. Formerly they had served as instructors on board Navy ships, but their shipboard function ceased with the establishment of the Naval Academy at Annapolis in 1845, and some were employed at the Observatory. Worden and other passed midshipmen assisted the lieutenants and professors by performing meteorological observations, writing correspondence, keeping accounts, and reducing data into forms useful to mariners.[5]

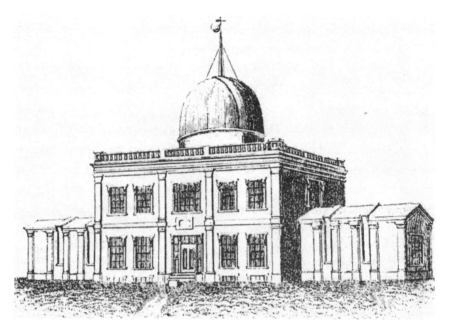

Photo 3.1 The U.S. Naval Observatory, circa 1845 *Naval Meteorology and Oceanography Command*

Calculations of a High Order

Maury reported that his officers were "fully occupied" in carrying out meteorological and magnetic observations; collecting hydrographic information; constructing charts; testing and rating chronometers; and ordering and supplying nautical books, maps, charts, and instruments for the Navy.[6] He informed the Bureau of Ordnance and Hydrography—his parent organization—that their work required "laborious & tedious calculations, involving mathematical attainments of a high order," despite the fact that they initially were "unpracticed & without experience." The inexperienced junior officers "had to learn the forms and figures & sources of error peculiar to the instruments" and the "rules for corrections." Their workload was heavy. "Formulas for a great variety of problems had to be proposed, and a number of Tables, some of them voluminous, had to be computed to facilitate the reduction of those formulas."[7] But they were Navy officers, Maury noted, and their work spoke "well for the scientific attainments which exist in this branch of the public service . . . [even though] they have not the advantage of an Academic education."

In March 1846 Secretary of the Navy George Bancroft acknowledged the tasks Maury set for his staff and referred to the men as an "able corps" producing "results important to maritime science and to the Navy." Bancroft also said he expected the Observatory would make "adequate contributions to astronomical science" and told Maury "to embrace in your catalogues all stars, even of the smallest magnitude" and to "determine with precision . . . the positions of the principal stars."[8]

Maury reported in 1846 that the principal duties of the astronomers were "to assist in perfecting and procuring the requisite data" for the forthcoming *Nautical Almanac*. They were to use their instruments to observe the sun, moon, planets, and selected fixed stars. He considered this the Observatory's "first duty."[9]

Worden was involved early on in making astronomical observations. But he and other passed midshipmen also were tasked with making meteorological observations every two hours, day and night. On even hours they used barometers affixed with thermometers, as well as sun-, shade-, radiating-, and wet-bulb thermometers. On odd hours they took dew point readings. They also recorded wind, clouds, rain, and other weather phenomena. In a single year they made between 30,000 and 40,000 such observations.[10]

When not engaged in recording meteorological observations, the passed midshipmen computed tables and calculated reductions from astronomical observations. Worden was assigned to assist Lt. William Herndon with the Pistor-and-Martin prime vertical transit, a seventy-seven-inch-long German-made instrument that Gilliss had acquired in Berlin during an 1842–43 trip to Europe. It remained in use until 1925. Herndon and Worden used the transit for their observations on fixed stars, particularly those in the constellation Lyra, which was nearer to the zenith of the Washington Observatory than to any other observatory in the world.[11] Using the Pistor-and-Martin transit was not easy. Observations were "both more tedious and laborious than with any other; the time elapsing between the beginning and the end of a complete observation, varying from a few minutes to few hours."[12]

During each session, the observer had to climb a flight of five steps and elevate the thousand-pound instrument twice by screw and lever, and reverse it by hand. Observations were performed in a recumbent position. This meant Worden had to sit up each time to make upward of one hundred entries in his notebook, each consisting of three or more figures. An observer working from dark until daylight was able to make—and then only rarely—no more than twelve complete observations.[13]

When the observations were complete, the readings had to be computed and reduced mathematically into usable forms. Then the data were compared with those from the Observatory's other instruments: the mural circle and meridian circle telescopes. According to Maury, reduction work was "still more tedious"; certainly it was a test of Worden's mathematical acumen.

The first volume of *Astronomical Observations* lists Worden as having made the nighttime observations using the prime vertical transit four times between 2 June and 31 December 1845. He observed the Lyrae (the stars within the Lyra constellation), Lacertae, and Andromedae several times each during this period. He was joined in this work by Maury himself and occasionally by Lieutenant Herndon.[14]

Worden prepared four handwritten journals in 1845–46 that are preserved at the National Archives in Washington. They reveal the detailed work needed to use the prime vertical transit, starting with finding the star being observed, followed by measurements taken for leveling the telescope at its north upper end and its south lower end as it was used to peer into the galaxies at various time intervals. His notes reveal his attention to detail but also his impatience when weather conditions were not conducive to observing the heavens or the equipment did not perform as he wanted. Worden entered his data in ink on preprinted journal pages; on facing pages he recorded clock errors—measured in hundredths of seconds—and made notes on obscuring clouds, vibrations experienced, and other relevant data. He recorded the readings by hour, minutes, and seconds of the Northern Hemisphere constellations Andromeda, Cygnus, Hercules, Lyra, Lynx, and Perseus. Sometimes all that work went for naught. Although Worden made numerous notations on 31 July 1845, while trying to observe 8^2 Lyrae 2191 East, for example, he noted that the night's effort was "not worth a damn." But, he added, "if you will look over this & the preceding sights you will readily discover why I did not complete them in the West—I came up before sunset but as I had no assistant, did not undertake the Hercules stars—With 61 Cygni I lost my patience, the tang screws having broke adrift in the middle of obs[servation]. An unprofitable evening's work. Time spent to no purpose."[15]

Another night he could not find Lacerta, and on still another he recorded 28 Cygnus West but noted "star doubtful" and that the tang screw, used to tighten the instrument's sighting device, had "broke adrift" again. Another of his ledgers includes a comparison of readings made with the observatory's No. 1516 chronometer and the east- and west-wing clocks. On 9 October, he thought he spotted a star in the Perseus constellation but changed his mind, noting, "Not P Persei, but a fine star of 5th mag[nitude]." But the time wasn't wasted. His Observatory experiences would serve him well in the future when he was required to assess warship design and engine capabilities.[16]

Worden spent most of his time at the Observatory with other duties, which, Maury reported to Bancroft, "only allowed him to observe occasionally." Furthermore, Maury noted that "as the calls on my time admitted I relieved Mr. Worden at this instrument, and have continued with Lieut. Herndon to observe with it whenever my engagements admitted."[17] The nature of Worden's other duties is implied by Maury's notes that a passed midshipman "is always on duty, day and night, engaged with meteorological observations. He is required to set up all night and take observations, per annexed form, which is filled up with the rough entries of a single day, copied from the Journal."[18]

The second edition of *Astronomical Observations* lists Worden's prime-vertical transit observations made between March and May 1846. He also was one of seven officers who observed a solar eclipse on 24–25 April 1846, each man using a different instrument. While Herndon employed the prime vertical transit, Worden used the "Comet Searcher." On 11 May, he also made observations of occultations of the star Scorpii using the "5 ft. Telescope." In addition to the prime vertical transit, Worden made observations of Mercury, Venus, Sagittarius, the comet Aguilar, and many other celestial objects on the meridian circle transit.[19]

In August 1844 Worden was sent to the Brooklyn Navy Yard on a temporary duty assignment to deliver navigation charts and instruments to *Yorktown*, which had just been reactivated for service with the Africa Squadron. Worden was supposed to make a similar trip to deliver charts and instruments for a ship that would someday be his, *Cumberland*, then at Charleston, South Carolina, in December 1845, but apparently, that order was canceled.[20]

Marriage and Search for Equity

Several important events in Worden's personal life occurred during his Observatory assignment. One was his marriage to Olivia Akin Toffey, the twenty-three-year-old daughter of Daniel Toffey and Betsey Hollaway Toffey of Quaker Hill, a hamlet in the Town of Pawling in Dutchess County. Her family was of the local gentry in Quaker Hill with important business dealings in New York City. Olivia's father was a prominent farmer, a speculator in the New York City cattle market, and, in 1839–40, a one-term Whig Party member in the New York State Assembly.[21]

Worden wrote to Olivia on 19 March 1844 that he had just met with her father in Manhattan and had glorious news.

> I have just returned . . . as *"Envoy extraordinary"* from the Court of "Cupid," entrusted by his little Godship with negotiations of a highly interesting and delicate nature, which I am happy to inform you have been brought to a *successful* and *satisfactory* termination—Yes, my *own* truly loved one, your good Father gave his consent to our engagement without a moments hesitation, remarking that as it was a matter which particularly interested you, he would allow you to judge for yourself. . . . I was so completely *unstrung* by a rush of emotions to my heart when he gave so prompt a counsel, that I found it quite out of my power to explain my situation and circumstances as fully as I wished to.[22]

Fishkill and Quaker Hill are only twenty-five miles apart, but John and Olivia probably first met in New York City, where Daniel Toffey had business dealings. Worden's romantic note reporting her father's approval was written in New York City, where John was on a two-day business trip. He took the opportunity to hold his audience with Daniel Toffey at the Bull's Head, a tavern at Third Avenue and Twenty-Fourth Street in Manhattan. He was to leave the next day for Sing Sing, a village adjacent to his birthplace in Westchester County, and then planned to go "home" to Fishkill, where he anticipated Olivia joining him, presumably to meet his parents.

Unfortunately, no other letters survive from this period, and few from later, that provide insights into the relationship between John and Olivia and her influence on his career. He was clearly smitten with Olivia, whom he called Olive. His March 1844 letter to her reveals that Daniel Toffey allowed Olivia "to judge for yourself" in the matter of marriage, indicating that he considered her a woman of mature, reliable thinking. Their marriage survived fifty-three years of the rigors and absences of her husband's naval service.

After their wedding at Quaker Hill on 16 September 1844, the newlyweds set up housekeeping in Washington near the Observatory, supported by a passed midshipman's annual salary of $750. Their first child, John Lorimer Worden Jr., was born in Washington on 3 August 1845. Their second child, Daniel Toffey Worden, was born in Manhattan on 27 April 1847, after Worden left for the Mexican war front. Also around this time, Worden's cousin Curtis Burr Graham received a contract as an agent of the Bureau of Ordnance and Hydrography to work as a lithographer for the Coast Survey. This was the first of several federal appointments for family members.[23]

Worden's name appeared in congressional records and in newspapers concerning a matter of personal interest during this time. Worden averred that from 1 December 1840 to 30 May 1842 he was required to perform duties on *Relief* above his grade of sailing master, specifically those of a lieutenant, without receiving commensurate pay. When the Navy denied his request for the back pay he felt he deserved, Worden took his appeal to Congress. In January 1846 Senator Reverdy Johnson, a Whig Party member from Maryland, submitted a petition on Worden's behalf requesting "compensation for the performance of duties belonging to officers of higher grade than that which he holds." The petition was referred to the Committee on Naval Affairs. A similar petition was submitted the next day in the House of Representatives by Richard Platt Herrick, a New York Whig, and referred to the House Committee on Naval Affairs. His petition was reported on favorably by the House Committee on Naval Affairs to the whole House on 26 March 1846. But the war with Mexico intervened, and nothing more happened with the petition until 3 March 1847, when Senator Jacob Welsh Miller, a New Jersey Whig, ordered the Senate Committee on Naval Affairs to give no further consideration to Worden's petition. However, his earlier champion, Senator Johnson, again referred the matter to committee on 20 December 1847. On 5 May 1848 the committee ordered a report to be printed, but eight years would pass before the matter was adjudicated. During most of that time Worden was deployed overseas (see chapter 5).[24]

Onset of War

Worden's Naval Observatory assignment ended at the outbreak of the war with Mexico. He sent a letter to Secretary Bancroft on 26 May requesting to be detached and granted a leave of absence until called to sea duty. He was promoted to lieutenant effective 30 November 1846, and in January 1847 he was assigned to the Pacific Squadron's storeship *Southampton*.[25] Although Worden learned seamanship during his long, hard years on board Navy ships, his early education, innate intelligence, and patience during this formative period made him particularly well suited for scientific endeavors. His sea service and Naval Observatory assignments provided practical experiences that benefitted his career both at sea and on shore. He would later approach his Civil War commands as an intrepid experimental scientist and unflappable commander of ships and men. His long hours in the dark Observatory dome looking at stars would serve him well when he directed devastating artillery fire from inside the poorly illuminated iron pilothouses of *Monitor* and *Montauk*.

CHAPTER 4

FROM STORESHIP TO WARSHIP

The manifest destiny concept of western expansion moved the United States ever closer to war with Mexico. The annexation of Texas in 1845 did not resolve the issue of the disputed border between Texas and Mexico. The Mexicans claimed the border was along the Nueces River, while Texans believed that the border should be the Rio Grande. The dispute prompted President James K. Polk to send an army of occupation commanded by Brig. Gen. Zachary Taylor to the Rio Grande. When Taylor established Fort Texas, a star defensive installation overlooking the river, the Mexicans viewed this as a threat to their sovereignty and responded accordingly. On 25 April 1846, units of the Mexican army commanded by General José Mariano Arista attacked and captured a small American scouting party and then besieged the fort. Taylor counterattacked with his 3,400-man force and defeated Arista's army on 8 May in the Battle of Palo Alto, and again on 9 May at Resaca de la Palma. The Mexicans retreated. Upon hearing news of Taylor's victories, Polk sent a message to Congress claiming Mexico had invaded U.S. territory. A declaration of war followed on 13 May 1846. Taylor's victories created war fever throughout the nation, and many men volunteered to fight to expand the nation's "rightful" boundaries to the Pacific Ocean.

The U.S. Navy was already on the front lines when war was declared, and it only required reinforcements to help fulfill the dreams of manifest destiny and ensure the occupation of the coveted western lands. The Pacific Squadron had temporarily occupied Monterey in 1842 to forestall a rumored British takeover of California (see chapter 2). Thus the Navy was well placed and well prepared to support America's expansionist goals.

On the Way to War

When war was declared, Worden, like most young officers, sought active service. The war being fought along the Atlantic and Pacific coasts presented a grand opportunity for a naval officer to attain laurels that could advance his career. After he was detached from the Naval Observatory, Worden remained on leave until he was called for sea duty. He moved his family to Quaker Hill, where they spent time together before he left for the war front.[1]

Worden was among those President Polk nominated on 4 August 1846 for promotion to lieutenant to fill the vacancies occasioned by the promotions of others to commander. The Navy needed more officers to staff the ships and crews necessary to blockade Mexico's coasts. Meanwhile, Worden was warranted a master, in line for promotion, on 15 August. Polk signed Worden's promotion to lieutenant on 17 January 1847, with an effective date of 30 November 1846, to fill the slot vacated by the death of Lt. Charles Morris of the frigate *Cumberland*. Morris had died from wounds received during the abortive attack on Tabasco, Mexico, on 26 October 1846 led by *Cumberland*'s commander, Capt. French Forrest.[2]

Newly minted Lieutenant Worden was detailed to the storeship *Southampton*, berthed at Gosport Navy Yard in Portsmouth, Virginia, across the Elizabeth River from Norfolk. He reported to Gosport commandant Commo. Charles W. Skinner on 3 February 1847 and assumed his position as executive officer of *Southampton*, Lt. Robert D. Thornton commanding, two days later. The ship stood out to sea on 17 February, but contrary winds kept it from clearing the Chesapeake Capes until 23 February.[3]

Worden left no written reflections about his assignment to a storeship rather than a frigate or sloop of war. He was well aware that storeships played an important role in all aspects of fleet operations, and he knew that the lightly armed *Southampton* would be involved in dangerous operations when it reached the waters of California. His role as the storeship's executive officer was to keep the fleet properly supplied in a combat zone, and this would probably bring him contact with the enemy. He stood ready to perform whatever was required to achieve victory. Because the U.S. Army had no way to rush a large number of troops to the Pacific coast, it would be up to the Pacific Squadron, Worden included, to conquer Alta and Baja California. The Navy's ability to quickly move up and down the Mexican Atlantic and Pacific coasts with no opposition gave the Americans a distinct advantage. Ships, whether steamers or sail-powered, could position bluejackets, Marines, and artillery at multiple sites to maintain the blockade and capture port cities on the Gulf of Mexico and the Gulf of California.

While Worden was in Norfolk awaiting *Southampton*'s departure, he is said to have attended a New Year's Day reception where he encountered Nellie, a precocious nine-year-old. Nellie—a pseudonym adopted by the author Myrta Avary—later claimed she had met one of the "gallant 'boys in blue' " at the reception, which was hosted by her parents, and intimated that "the ardor of [her] affections prevented a young officer ... from exchanging a word with anybody unhampered by my close attendance." Nellie revealed years later, "I proposed to him and was promptly accepted; I made him drink punch with me.... Through a long day, he did not once escape me. This young officer was Lt. John L. Worden."[4] This episode was one of the "history told over tea-cups" stories that Myrta Lockett Avary included in her book *A Virginia Girl in the Civil War, 1861–1865: Being a Record of the Actual Experiences of the Wife of a Confederate Officer*. The volume offers sweet memories of a world later caught up in the Civil War.

Bound for the Pacific

Southampton's outbound cruise was uneventful until the vessel reached Rio de Janeiro on 12 April and met up with the fifty-gun frigate *Columbia*, the flagship of Commo. George Washington Storer, commander of the Brazil Squadron. After giving a thirteen-gun salute in honor of the commodore, *Southampton* hoisted the Brazilian flag at its foremast, which called for a twenty-one-gun salute from the American warships. In return, the city fired a twenty-one-gun salute. When the smoke cleared, the U.S. minister to Brazil, Henry Alexander Wise of Virginia, toured *Southampton*.

As part of his duties Worden coordinated the reconstruction of the storeship's staterooms, which were in a "very leaky condition." He also organized the receipt of fresh provisions and three cases of wine for delivery to the ship's next port, Valparaíso. Several men deserted in Rio de Janeiro, but Worden was able to recruit replacements.[5]

Southampton left Rio on 21 April 1847, destination Valparaíso, Chile, a common port of call for U.S. naval vessels to resupply before and after rounding Cape Horn. Rounding the Cape was often an extremely rough and dangerous voyage. Old sailors would say they were near the end of the earth. Fortunately for *Southampton* and those on board, the weather was "moderate breezes and cloudy with snow and rain" on the approach to the Cape on 14 May. On entering the Pacific Ocean on 20 May, *Southampton* encountered "light variable breezes and foggy damp weather." The last six days of the voyage passed quickly and without incident. Lieutenant Worden was standing watch as the ship stood in for Valparaíso's harbor on 17 June 1847. The voyage had taken four months, during which time *Southampton* was out of touch with the Navy Department in Washington and the other ships of the Pacific Squadron.[6]

Between 17 and 22 June, *Southampton* took on fresh beef and vegetables as well as 4,000 gallons of water and 8,050 sticks of firewood for the final leg of the voyage to Alta California. Crewmembers were permitted liberty, which Worden oversaw, because Valparaíso was the last solid ground they would walk on for another two months. The storeship stood out from the Chilean port, with Worden standing watch, on 24 June.

Supplying the War Front

Much had occurred in Alta and Baja California while *Southampton* was en route to Monterey. When the Pacific Squadron commander, Commo. John Drake Sloat, learned on 7 July 1846 that war had erupted with Mexico, his forces immediately captured Monterey. On 9 July, the same day the sloop of war *Portsmouth* occupied Yerba Buena (San Francisco today), Secretary of the Navy George Bancroft dispatched Capt. Robert Field Stockton to command the Pacific Squadron. Bancroft wanted Stockton to act more aggressively than Sloat had done, and to work in conjunction with the explorer U.S. Army captain John C. Frémont's three-hundred-man California Battalion. With the support of Stockton's ships and personnel, Frémont's battalion conquered northern Alta California. The Americans then focused on Los

Angeles in southern Alta California. The Californios—Hispanic Californians loyal to Mexico—had briefly abandoned Los Angeles, but they reorganized and pushed Stockton's forces back to their ships. Brig. Gen. Stephen Watts Kearny arrived on the scene after a hard march from Santa Fe, New Mexico, and joined forces with Stockton's bluejackets to defeat the Californios during the Battle of Rio San Gabriel on 8 January 1847. The next day, all Californio resistance was crushed at the Battle of La Mesa. These engagements ended the military conflict in Alta California, as confirmed on 13 January with the Treaty of Cahuenga between the United States and the Californios.[7]

After the Americans suppressed the Californios a new conflict arose, this time between Commodore Stockton and General Kearny about the governance of California. Kearny's orders called for him to assume the position of military governor of Alta California, but the commodore disagreed.[8] When Commo. William Branford Shubrick arrived to replace Stockton as the Pacific Squadron's commander, Kearny hastened to Monterey to meet him, and they agreed to work together. Kearny and Shubrick issued a joint proclamation on 1 March detailing that the Navy would be responsible for customs and port duties, and the Army would be in charge of civil governance.[9]

The Pacific Squadron was now on the move, and *Southampton* would soon play an active role in Baja California. Meanwhile, however, the storeship had to perform its purpose. As soon as *Southampton* arrived in Monterey, Worden organized the receipt of fresh beef and vegetables for his ship's crew and the squadron's other ships from Monterey's large naval storehouse. First to receive supplies was the frigate *Independence*. *Southampton* supplied *Portsmouth* with 12 barrels containing 431 gallons of whiskey and 933 pounds of rice, as well as providing *Congress* with 2 barrels containing 2,991 pounds of bread.[10]

In addition to resupplying the squadron and keeping the Monterey storehouse stocked, Worden had to ensure that *Southampton* completed essential maintenance. He secured the services of *Warren*'s sailmaker on 25 and 31 August to mend *Southampton*'s foresail. The next week he put the crew to work painting yards and mast heads. Later in September he had the crew get up a new main trysail gaff. He also drew twenty-five pounds of nails and fifty gallons of white paint from the storehouse for future ship repairs.[11]

Although it was a storeship, *Southampton* was also a warship serving in hostile territory. Even though the vessel was armed with only two 42-pounder carronades, Worden mustered the crew at quarters to practice working the guns. After he felt they had received significant training on the heavy, short-barreled carronades, Worden had the guns secured. During the time spent in Monterey, he also trained some crewmembers with small arms, a skill useful both for defending the ship and for bluejackets sent on shore excursions.[12]

Even though many on board expected *Southampton* to head south on leaving Monterey, the loaded storeship set sail north to San Francisco on 12 October 1847. Two days later *Southampton* encountered an unknown schooner. Worden ordered his ship's colors raised and a shot fired across the bow of the mystery ship, which quickly displayed the French tricolor. *Southampton* arrived at San Francisco and anchored in Yerba Buena Cove the next day, and Worden immediately put the crew to work securing ordnance for future use in Baja California. Commodore Shubrick, then cruising with elements of the Pacific Squadron in the Gulf of California, had asked U.S. Army colonel Richard Mason to provide seacoast mortars to support the squadron's operations. *Southampton* received two 10-inch mortars, and Worden assigned enlisted men to rig block and tackle to haul the artillery on board—arduous work since each mortar weighed nearly 5,800 pounds. In addition to bringing these huge guns on board, Worden guided the men in loading other ordnance and gunnery matériel that included hand spikes, wheelbarrows, water buckets, spades, pickaxes, pickax handles, crowbars, piercing wires, gunners' gimlets, fuse saws, wooden fuse setters, fuse extractors, fuse mallets, powder measurers, and gunner's quadrants. The next day brought 200 mortar cartridges, 200 10-inch shells, and 200 10-inch fuses. *Southampton* stood out from San Francisco on 19 October and reached San Diego on 5 November. The next stop would be the Gulf of California combat zone.[13]

Once Alta California was completely controlled by U.S. forces, Secretary of the Navy John Y. Mason ordered Commodore Stockton, still in command before Shubrick arrived, to occupy Baja California and blockade Mexico's Pacific coast ports. One of the Polk administration's war aims was to annex Baja California and the mainland Mexican state of Sonora. Stockton intended to fulfill these expansionist dreams. Believing that all of Alta California was under American control, Commodore Stockton proclaimed that "having by right of conquest taken possession of that territory by the name of Upper and

Lower California [I] do now declare it to be a territory of the United States under the name of the territory of California."[14] He was a bit premature.

Trouble in Baja

The captain of the sloop of war *Portsmouth*, Cdr. John B. Montgomery, then at Mazatlán, Sinaloa State, was ordered to show an American presence on the southern Baja California peninsula on the west side of the Gulf of California. *Portsmouth* captured San José del Cabo, a small farming and fishing village in southern Baja, on 30 March 1847, then moved down the coast to the peninsula's tip and forced Cabo San Lucas to surrender. Unfortunately, Montgomery lacked sufficient manpower to leave a garrison at either of these Gulf Coast towns. *Portsmouth* reached La Paz, the capital of Baja, farther north on 13 April. The next day, Colonel Francisco Palacios Miranda, the governor and military commandant of Baja California, surrendered La Paz, and the local authorities signed the articles of capitulation. This document had rather unusual provisions that granted the inhabitants U.S. citizenship rights but allowed them to retain their officials and laws. Not all Baja Californios accepted this collaboration. Loyalists gathered at Santa Anita, about twenty miles north of San José del Cabo, declared Miranda a traitor, and proclaimed Mauricio Castro the new governor, with volunteer troops placed under the command of Captain Manuel Pineda Muñoz.[15]

General Kearny was preoccupied with securing the safety of the American positions in Alta California during much of this time. When he received orders on 23 April to send troops to occupy a portion of Baja California, he delayed because he lacked a sufficient number of soldiers and also wanted to confirm the political discord in Mexico. The First Regiment of New York Volunteers arrived just before Kearny returned home. This unit, recruited by New York state legislator Jonathan D. Stevenson and referred to as the New York Legion or California Guard, had traveled from New York City around Cape Horn to Monterey in four vessels. Stevenson was the regiment's colonel, and Lt. Col. Henry Stanton Burton was his executive officer. On 30 April 1847 Kearny ordered Burton and Companies A and B of the First New York Volunteers to embark on the storeship *Lexington*, commanded by Lt. Theodorus Bailey. *Lexington* left Alta California on 4 July 1847 and reached La Paz seventeen days later. Burton's men waded ashore and quickly

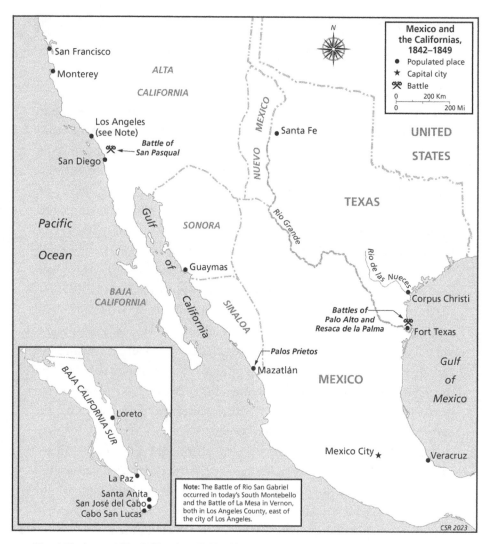

Map 1 Mexico and the Californias, 1842–49

established an outpost on a rise outlooking the town and harbor, and Burton reinstated the civil government.[16]

Burton's men enjoyed La Paz. Lt. Edward Gould Buffum thought the village was the prettiest he had ever seen in California, noting that the "houses were all adobe, plastered white, and thatched with the leaves of the palm tree, and were delightfully cool. The whole beach was lined with palms, dates, fig, tamarind and coconut trees, their delicious fruit hanging down on them in clusters."[17] While duty in La Paz seemed almost idyllic, serious trouble was brewing to the north.

In the meantime, Commodore Shubrick sortied from Monterey with *Independence* and *Cyane*. On 29 October the two ships joined with *Congress* at San José del Cabo to establish U.S. control over the peninsula. On 4 November Shubrick proclaimed his intent to conquer Baja California permanently. Much of the local population actively supported the American occupation. Shubrick left behind a small garrison of Marines commanded by Lt. Charles Heywood in San José del Cabo to enforce U.S. control. Heywood established his force in a run-down old mission building and house overlooking the village.[18]

After leaving Heywood, Shubrick moved *Independence*, *Congress*, and *Cyane* across the Gulf to Mazatlán and demanded its surrender on 11 November. Lieutenant Colonel Rafael Telles commanded a defensive force of some 560 soldiers there but had built no fortifications to protect the town from the Americans. Accordingly, he withdrew from Mazatlán when the U.S. warships appeared at its port, Palos Prietos, and refused Shubrick's demand that his force surrender. On 11 November Capt. Elie A. F. La Vallette, commander of *Congress*, took a 730-man landing party ashore, quickly occupied Mazatlán, and raised the U.S. flag. La Vallette issued military regulations, including the collection of customs duties, but did not otherwise disturb the local citizenry. Lt. Henry Wager Halleck, an 1831 graduate of the U.S. Military Academy, went ashore with the landing force and laid out fortifications. Four hundred sailors and Marines were left to garrison the town.[19]

Southampton Arrives in the Gulf

Southampton neared the Gulf of California on 11 November 1847. While at sea, Worden had continued to drill the crew in small arms techniques in preparation for duty in a war zone. He noted in the ship's log on 11 November that the ship passed an American whaler and he met Lt. Washington Allon Barlett of the brig *Caroline*. Barlett had been the first American *alcalde* (mayor) of Yerba Buena, and it was Barlett who had renamed the town San Francisco in January 1847.[20]

Southampton reached San José del Cabo on 14 November and anchored in the harbor. Lieutenant Worden took the No. 2 cutter to shore to communicate with Lieutenant Heywood, whom he knew from his prior European cruise in *Cyane*. Seeing that all seemed well, Worden returned to the ship. He ordered *Southampton* to raise anchor and stood out for Mazatlán the same day.[21] When *Southampton* arrived in the port's large anchorage, Worden immediately noticed the U.S. flag flying over the Mexican army barracks. All of Shubrick's squadron was now at Mazatlán, including *Independence*, *Congress*, *Portsmouth*, and *Cyane*. The commodore sent signals to *Southampton* noting that the squadron had added the brig steamer *Scorpion* and several bomb gun (mortar) vessels, including *Vesuvius* and *Hecla*, as well as some smaller support vessels.[22]

Worden was kept busy for the next ten days organizing the resupply of the squadron. On 17 November *Cyane* received 399 pounds of tobacco and 3 barrels of whiskey. *Southampton* delivered to *Congress* 10 barrels of bread, 2 barrels of flour, 34 half-barrels and 34 full barrels of beef, 18 barrels of pork, 372 pounds of tea, 7,047 pounds of sugar, 3 barrels of flour, 713 pounds of butter, and 1,144 pounds of rice. The frigate's personnel serving on shore received 431 gallons of whiskey, 25 barrels of beef, and another 25 barrels of pork. *Congress* was given still more supplies on 21 November, including 632 pounds of butter, 1,785 pounds of rice, 352 gallons of vinegar, 8 barrels of molasses, 16 barrels of pork, and 4 half-barrels of beef.[23]

By 23 November Commodore Shubrick had learned that loyalist Californios had attacked Lieutenant Heywood's position in San José del Cabo, and ordered *Southampton* to return there to support Heywood. As the storeship was being hauled out of Mazatlán's harbor, eight Marines, a sergeant, and seven privates from *Portsmouth* came on board as supernumeraries along with a quantity of grape and canister shot, musket cartridges, and other ammunition to resupply the fortification at San José del Cabo. As *Southampton* sailed west on 25–27 November 1847, Worden exercised the crew with small arms and supervised the repair of the ship's pistols and muskets. He knew that his ship was headed toward a possibly dangerous situation and wanted the crew ready for any circumstance that might occur.[24]

Taking the Lead

Southampton's arrival off San José del Cabo on 28 November was a welcome sight for Lieutenant Heywood and his garrison of twenty-eight Marines, four passed midshipmen, and twenty Californio volunteers. His fortified position in "Mr. Mott's house" and the old mission overlooked the town, and he likely had a good view of the loyalist Californios who were pressing his defenses. Heywood had only one 9-pounder gun and a four-week supply of provisions. Captain Pineda Muñoz had decided to strike against the Americans at both San José del Cabo and farther north at La Paz. On 19 November he sent a force of 150 irregulars under the command of Lieutenant Vicente Mejía against Heywood's position to demand Heywood's surrender. Heywood refused. The Mexicans attacked later that day but were forced to retreat. The next night Mejía led an assault to capture the 9-pounder gun position. The assault failed, and Meíja and three of his men were killed; three Americans were wounded. Pineda then decided to besiege the American position, but the appearance of two American whalers, *Magnolia* and *Edward*, in the harbor changed his mind. Pineda thought they were American warships with heavy guns and decided to give up on taking Heywood's outposts and combine his forces with the hope of capturing La Paz.[25]

When *Southampton* arrived at San José del Cabo to reinforce and resupply Heywood's garrison, Worden took a cutter ashore to assess the situation. He brought along the ship's surgeon, Dr. James McClellan, to attend the garrison's sick and wounded. After speaking with Heywood, Worden mustered ten Marines and began the process of transferring a 12-pounder carriage gun; twenty-nine 12-pounder cartridges; ten round shot; ten stands of grape shot and five of canister shot; plus rammers, spongers, powder horn, and priming wires to support Heywood's defenses. He detailed Carpenter's Mate Anthony Woodhouse ashore to mount the gun atop the Mott house properly and to make other improvements to the American defenses. To further reinforce Heywood, Worden sent Passed Midshipman Henry K. Stevens with sixty bluejackets along with food, candles, and other necessities, including 343 gallons of whiskey.[26]

Once the situation in San José del Cabo was stabilized, *Southampton* was detailed to resupply Lt. Col. Henry Burton and Companies A and B of the First New York Volunteers at La Paz. Burton's troops had been the first to arrive in the Gulf of California combat zone, and Commodore Shubrick had quickly assigned them to the defense of La Paz. Pineda's forces were pressuring the American position. *Southampton* left San José del Cabo on 6

Photo 4.1 Worden's former ship *Dale* off San José del Cabo, 1847, painting by Gunner William H. Meyers *NARA, U.S. Navy Subject File, Box 458, entry 502, RG 45*

December for Guaymas, Sonora, and arrived there on 20 December. With assistance from *Dale*'s boats, *Southampton* was towed into the harbor. Heavy weather encountered en route to Guaymas had done some damage, and the storeship required significant repairs to its sails. Once in the harbor, *Southampton* began resupplying *Dale*. Even as *Dale* was receiving supplies, it sent several shells toward the enemy troops in town.[27]

Worden also organized the transfer of two 32-pounder shell guns with associated equipment from *Dale* to *Southampton* to be mounted on the port side of the storeship. Simultaneously, Worden guided the hoisting of a 10-inch mortar out of *Southampton* and onto one of *Dale*'s launches. The mortar was transported to Isle Almagre Chico near the entrance to Guaymas' harbor. All the supplies, equipment, and ammunition needed to operate the large siege weapon were also off-loaded. When the gun was in position, the bluejackets test-fired it and one of the trunnions broke off. The broken trunnion was returned to *Southampton*, and a second 10-inch mortar was sent to the island. Under Worden's command, Gunner William Myers managed the replacement mortar, which sent three shells into Guaymas on 24 December and three more the next day.[28]

On 20 January Worden was given command of the prize schooner *Fortuna*—his first ship command. He armed *Fortuna* with a medium 12-pounder and, along with a purser's clerk, a pilot, and a crew of ten well-armed bluejackets, got under way for a short cruise along the coast, towing *Southampton*'s third cutter. A week later, leaving *Fortuna* in a secure anchorage, Worden, his crew, and the armaments returned to *Southampton*.[29]

After crossing the gulf to Baja, on 2 March 1848, at La Paz, Worden was placed in command of *Southampton*'s launch. Lieutenant Halleck was attached to his command along with an eight-man crew and a pilot. They reached Loreto about 200 miles north the next day on a mission to harass Mexican shipping. Worden soon captured the schooner *Rosita* and returned it to La Paz on 9 March. Between 1 and 6 April Worden commanded several daily shore expeditions of fifteen to twenty men from *Southampton* to defend La Paz and guard the public stores. *Southampton* left La Paz on 17 April and dropped supplies at San José del Cabo on the way to Mazatlán, where it remained until 4 May. At this point, "in consequence of ill health," Shubrick ordered Worden transferred to the ship of the line *Independence* to be treated in its infirmary for gastric derangement. This painful but not uncommon malady among shipboard sailors of the era was caused by an obstruction of the gastric outlet and often accompanied by vomiting, a feeling of being overfed, and weight loss (see appendix C for a list of Worden's medical maladies). The Mexican War was over for John Worden, but his time on the Pacific Coast was not.[30]

CHAPTER 5

BETWEEN THE WARS

The Mexican-American War was effectively over in September 1847 when Mexican forces surrendered Mexico City, but the official end came with the signing of the Treaty of Guadalupe Hidalgo on 2 February 1848. Under the terms of the treaty Mexico ceded 55 percent of its territory to the United States. Americans were eager to expand into the space and fulfill the nation's manifest destiny. The New York volunteers had been mustered out and were anxious to return home, and Lieutenant Worden, occasionally in ill health, was ready to return to his family and meet the infant son he had never seen. But the Navy's Pacific Squadron had a critical postwar role to play. Worden's commodore from his service in California in 1842–43, Thomas ap Catesby Jones, was in command again.

When the hostilities ended, the Navy ceased blockading Mexican ports and the Army began to remove its troops from Mexico. Baja California was not included in the territory ceded to the United States, as some had hoped it would be, but American forces still occupied it. The Navy was tasked with moving the American troops out of the war zone and relocating Baja California residents who had aided the United States during the war to Alta California because the Mexican authorities threatened to seize their property and arrest them for treason. In the meantime, Alta California needed a government. While initially this was the Army's task, the Navy provided critical logistical support in moving troops and matériel and guarding the coast and government stores and funds.[1]

The discovery of gold at Sutter's Mill near Sacramento in January 1848 complicated the situation. The opportunity to gain instant wealth brought about a huge influx from the East of prospectors with gold fever. Men deserted en masse from merchant ships and from Army and Navy forces as well. Gold seekers arrived from all around the globe. The impact of all this on Navy force strength and operational capabilities was considerable.[2]

Although he had been away for only seven months and might reasonably have expected to serve in the Pacific for at least two years, Worden nevertheless made two formal requests to return home. The first request was denied, and the second took many months for approval. The end of the war and the gold rush created a shortage of officers and crews in the Pacific Squadron, and he could not be spared. Although the war and life at sea had taken a toll on Worden's health, he would not return home for another two years. He sailed on four Navy vessels during and after the war before returning to Boston in April 1850.

Worden had important reasons for returning home. He had been very ill, and his second son, Daniel Toffey Worden, had been born. His parents had moved to Michigan and may have needed financial assistance. But in his fervent efforts to get home Worden ignored proper channels and learned a hard lesson as a result. On 15 August 1848 he wrote directly to the Secretary of the Navy asking to be sent home for reasons "absolutely necessary to my personal interest." His request was denied simply because he had not gone through the chain of command. Thirteen months would pass before a second request—sent through proper channels—was approved and he could start for home.[3]

Worden's time in *Independence* brought him some consolation. Not only did the squadron's flagship have better medical facilities than *Southampton*'s, but his old friend Lt. Henry Wise arrived on board as a transient passenger on 8 May, four days after Worden was admitted to the sick bay. Worden was well enough to stand watch on 13 June, and he continued to do so, often alternating with Wise and Charles Heywood, until 14 July, when he was transferred to the storeship *Warren*.[4]

While he waited for permission to go home, Worden was fully engaged on *Warren*. He was involved in relocating war refugees—both American expatriates and native Mexicans who had sided with the Americans during the war—from Baja California to Monterey. *Warren* also transported large amounts of Army specie and three companies of mutiny-prone New York Volunteers from Mexico to Monterey. Shipboard discipline was difficult to maintain. With the war over and little prospect of returning home soon, sailors and Marines were drinking heavily, fighting, shirking their duties, disobeying orders, and acting insolently toward officers. By the time *Warren* and other ships reached Monterey, insubordination was rife. Some of *Warren*'s enlistments had expired, and those men were free to go prospecting; others whose terms had not ended simply deserted. Squadron commander Commo. Thomas ap Catesby Jones reported a "whirlwind of anarchy" in California; even some of his officers were "restive" and wanted to go to the gold fields.[5] During the five months *Warren* was at anchor at Monterey, Worden sometimes stood watch three times a day directing the ship's day-to-day activities. He was on watch on at least one occasion when a man was caught trying to desert and was returned as a prisoner.[6]

On 23 March 1849 Worden made his second request to be sent home "by the most convenient and expeditious route." This time, he sent it through *Warren*'s captain (Cdr. Andrew Kennedy Long) and the squadron commander (Jones), both of whom agreed to "this reasonable request." He told the Navy Department that he had completed his second cruise of three years on the Pacific station, diplomatically noting that because of the shortage of officers, "the necessities of the service may render my detention to an indefinite period unavoidable." But he ended by asking the department for its "early and favorable attention to my request, as I make it under the strongest necessity for a speedy return to my family."[7]

During the final months of Worden's time on board—from June to September 1849—*Warren* became a floating prison. Initially, the prisoners had been Army and Navy deserters. Many were from *Warren* itself, some having slipped away while the ship was still at La Paz. Commodore Jones tried to coax deserters back with offers of leniency and threatened action against officers who did not do enough to stem the rate of desertions. Three sailors who deserted from *Warren* were captured, tried for murder, and executed in January 1849.[8]

Later, *Warren* took on civilian seamen who refused to perform their duties, as well as mutineers and deserters from American, British, Chilean, and Ecuadorean merchant ships. During one of Worden's watches in July, the San Francisco police, lacking jail space on shore, brought on board seventeen prisoners charged with robbery and attempted murder of "defenceless and ignorant foreigners." More prisoners arrived the next day as naval and civilian authorities did what they could to stem riotous and violent behavior.[9]

When he was standing watch, Worden had to deal with situations even a healthy man would have found difficult. One modern historian notes that the deck officer had a "sea watch by day and a double watch by night," and concluded that the situation at San Francisco was "tantamount to turning the Pacific Fleet into a squadron of prison ships."[10]

Ohio and Home

On 12 September 1849, while still at San Francisco, Worden was detached from *Warren* to *Ohio*. *Ohio* had served in the Atlantic and Pacific during the war and had been the Pacific Squadron's flagship since May 1848. With its deployment ending, *Ohio* was directed to return to the East Coast by way of Cape Horn. The vessel's commander, Capt. Cornelius Kincheloe Stribling, ran a tight ship, keeping it well painted and clean, and frequently exercising the crew with small arms and at the guns. Prayers were read daily, some twice a day, and divine service was held every Sunday. When scurvy erupted in July 1849, Stribling sailed to Honolulu for fresh vegetables and fruit. Although the crew regained their health, the ship was significantly shorthanded when it departed for Boston on 15 September. After only five days at sea, scurvy reappeared and the sick list swelled. Rather than sailing to Valparaíso as planned, Stribling took *Ohio* to Hilo for fresh fruit and vegetables.[11]

Worden was no passive passenger on his way home. He stood watch on a nearly daily basis and was watch officer for thirteen of the sixteen days at Hilo. Back at sea on the way to Valparaíso, sick calls continued at a high rate, and crew discontent was evident with an uptick in punishments. Two cases involved Worden. Stribling ordered ten lashes with the cat-o'-nine-tails for an ordinary seaman who neglected duty and showed disrespect to Lieutenant Worden. Another offense resulted in seven lashes for a first-class boy—with the "boy's cats"—for displaying insolence to Worden. Just after midnight on

23 November, Worden was standing watch when he saw seaman John Gormson fall overboard from aloft. He immediately ordered life buoys cut away, brought the ship into the wind, and took in sails while a boat was lowered and a search conducted. The boat returned at 1:45 a.m. without Gormson. "It is said," wrote Worden in the log, "that he struck the spare spars in the chains as he fell. If so, he must have sunk immediately."[12]

At Valparaíso on 28 December, Stribling wrote to the Navy Department that "every indication of scurvy has disappeared from our crew and . . . we now may be said to be healthy." Despite this claim, thirty-nine men had been sick when *Ohio* arrived three days earlier, and forty-one were ill when *Ohio* left on 4 January 1850. More illness lay ahead.[13]

Ohio rounded Cape Horn with relative ease on 24–27 January. Three weeks later, on 17 February when *Ohio* was about one hundred miles south of Rio de Janeiro, the log reported that Pvt. Edward Best, USMC, died of consumption and was buried at sea. The ship reached Rio two days later and remained until 28 February. Yellow fever was "prevailing" in the area, particularly in ships at Rio and Bahia. During the stay in Rio, an average of forty-one men per day were sick.[14] Any captain would have been wary of the situation in Rio.

Ohio departed Rio on 28 February. Within two weeks fifty men had fallen ill from yellow fever; sixteen died. The disease killed three officers (executive officer Lt. Charles Armstrong, Lt. Henry Eld Jr., and Midn. Joseph B. Miller); one of the surgeons, Dr. Ephraim J. Bee; ten sailors; the purser's clerk; and a civilian passenger. Their remains were committed to the deep as the ship made its way north. When *Ohio* reached Boston on 26 April, Worden's family must have been relieved to see his name on the list of survivors reported in the press. Twenty-five men were sent straight to the Charlestown Navy Yard hospital. Worden was the last officer of the watch on *Ohio* when it was decommissioned on 3 May. Afterward he and the other officers were granted three months' leave.[15]

After first rejoining his wife, sons, and in-laws at Quaker Hill, Worden made his way west. He stopped first in Buffalo, New York, where he wrote to the Secretary of the Navy to ask that communications be forwarded to him at his parents' home in Courtland, Michigan. He was back in New York City by 9 July and then spent part of the summer in Southport, Connecticut, on Long Island Sound. While he was in Southport, he wrote to Lieutenant Maury asking if a position was available for him at the Naval Observatory. After receiving Maury's enthusiastic and positive reply, Worden wrote to the Navy Department asking for orders to Washington. In anticipation of receiving them, Worden moved to Brown's Hotel on Pennsylvania Avenue in Washington. Four years and four months after last serving at the Observatory, Worden reported for duty on 15 September 1850.[16]

Second Naval Observatory Tour

Worden was one of seven lieutenants at the Observatory, including Maury; seven professors of mathematics; eight passed midshipmen; and seven civilian employees. One of the professors was William P. Flye, who would later serve on the ironclad *Monitor* after Worden had left it (see chapter 7). Worden's cousin, Curtis Graham, was reassigned from the Coast Survey to the Observatory as a lithographer two months later.[17]

Worden took up his old duties at the Observatory. He surveyed nautical instruments, books, charts, and other public property, condemning some items, sending others for repair, and adding new instruments to the inventory. He was dispatched to New York City in October to confer with Arthur Stewart, a clock dealer who repaired and rated marine chronometers for the Navy. Worden hand-carried a gridiron regulator, a specialized pendulum used in timing devices. Maury later told Stewart that Worden had been "much pleased with his interview." Worden was in the Observatory hospital for catarrh early in the new year but was released after four days to return to duty.[18]

At this point, Maury was several years behind in publishing *Astronomical Observations*. The volume published in 1853 credited Worden as one of the officers "who from time to time could be detailed for the purpose" of assisting the civilian professors with their observations. In this regard, Worden worked with his professor from *Cyane*, James Major, on the 4.5-inch meridian circle telescope. While Major measured declinations, Worden computed refractions. Subsequent volumes of *Astronomical Observations* reported that Worden had been engaged in computing both refractions and declinations from observations made by others in 1848–50 using the prime vertical and meridian circle instruments. He worked with Major and Professor Joseph S. Hubbard in making these calculations.[19]

An example of Worden's work from this period preserved at the National Archives is a tabulation he cowrote with Passed Midn. Colville Terrett: "Computations of Reductions to Mean Places 1850.0 of Stars Observed with the Prime Vertical, 1848." The handwritten document includes the reduction of data collected from hundreds of hours of observations of stars using this instrument. Worden and Terrett meticulously reduced data from notes made by earlier observers and filled in, on duplicate forms, upward of thirty-five lines of data per page from their own readings, using dozens of preprinted ledger pages.[20]

Worden's other duties in 1850–52 remain obscure. The production of *Astronomical Observations* fell behind, and records from the later Maury years are scant. The volume covering 1851–52 was published out of sequence and did not appear until 1867. Maury's predecessor, Lt. James Gilliss, returned to the Observatory in 1861, three days after Maury left to join the Confederacy, and annual publications of *Astronomical Observations* resumed. The 1851–52 volume reported that Worden had been present at the Observatory for one year, two months, and seventeen days, which does not include his time in 1850. "The records do not show in what manner the others were employed," declared Gilliss, "but it is believed that at least three of [the officers] were charged with the care and distribution of the instruments and charts for the naval service, and the remainder upon investigations for the 'Wind and Current Charts.'" However, a volume published in 1880 providing retrospective information indicates that Worden, working with Hubbard, was a prime vertical observer in 1849 and 1850. Since Worden did not arrive until September 1850, it is more likely that he and Hubbard were observers in 1850 and 1851.[21]

A Navy reform bill introduced in the Senate in February 1856 included a proposal to establish a National Scientific Corps. It was not a new concept. Twenty years earlier, then-Cdr. Thomas ap Catesby Jones had been appointed to lead an exploring expedition to the Pacific Ocean as a way to increase the Navy's participation in America's western expansion. Jones did not go on the expedition because he felt the Navy did not have sufficient authority over the proposed corps, but his nephew, then-Midn. Catesby ap Roger Jones—whom Worden would face during the Battle of Hampton Roads in 1862—did briefly participate in such an expedition. The 1856 bill would have included the Naval Observatory, the production of *Nautical Almanac*, aspects of the Hydrographical Department, and "such other scientific duties connected with the naval service as the Secretary of the Navy may, from time to time, prescribe, or as may be prescribed by law" in the National Scientific Corps. The officers assigned to the proposed corps would be Naval Academy graduates and would not be entitled to military command. Although this requirement seemingly disqualified Maury (perhaps by intention), Gilliss, Worden, and other scientific officers, Maury approved of the concept "with some slight alterations" and anticipated being selected as the corps' captain in charge. The National Scientific Corps concept was similar to John Dahlgren's successful push around the same time to establish a specialized ordnance officer category. The scientific corps proposal met opposition in the Senate from those who did not want the government invested in scientific pursuits, and it was not included in the final bill.[22]

At Sea Again

After eighteen months at the Naval Observatory, Worden was ready to develop his leadership skills further. He wanted a sea assignment, and not on just any ship. He specifically requested the *Raritan*-class frigate *Cumberland*. "In support of my application," he told the Secretary of the Navy, "my 11 years of service at sea has been almost exclusively in sloops of war and store ships." An additional incentive for Worden's request, not mentioned, was to sail again with his old friend Henry Wise, who had been assigned as flag lieutenant for the vessel's forthcoming cruise to the Mediterranean.[23]

Before *Cumberland* left the Charlestown Navy Yard on 15 May 1852, Worden arranged for eighty-three dollars of his monthly pay to be allotted directly to his family, which was about to increase by one. His third child, Grace, was born in Washington on 16 June; Worden would not meet her until 1855.[24]

Worden served under three commanders during his *Cumberland* assignment: Capt. Louis Malesherbes Goldsborough (1852), Capt. Charles C. Turner (1852–53), and Cdr. Andrew Allen Harwood (1853–55). The squadron commander was Commo. Silas Horton Stringham. Worden was one of four lieutenants initially assigned to *Cumberland*, and was the most junior among them and the one with the least sea service. The senior-ranking lieutenant was John Randolph Tucker, who in ten years would command the Confederates' James River Squadron during the Battle of Hampton Roads. (The other lieutenants, John Bonnett Marchand and William Ronckendorff, remained loyal to the Union.) The lieutenants rotated as watch officers.[25]

Worden's duties on *Cumberland* were routine, and his name does not appear in the deck log other than for his watch signatures. Although he was mentioned numerous times in Henry Wise's private journals on earlier cruises, Worden's name appears only once in Wise's *Cumberland* journal, when Wise invited Worden, other married messmates, and his pit-mates to a late-night thirty-third-birthday party he hosted for himself. Wise often used "we" to describe his companions when going ashore, so there is no clear record of when Worden accompanied Wise on the latter's many excursions.[26]

A bout of parotitis put Worden in sick bay for five days during the passage from Gibraltar to La Spezia, Sardinia. Later in 1852 he was on the sick list three times for orchitis. It was a "subacute" case, enough to keep him

Photo 5.1 Frigate *Cumberland*, lithograph by Nathaniel Currier, 1843 *Naval History and Heritage Command NH 64089-KN*

listed as sick for thirty-one days, but not enough to keep him from taking his turn on watch day and night. With Worden and other lieutenants so often on the sick list, Stringham requested two additional lieutenants for *Cumberland*. Although Worden was not infected, cholera caused two deaths on *Cumberland* during the latter part of Worden's deployment, and the ship remained offshore of Sicily and Spain when outbreaks of the disease were reported there.[27]

Worden's main duty was to help manage the sailing of the ship. *Cumberland* was a slow-moving vessel that sometimes had to be towed from port to port. Stringham requested an additional steamer that "could be relied upon in all emergencies" when the Crimean War began in 1853. *Cumberland* spent prolonged periods in ports, especially at the U.S. Navy depot at La Spezia. When not at La Spezia or at the Navy's Port Mahón depot on Menorca, *Cumberland* cruised throughout the Mediterranean. The official duties during port calls involved firing salutes to the host country and receiving visits from foreign naval officers, occasional royalty, local dignitaries, and, invariably, the U.S. consul bringing long-delayed orders from Washington.[28]

Key to *Cumberland*'s mission was observing political and economic developments in the Mediterranean's littoral nations, protecting American commerce, and providing aid to U.S. citizens as needed. The squadron was specifically tasked with observing preparations for and acts of war between Mediterranean powers while maintaining "strict neutrality." Stringham told his captains that "nothing but necessity of prompt and effectual protection to the honor and interests of the United States will justify you in either provoking hostilities or committing any act of violence towards a belligerent, and more especially against a state with which our country is at peace." The need for such activities demonstrated how critical it was for the Navy to have steam-powered ships that could move quickly to where observation or action was needed. Stringham occasionally moved his flag to faster-moving vessels to place himself closer to the action. He also used his ships to convey U.S. consular officials from port to port as needed. But maintenance, repairs, and costs of the steam engines greatly limited the squadron's flexibility.[29]

Early in the deployment, its duty to protect American citizens took *Cumberland* to Greece so Stringham and U.S. Minister to Turkey George Marsh could remonstrate with Greek authorities in Athens over the brief imprisonment of Jonas King and the destruction of his property. King was the U.S. consul in Athens, but he was also a missionary whose Protestant church activities were of concern to Greek Orthodox conservatives. The squadron's ships also patrolled the Aegean Archipelago to suppress piracy. They were anchored at Piraeus, Athens' port, when tension between Turkey and Russia began increasing in 1852–53. In May 1853 *Cumberland*'s officers learned that Russian residents in Turkey had departed for safer countries and Russian troops and ships were moving toward Constantinople. In June, the British and French fleets were on the move and Turkey was mobilizing tens of thousands of troops.[30]

On 5 June 1853 *Cumberland* sailed through the Dardanelles and anchored at Constantinople for ten days. During this stop, Stringham became involved in an international incident that embarrassed Turkey and attracted negative publicity back home. It started on 14 June when the Austrian internuncio to the Ottoman court, Baron Karl Ludwig de Brück, visited *Cumberland* and was saluted with seventeen guns. The U.S. government had earlier considered recognizing Hungary's independence from Austria, so U.S.-Austrian relations were at a low ebb. The American press criticized Stringham for honoring the representative of "the bloody Austrian tyrant." Stringham defended the salute, which, he said, was done according to standard Navy customs. The next day, Stringham and "a large number" of *Cumberland*'s officers were received by the Ottoman sultan. Worden was left in charge of the ship to prepare for departure as soon as they returned.[31]

Cumberland was at La Spezia on 4 October 1853 when Turkey declared war against Russia and the Crimean War began. *Cumberland* headed away from the conflict, going to Port Mahón for two months of maintenance. The ship was at Naples when Britain and France declared war on Russia on 28 March 1854. American public opinion tended to favor Russia over Turkey, and diplomatic relations between the United States and Britain, according to historian Trevor Royle, "were in one of their seasonal troughs." But Americans on the scene were pro-Turkey, and during a second visit to the sultan in Constantinople, Stringham expressed support for the Ottoman Empire. He moved *Cumberland* close to the war zone, but only for a little more than two weeks. Officially, the United States was neutral—but not isolationist—and piracy in the Aegean Sea was more pressing. *Levant* and *St. Louis* were left behind to continue monitoring the war. Thereafter *Cumberland* cruised in the western Mediterranean, spending most of the time at Villefranche, Genoa, and La Spezia. While the vessel was at Villefranche in December 1854, former president Martin Van Buren and his traveling companions visited the ship.[32]

Worden was detached from *Cumberland* at La Spezia on 14 February 1855 and reported to the homeward-bound sloop *Levant* the same day. He declined to cross the Atlantic as a passenger and instead insisted on taking his turn as watch officer. This allowed another *Levant* lieutenant, William Francis Spicer, to remain in Europe on leave. *Levant* arrived at New York on 4 May, and Worden was detached on 7 May. He was granted three months' leave, which he spent with family at Quaker Hill and in Michigan. He wrote from Michigan on 7 August requesting orders for the Naval Observatory.[33]

Return to Washington

Worden's third and final assignment to the Naval Observatory lasted only from October 1855 to March 1856. He arrived there at a time of major turmoil. Secretary of the Navy James Cochran Dobbin had informed Commander Maury (he had been promoted in September 1855) that a board of officers had recommended—and President Franklin Pierce had approved—that he be placed on the Navy's Reserve list with absent-duty pay; in the meantime he was allowed to continue as superintendent. Maury was furious with this de facto dismissal and demanded to know who was on the board that made the decision. He wrote numerous letters to suspected board members, members of Congress, family, friends, and colleagues at home and abroad pleading his case. In the end, he retained his active-duty status.[34] Maury's threatened dismissal must surely have disconcerted his staff, but their reactions have not been found. The publication cycle of *Astronomical Observations*, which might have revealed more about Worden's activities, was delayed in the mid-1850s, and no detailed reports for much of the decade were ever published.

Worden's assignment in Washington gave him the opportunity to reopen his claim against the federal government for the pay he believed he had earned during his 1840–42 deployment on *Relief* (see chapter 3). Up to this time, Congress had adjudicated claims against the government, but that had become burdensome, so a new federal court—the U.S. Court of Claims—was established in 1855. To pursue his case further, Worden hired attorney Josiah F. Polk and asked the Senate to withdraw his 1846 claim so that he could file a new one, which he did on 4 June 1856. When *Worden v. United States* was finally heard two years later, the government's solicitor argued that no evidence had been presented to prove or disprove that *Relief*'s commander had the authority to appoint Worden as acting lieutenant. He also pointed out the precedent of an almost identical 1857 case (*McIntosh v. United States*) that was decided for the government. On 19 April 1858 the Court of Claims found Worden "was not entitled to relief."[35]

Worden meanwhile went on sick call on 1 April 1856 for an ulcerated throat, but that did not deter him from moving on. He was detached from the Observatory on 14 April, with orders attaching him to the Brooklyn Navy Yard in New York.[36]

A Change of Course

Worden's assignment to the Brooklyn Navy Yard came about in an unusual way. In the past, he had requested and received orders for a particular assignment. This time he arranged a job swap with Lt. Thomas Brasher, the Yard's executive officer. Brasher had been at the Yard only about a year but agreed to the swap. Worden sent his request for reassignment to Secretary Dobbin through Maury and Capt. Joseph Smith, acting chief of Bureau of Ordnance and Hydrography. It read, "With the consent of Lieut. Thos. Brasher, 1st Lieutenant of the Navy Yard at Brooklyn, I respectfully request permission to exchange positions with him."[37]

Neither Maury nor Smith commented on the propriety of the request. But Dobbin did. He replied, "As this transfer is for the individual benefit of yourself and Lieut. Brasher, and not for the convenience of the Service; the Department declines to order you to New York." Brasher and Worden had apparently committed a bureaucratic faux pas. But in the next sentence Dobbin wrote that the department "will[,] however, detach you from the Observatory, and on your reporting yourself at New York, will give you orders to that Yard, and so to Lieut. Brasher, to the Observatory." Worden quickly followed up with a formal request to be detached from the Observatory and attached to the Navy Yard.[38]

Worden reported for duty on 16 April 1856 and subsequently earned praise as "one of the most industrious and efficient officers at the Navy-Yard." The assignment gave him a new level of management experience. As executive officer, he interacted with Dahlgren's assistant inspectors of ordnance and the directors of the departments for construction and repair, steam engineering, yards and docks, equipment, and ordnance. He also administered applications for leave from the professional civilian staff; determined writing skills and pay of foremen, clerks, and laborers; and kept track of the various classes of mechanics and their salaries.[39]

His immediate superiors when he arrived were the War of 1812 veteran commandant of the Yard, Flag Officer Abraham Bigelow, and Bigelow's deputy, Cdr. John De Camp. Two other lieutenants, a purser, a surgeon, a chaplain, and ten Navy petty officers reported directly to Yard headquarters. Numerous other lieutenants, surgeons, chaplains, and petty officers were assigned to ships stationed or in ordinary at the Yard, or to the hospital or laboratory, each with its own complement of professional and clerical staff. Worden had collaborated with civilian scientists at the Naval Observatory, but the Navy Yard had many more civilian professionals: engineers, constructors, inspectors, storekeepers, and their assistants. There also were civilian day laborers who performed the Yard's labor as sail and block makers, blacksmiths, painters, caulkers, and coopers. As the Navy's preeminent station in New York State, Yard headquarters also kept track of the status of officers assigned in or on leave in the state.[40]

Just before and during Worden's tenure, the Yard underwent major renovations, with more land and new buildings added. Changes included enlarging the hospital and laboratory and building new Marine barracks, a watchmen's building, and various workshops. To accommodate the expansion, the Yard was enlarged with land reclaimed from the East River. The Yard also had been home since 1833 to the Naval Lyceum. Worden likely visited this precursor to the U.S. Naval Institute, and it might have been an inspiration to him some seventeen years later when the institute was founded during his superintendency of the U.S. Naval Academy (see chapter 13). Only two new ships—*Niagara* and *Iroquois*—were launched during Worden's time at the Navy Yard, and of those only *Niagara* was commissioned.[41]

Worden also served on boards of investigation concerning civilian employee misbehavior and on several court-martial boards. He accompanied a draft of seamen to Norfolk to join their ship bound for the East Indies Squadron. Perhaps in recognition of his work at the Naval Observatory, Worden was directed to examine and test a newly patented tripod used for zenith observations on board the mail steamer *Adriatic*. The detail was issued, however, while Worden was on three weeks' leave of absence, and a Coast Survey lieutenant performed the test instead. When the commandant and second in command were absent, Worden served as commandant pro tempore or signed documents "for the Commandant." In this capacity he had to deal with myriad routine matters ranging from roof repairs to inferior granite received for the quay wall, magazine improvements, and storehouse inventories.[42]

He even gained some experience in the political realm when he and Navy Yard civil engineer Charles Kinnaird Graham (not a relative) were asked to accompany U.S. District Attorney for New York City Theodore Sedgwick to "assist in defeating" a bill before the state legislature. In 1852 the state had granted Brooklyn lawyer Henry Ruggles the right to build a dock on land under water on the north side of the Navy Yard. Now Ruggles wanted to amend the grant so he could build a pier or piers on the site, something the new Yard commandant, Capt. Lawrence Kearny, said would "disadvantage" the Navy Yard. By the time Worden and Graham were alerted on 29 March 1858, the bill had been unanimously passed by the state Senate and forwarded to the Assembly. Sedgwick's scheme was unsuccessful, however, as the bill was reported out adversely by an Assembly committee.[43]

Poor health continued to plague Worden at his new post. In May 1857 he was treated for intermittent fever, and later in the year he suffered from jaundice. Autumn brought Worden and Olivia their fourth child, Olivia "Lilly" Steele Worden, who was born in Brooklyn on 14 November 1857.[44]

Worden's time at the Brooklyn Navy Yard was cut short by Navy Department orders issued on 18 June 1858 detailing him to be the first lieutenant on *Savannah*, flagship of the Home Squadron. He was familiar with *Savannah* because it had undergone repair at the Yard. But he did not want this assignment.[45]

CHAPTER 6

ON THE EDGE OF WAR

Lt. John Worden's Brooklyn Navy Yard assignment was both personally rewarding and career enhancing. Worden expanded his management skills as he made use of all his previous sea service, combat, and Naval Observatory experiences to support the Navy Yard's operations. He also learned a great deal about ship design, maintenance, management, repair, and construction. He was hoping next for an assignment to the U.S. Coast Survey based on his experience mapping the harbor at Monterey, California, in 1843. As was often the case, however, the Navy Department had other plans. On 18 June 1858 Worden was directed to report as first lieutenant on board the Home Squadron's *Savannah*.[1] His dissatisfaction with the assignment became so well known that even the *New York Times* noted it: "Lieutenant Worden . . . has been ordered to the *Savannah*. . . . This change comes upon Lieutenant W. at a peculiarly unfortunate time; and if he had to leave home now it would be a great hardship."[2]

The "great hardship" seems to have been related to his pique at not getting the assignment he wanted. On 1 July, however, he dutifully reported on board *Savannah*, then berthed at the Brooklyn Navy Yard, although he was still pressing the department for a different billet. On the day he reported to *Savannah*, Worden wrote the Secretary of the Navy, "I respectfully & earnestly request that I may be detached from the 'Savannah' & ordered to the U.S. Coast Survey." The request was denied. The *Times* later noted that "Lieut. W. has been twenty-four years in the Navy, and is esteemed as one of its most efficient and honorable servants." A man such as that was needed on *Savannah*.[3]

From the Mosquito Coast to Veracruz

The shipboard assignment might have been much worse. *Savannah* was virtually a new ship, having been razeed in 1857–58 from a 44-gun frigate into a 24-gun sloop of war, and it was considered one of the Navy's best vessels.[4] Capt. Joseph R. Jarvis was *Savannah*'s commander, with John L. Worden as his first lieutenant. The sloop left New York on 5 August 1858 and headed for the Gulf of Mexico with a mission to protect U.S. citizens and American political and economic interests in the region. Jarvis ran a tight ship, with nearly daily drills with the great guns, howitzers, small arms, and occasional live-fire target practice. Worden and *Savannah* would confront two potentially explosive diplomatic situations during the next two years.

From August 1858 to January 1859, *Savannah* anchored at San Juan del Norte on Nicaragua's Mosquito Coast. Its mission was to observe the movement of ships suspected of transporting soldiers of fortune who were hoping to topple the legitimate government and reinstall the mercenary filibuster William Walker as president. Walker had been repatriated to the United States by the U.S. Navy in 1857, but the Nicaraguan authorities feared his return. The presence of *Savannah* and its consort, the sloop of war *Jamestown*, apparently discouraged the subversive activities. In February 1860, following a brief visit to Aspinwall, Panama, *Savannah* was sent to Veracruz, Mexico. During this period and afterward Worden served as commander pro tempore during Jarvis' absences.[5]

Mexico was embroiled in a civil war between the Liberals, led by the elected president Benito Juárez, and the Conservatives, led by General Miguel Miramón. Liberal-controlled Veracruz was under siege by Conservative forces when *Savannah* and the sloop of war *Saratoga* arrived on 25 February 1859. *Savannah* maintained combat readiness but mostly sat back and observed the movements of American and foreign vessels. The ship took a five-month break for maintenance at Warrington Navy Yard, Pensacola, and Charlestown Navy Yard, then returned to Veracruz on 5 February 1860.[6]

In early March, Juárez asked for U.S. naval assistance in capturing a rebellious Mexican naval officer, Rear Admiral Tomás M. Marin, who was supporting a renewed siege of Veracruz. When Marin's force failed to respond to *Savannah*'s request for identification on 6 March, Jarvis directed *Saratoga* to investigate. After a brief exchange of gunfire—known as the Battle of Anton Lizardo—Marin's ships surrendered. *Savannah* took prisoners on board and organized prize crews for two captured steamers.[7]

Savannah departed Veracruz on 20 October 1860 and reached the Brooklyn Navy Yard on 16 November, where it was decommissioned. Worden went on leave at Quaker Hill. He needed it. His right foot had been injured on 22 March 1859 during practice with a shell gun, resulting in a six-day stay in the ship's infirmary. Less than a month later he reinjured the foot and was relieved from duty for eleven days. But the foot was not his only medical problem. He made recurring visits to the infirmary during his time on *Savannah*. In March 1858 he was treated for a bacterial infection on the right hip. The following November he was treated for abdominal pains, probably kidney-related, which recurred in February 1860. He was off duty for a week each time.[8]

Urgent Mission to Pensacola

While Worden was resting at home, the Deep South states seceded from the Union and banded together as the Confederate States of America. War was inevitable. In January 1861 Worden wrote to the Navy Department requesting assignment to the Naval Rendezvous at New York.[9]

As tempers flared throughout the South, state militias took over federal post offices, customs houses, arsenals, and forts. Two key forts, one guarding Pensacola and the other defending Charleston, became flashpoints. When Florida seceded on 10 January 1861, the state's militia demanded control of federal resources in their state. When Alabamians seized the forts guarding the entrance to Mobile Bay, federal authorities feared Pensacola would be next. The Gulf Coast city was a valuable prize with its three prominent brick forts—Barrancas, McRee, and Pickens—and the Warrington Navy Yard. Warrington had produced the *Narragansett*-class steam gunboat *Seminole* and the *Hartford*-class steam-screw sloop of war *Pensacola* in 1859, and constructed, supplied, serviced, and repaired many of the Navy's finest vessels. The storeship *Supply* and five-gun steamer gunboat *Wyandotte* were currently in the Yard. If rebel forces succeeded in capturing the forts and Navy Yard, Pensacola would become a major asset for the new Confederate Navy. Of the three forts, Pickens—the most important in defending the Navy Yard and Pensacola—was unoccupied, McRee had only a caretaker ordnance sergeant, and Barrancas was a barracks. A mere forty-six men under the command of Lt. Adam Jacoby Slemmer manned the three forts.[10]

Aware that Florida was about to secede, Slemmer sought guidance from Warrington's commandant, Flag Officer James Armstrong. Both men had heard rumors of an attack and knew they needed to take steps to preserve federal property. Secessionist officers on Armstrong's staff harried him to surrender the Yard to local authorities. On 9 January Slemmer received instructions from General of the Army Lt. Gen. Winfield Scott to prevent the seizure of Pensacola's forts. Armstrong received similar instructions from the Secretary of the Navy, and he and Slemmer agreed to shift their available resources to Fort Pickens. The fort was a likely choice. Situated, on Santa Rosa Island, it commanded the harbor and could be easily reinforced via the Gulf of Mexico. Armstrong offered Slemmer some ordinary seamen from the Yard and the support of *Supply* and *Wyandotte*.

Photo 6.1 Fort Pickens, Pensacola Harbor, Florida, by Currier & Ives, New York, circa 1860–70 *Library of Congress Digital ID 00360*

Slemmer moved all his resources to Fort Pickens as agreed, but two days later, on 12 January, Armstrong surrendered the Warrington Navy Yard without sending the promised support.[11] The Confederates demanded Pickens' surrender, but Slemmer refused, certain that help was en route, and for the time being the two sides maintained an informal truce. The 44-gun frigate *Sabine*, the sloop *St. Louis*, and *Wyandotte* were anchored off Pensacola Pass. *Star of the West*, supported by the sloop *Brooklyn*, steamed to Fort Monroe, Virginia, and embarked Capt. Israel Vogdes and a company of artillerists to reinforce Pickens. When *Brooklyn* and *Star of the West* arrived in Pensacola, an armistice was reached whereby local volunteers agreed not to attack the fort as long as the federal Navy agreed not to reinforce it.[12]

Lincoln's inauguration disrupted this stalemate. The new president was determined to hold the southern forts for the Union and was considering several schemes for doing so. Assistant Secretary of the Navy Gustavus Vasa Fox, a former naval officer, recommended creating a fleet of tugs and supply ships protected by the steam frigate *Powhatan* to relieve Fort Sumter. But *Powhatan* had already been promised to Lt. David Dixon Porter to resupply and reinforce Fort Taylor at Key West, Fort Jefferson on the Dry Tortugas, and Fort Pickens, with the defense of Pickens being the expedition's primary goal. The confusion surrounding the various orders convinced the new administration of the need for cabinet members to concentrate on their assigned duties. Furthermore, it proved that the Navy, which had lost some of its best personnel to the South, had to expand and discover new leaders quickly.[13]

The Confederacy responded to Lincoln's inauguration by sending General P. G. T. Beauregard to Charleston and General Braxton Bragg to Pensacola. Bragg immediately cut off Fort Pickens and kept the Union warships from obtaining provisions.[14] The situation in Pensacola was explosive. Bragg was strengthening the abandoned forts, Barrancas and McRee, to counter Pickens and the Union fleet. Vogdes and his company remained on board *Brooklyn* even though he had orders from General Scott to reinforce Pickens. Capt. Henry A. Adams, captain of *Sabine* and commander of the Pensacola station, was aware of the truce between the Union forces and local Confederates and refused to land the soldiers, even though he had received orders from the previous Secretary of the Navy, Isaac Toucey, to do so. The new Secretary, Gideon Welles, took immediate action to resolve the impasse.[15]

Lieutenant Worden, now posted at the Naval Rendezvous, had been suffering from kidney problems since returning from his service on *Savannah*. Olivia Worden later told a friend that her husband's health had been greatly impaired by his last cruise in the gulf: "He had been home with me but a little over 3 months, during that time he was sick, yes very sick for four weeks."[16]

Worden was still recuperating at Quaker Hill on 2 April 1861 when he received an urgent message from Welles to report "in person to the Department for special duty connected with the discipline and efficiency of the Naval Service." Worden reported to Capt. Silas Horton Stringham on 6 April. He was relieved from duty at the New York Rendezvous and told to be ready for sea service. That evening, near midnight, he received a summons from Welles for a special assignment. Paymaster Henry V. Etting, a veteran of forty-three years of naval service and a man Welles trusted, had assured Welles that Worden was "untainted by treason, and as possessed of the necessary qualifications for the mission."[17] Welles told Worden that he needed an officer to leave at once on a "secret, responsible, and somewhat dangerous duty through the South." He was to carry a dispatch to Captain Adams on *Sabine*. Worden replied that he could leave within two hours. Welles directed Worden to "make no mention of his . . . journey to any one, not even his wife." He added that Worden, as "an officer of the Navy traveling south to Pensacola, and yet not a secessionist or in sympathy with them, would likely be challenged and perhaps searched."[18] He wrote a brief dispatch to Adams and gave it to Worden unsealed, advising Worden that if he feared capture, he should commit its contents to memory and then destroy it.

Worden left Washington on 7 April, traveling by railroad via Richmond and Atlanta. In Atlanta he boarded a train filled with Confederate soldiers bound for Pensacola. Worden later wrote, "I went into the water closet, opened, read & destroyed the despatch."[19] He arrived at Montgomery, Alabama, on 9 April and at Pensacola near midnight on the tenth. On the morning of 11April he went to the wharf to find a boat to take him to *Wyandotte* but was approached by "a citizen of Pensacola" who told him he needed first to report to General Bragg. A Confederate officer took Worden by steamer to the naval hospital at Warrington, where he had an "interview" with Bragg. As he gave Worden a pass, Bragg asked Worden if he was carrying any dispatches. "Not a written one," Worden replied, which was true because he had destroyed it, "but [I] have a verbal communication to make to [Adams] from the Navy Dept." Bragg did not ask about the message's purpose. Worden inquired if he "would be permitted to land on my return toward Washington." Bragg told him that he would, "provided that Capt. Adams or myself did nothing in violation of the agreement existing between them."[20]

Worden was not yet aware of the tenuous agreement between federal and Confederate forces to leave Pickens alone as long as the Union did not land any reinforcements to strengthen the fort. The very order Worden was sent to relay to Adams—if Adams complied—would break that truce. Worden was heading into a situation with potentially severe consequences. After meeting with Bragg, Worden went to the Warrington Navy Yard but was delayed by "blowing hard" weather. He finally boarded *Wyandotte*, which delivered him to *Sabine* about noon on 12 April. He verbally gave Adams the order to land troops in support of Fort Pickens and in return received a dispatch from Adams to Welles. Anxious to return to Washington, Worden asked Adams if it was necessary for him to report to Bragg before beginning his trip north. Adams advised him that he did not need to do so. At 10 p.m. and still in uniform, Worden boarded the train that would take him from Pensacola to Montgomery, unaware that the war had erupted in Charleston earlier that morning or that Bragg had been ordered to intercept him. When Worden arrived at the first station south of Montgomery around 4 p.m. on 13 April, he was arrested by Confederate officers. The next day he was confined in the Montgomery city jail.

First Prisoner of War

According to Confederate attorney general Judah Benjamin, Worden was arrested because he had "violated his promise to report to Gen. Bragg, carried into Fort Pickens secret dispatches, while he showed General Bragg opened dispatches; and further, to report himself on returning from Fort Pickens."[21] Worden denied these charges. He later stated, "On my return to the harbor of Pensacola I did not stop at Genl. Bragg's headquarters because . . . there was nothing said by Genl. Bragg requiring me to do so. Of course, if I had understood it had been required of me, I would have done so."[22]

Worden insisted he had done nothing wrong and felt his honor had been impugned by the arrest. He immediately wrote to Welles explaining the circumstances. Olivia learned of his imprisonment in a telegram Worden sent to her via the Brooklyn Navy Yard stating that he was "well & comfortable" and that he hoped to see her "in a few days." In his follow-up letter to Olivia, Worden was less optimistic: "I cannot tell you how long I shall be detained.... I pray you to keep up good spirits & a cheerful heart. Kiss the little ones for me."[23]

Olivia Worden immediately got to work to free her husband. She wrote first to Gideon Welles for assistance. Welles responded that he could do nothing about it. "His conduct has always been that of an Officer of high standing, and I sincerely regret that at present there appears no way of releasing him from his unjust detention. Rest assured the first opportunity of relieving him will be embraced."[24]

Olivia also contacted Worden's good friend Lt. Henry A. Wise, then assistant chief of the Navy's Bureau of Ordnance in Washington, to ask his help in gaining Worden's release. Wise replied on 8 May that he had spoken with Secretary Welles, Commo. Hiram Paulding, Captain Stringham, and his father-in-law, former secretary of state Edward Everett, about the situation. He believed the case was being "well considered" and that Worden would "shortly be released." He also cautioned that "retaliation would not be judicious & might make Jack's position worse." Olivia asked if Wise's wife, Charlotte Brooks Everett Wise, could send a letter to Varina Davis, wife of Confederate president Jefferson Davis, to aid in her husband's release. Wise advised, "My wife will back you."[25] No evidence survives of Charlotte Wise writing to Varina Davis.

John Worden's imprisonment became something of a cause célèbre in the North. The *National Republican* of Washington, DC, painted a gloomy picture: "Silently awaiting his doom, in the prison of Montgomery, is an officer of the United States Navy, whose existence seems to have been forgotten by his country and his friends ... one of the most efficient officers in the service."[26]

Olivia maintained a steady stream of letters to various officials, politicians, and business leaders expressing concerns for her husband's health and even suggesting candidates for exchange. She noted that her husband was "confined for simply obeying his orders in good faith entrusted to him by the Government" and was suffering terribly.[27] Although his chronic poor health probably did exacerbate his misery, Worden's prison conditions were

Photo 6.2 Jack Worden in Montgomery City Jail, drawing by Lt. Henry A. Wise in letter to Olivia Worden, 8 May 1861 *John Lorimer Worden Papers, Abraham Lincoln Library and Museum, Lincoln Memorial University, Harrogate, TN*

far better than those most Civil War prisoners of war had to endure. Worden later offered a few memories of his imprisonment in his five-page handwritten "Sketch of My Trip to Pensacola in 1861." He was privileged to eat meals with the jailor's family, although he covered the expense, and often received gifts of food from well-wishers. One such gift came from the widow of an old shipmate. He had pledged not to try to escape, and he was occasionally allowed to walk to the end of town and back. He was somewhat of a curiosity as he received visitors who just wanted to gape at him.[28]

Meanwhile, Olivia feverishly continued to press for his release. She shared passages from one of Worden's letters with her friend Margaret Marchand of Philadelphia, whose husband, Cdr. John Bonnett Marchand, had served with Worden in *Ohio* and *Cumberland*. "He had been sick," Olivia wrote to Margaret, "but was again quite well. He writes that he is treated kindly by the jailor's family and by those with whom he comes in contact but is not allowed parole. He is allowed to mess with the family of the jailor by paying board. So, in that particular way he is comfortable."[29]

Olivia feared the government would "abandon him and leave him there to die." Her pleas finally gained traction, and wealthy Philadelphia banker Jay Cooke took up Worden's cause. Cooke sent a message along with one of Olivia Worden's letters to Mrs. Marchand to Senator John Sherman of Ohio, stating, "Will you give a few moments that you may peruse the enclosed letter from the wife of Lieut. Jno. L. Worden now in a prison at Montgomery. . . . Surely something should be done at once to get Worden released. He is in bad health. . . . Can't an exchange be made or his release be obtained in some way. He saved Fort Pickens. Gov'ment should now save him. . . . Will try to have some action taken."[30]

Senator John Conover Ten Eyck of New Jersey wrote to Olivia Worden in mid-July to assure her that he had spoken with Secretary of War Simon Cameron about her husband's unfortunate circumstances. On 23 July Ten Eyck introduced a resolution in the Senate asking President Lincoln to do something about John Worden's imprisonment.[31] The fact that no formal exchange cartel had been established between the United States and the Confederacy was among the issues complicating Worden's release. Lincoln did not wish to adopt any position that implied recognition of the Confederate States as an independent nation.

It appears that neither side had devised a policy for the treatment of prisoners of war. When the Civil War erupted in April 1861, the entire Fort Sumter garrison marched out of the fort with colors flying. Rather than imprisoning them, the Confederate authorities sent them back to New York on the steamer *Baltic*, where they arrived to public acclaim. Likewise, after the 10 June 1861 Battle of Big Bethel, prisoners were simply returned. Olivia Worden's concerns about her husband's future could have been heightened by the capture of the privateer *Petrel* by the federal ship *St. Lawrence* on 20 July 1861. Thirty-six Confederate sailors were taken in the Union steamer *Flag* to Philadelphia, where they were charged with piracy. The charges were dropped, but the sailors were imprisoned in Philadelphia's Moyamensing Prison, where they remained for the rest of the war.[32]

After the First Battle of Manassas (21 July 1861), public outcry led various politicians to push for creating a prisoner-of-war release program. The management and transportation of prisoners was troublesome and required resources needed elsewhere. Worden's case eventually prompted Congress to pass a joint resolution on 11 December 1861 for the administration to organize an exchange system.[33]

Until then, Maj. Gen. Benjamin Huger, commander of the Confederate Department of Norfolk in Hampton Roads, Virginia, interacted with Maj. Gen. John Ellis Wool, commander of the Union Department of Virginia, headquartered at Fort Monroe, to enact limited prisoner trades and provide clothing for prisoners. Huger's willingness to complete these prisoner switches prompted Flag Officer Louis M. Goldsborough, then commander of the North Atlantic Blockading Squadron, to write to Huger asking him to execute an exchange for Worden. Huger proposed swapping Worden for Lt. William Southall Sharp, CSN, who had been captured at Hatteras Inlet, North Carolina, on 29 August.[34] Sharp had been assigned to the Gosport Navy Yard when Confederate forces captured it on 21 April 1861. He immediately joined the Virginia State Navy, and then the Confederate Navy. Worden and Sharp knew each other because both had served in *Cumberland* in 1853–55, but they did not speak to one another during the exchange process.

Still despondent about her husband's fate, Olivia wrote to Goldsborough about her concerns on 6 November. "Be of good cheer," he responded two days later. "Don't despond. I am working hard to accomplish the release of your worthy husband & think I have almost brought it about. . . . You may, I confidently think, soon see your husband. I have been working to accomplish his release & only requires one step more."[35]

Goldsborough's efforts were successful. Lieutenant Worden signed his parole on 13 November 1861, pledging "not to serve in any manner directly or indirectly against the Confederate States of America until . . . I have been exchanged."[36] Worden left Montgomery on 14 November and reached Richmond the next day. He reported to the adjutant general's office and was sent to General Huger in Norfolk on 18 November. Under a flag of truce, he was traded for William Sharp in the middle of Hampton Roads and then taken to Fort Monroe. The next day, he took the Old Bay Line steamer *Adelaide* to Baltimore, arriving on 20 November. He wrote to Gideon Welles and advised him that he was supposed to "report immediately to the Dept. in person, but for the last three days I have been feeling the approach of the disease which I suffered last winter greatly, and I therefore deem it most prudent to proceed at once to my home, that I may receive the necessary medical treatment under the care of my family."[37]

Welles noted at the bottom of this letter, "Congratulate him &c."

The former prisoner reached Quaker Hill on 21 November, "greatly to the joy of his friends."[38] On 3 December Worden wrote to Welles that he had reported for duty at the U.S. Naval Rendezvous New York.[39] Worden had worked at the Rendezvous for less than a month when he was selected for another mission that would make his name widely known and forever respected.

CHAPTER 7

TO PROVE *MONITOR* A SUCCESS

While Worden was imprisoned in Montgomery, great changes in naval warfare were under way. Confederate secretary of the navy Stephen Russell Mallory had initiated a construction program for a new kind of warship. Mallory believed that a fleet of iron-encased vessels armed with rifled cannon might tip the naval balance of power in favor of the South.[1] The fall of the Gosport Navy Yard on 21 April 1861 was a godsend for the fledgling Confederate Navy. It enabled the rebels to raise the charred hull of the former steam-screw frigate *Merrimack* and begin its transition into the ironclad ram CSS *Virginia*. News about *Merrimack* reached the North shortly after the conversion began via escaped slaves, deserters, Northern sympathizers, and the press. The *Mobile Register* proclaimed that "the hull of the *Merrimack* is being converted into an iron-cased battery.... [S]he would be a floating fortress that will be able to defeat the whole Navy of the United States and bombard its cities."[2]

Secretary of the Navy Gideon Welles had already begun to counter and outbuild the Confederate armorclad program. On 3 August 1861 he secured an appropriation of $1.5 million to construct three experimental ironclads. Congress also approved the establishment of the Ironclad Board to examine and select the appropriate designs. The first design selected, a European-style armored frigate, would be named *New Ironsides*. The other selection was a tumble-home design submitted by railroad magnate and Republican Party insider Cornelius Bushnell, to be named *Galena*. The Ironclad Board had questions about the latter's stability, so Bushnell asked New York City engineer and inventor John Ericsson to look at the plans. Ericsson advised Bushnell that the *Galena* design was acceptable, but then he showed Bushnell a ship model that he had made for Emperor Louis Napoleon of France. Overwhelmed by the brilliance of Ericsson's concept, Bushnell immediately went to see Secretary of the Navy Welles in Washington and convinced him that the "country was safe because I have found a battery which would make us the master . . . as far as the ocean was concerned."[3] Welles assured Bushnell that he would get President Lincoln's support for this iron battery project. When Ironclad Board members Flag Officer Joseph Smith, Flag Officer Hiram Paulding, and Capt. Charles Henry Davis questioned the feasibility of this new-style armor-clad, Ericsson himself went to Washington, gave a dramatic explanation of the little ship's abilities, and secured the board's approval. The keel of the experimental ironclad was laid at the Continental Iron Works in Greenpoint, New York, on 25 October 1861.

When Worden left the Confederate prison and returned home, he knew nothing about the new ironclads being built in Northern shipyards. He may have heard about the conversion of *Merrimack* while passing through Norfolk, but he did not mention it because that would have been a violation of his parole. After a brief recovery period he reported to the Brooklyn Navy Yard on 3 December to fulfill his duty with the Naval Rendezvous New York. There he surely heard about the strange new ironclad being constructed upriver at Greenpoint; but he had no notion that his career and the very course of his life would soon be intertwined with the new vessel.

On 12 January 1862 the one-hundred-day construction timetable for the completion of "Ericsson's Battery" had expired without completion, but the ship had already taken its unusual form, and the ship builders were sure it would be completed in a few weeks. That same day Lieutenant Worden received a private letter from Flag Officer Smith of the Ironclad Board, chief of the Navy's Bureau of Docks and Yards, detailing him as commander "of the battery under contract with Captain Ericsson, now nearly ready at New York. I believe that you are the right sort of officer to put in command of her."[4]

She May Prove a Success

Although Worden's family was concerned that he was still too weak to return to duty, he hurried to Greenpoint to see his new command. He advised Smith on 13 January: "I went immediately to see her, and, after a hasty examination of her, am induced to believe that she may prove a success. At all events, I am quite willing to be an agent in testing her capabilities & will readily devote whatever capacity & energy I have to that object."[5]

Following that, Worden was detached from the Rendezvous to "report to Commodore Paulding for the command of U.S. Iron clad steamer."[6] He formally assumed command of the experimental vessel on 16 January. He now faced the greatest challenge of his career, as always with the conviction that he would do his duty to the utmost of his ability. The responsibility that Flag Officer Smith had placed on his shoulders would reap great rewards for the Union.

The ironclad's new commander immediately went to work at the Brooklyn Navy Yard. He was familiar with the Yard, having served as its executive officer from 1856 to 1858, and understood the resources available to prepare Ericsson's battery (which Ericsson had named *Monitor* on 20 January) for service once the ship was turned over to the Navy. Among his most important tasks were assembling and training the crew and securing guns for the turret.

Ericsson specified that XV-inch Dahlgren guns, the largest shell gun in the Navy's inventory, should be mounted in the turret, believing that they could project shells capable of damaging a brick fort—or another ironclad. Assistant Secretary of the Navy Fox agreed with Ericsson's assessment. But few of the XV-inch smoothbores were available in January 1862. Eventually, Worden was forced to take XI-inch Dahlgren guns from the steam sloop *Dacotah*. The XI-inch guns could hurl a 187-pound solid shot or a 169-pound explosive shell more than 1,700 yards. The huge guns were installed in the confined space of *Monitor*'s turret in mid-February. Each XI-inch Dahlgren weighed more than eight tons, and their massive size left little room in the turret for the gun crews. Worden had to make other adjustments as well. The large pendulum port shutters that had been installed to protect the turret's interior would be impractical to operate during combat because of their weight. Further, with the pendulums in place, the limited space in the turret allowed only one shell gun to be fired at a time.[7]

Long before the gun issues were resolved, Worden reported to Gideon Welles on 22 January that he had received a copy of Ericsson's contract and had been in contact with Chief Engineer Alban Stimers, the first officer assigned to the ironclad project. At Ericsson's request, Stimers was the overseeing agent, but he was never an official crewmember.[8] Worden had received an application from Lt. Samuel Dana Greene on 20 January asking to be ordered to "Ericsson's Steam Battery." Worden passed the application along to Welles, stating, "I enclose herewith an application of Lieut. S. D. Greene for orders to the U.S. Iron Clad steamer building by Capt. Ericsson. If consistent with the views of the Department, would be gratified if Lieut. Greene's application be granted."[9]

Greene joined the ship's company on 24 January 1862. Acting Assistant Paymaster William Keeler was another early officer assignment. As paymaster, Keeler had to arrange all provisions, clothing, and other items to fulfill the crew's needs. Worden or his designee would deal with the ship's operation and fighting abilities. Keeler was taken aback by Worden's appearance at their first meeting. In a letter to his wife Keeler described Worden as "tall, thin & quite effeminate looking, notwithstanding a long beard hanging down his breast—he is white & delicate probably from long confinement & never was a lady the possessor of a smaller or more delicate hand, but if I am not very much mistaken, he will not hesitate to submit our iron sides to as severe a test as the most warlike could desire. He is a perfect gentleman in manner."[10]

On 27 January 1862 Lieutenant Worden reported to Welles that he had surveyed the vessel and understood the manpower required to operate it.

> In estimating the number of her crew, I allowed 15 men and a Quarter Gunner for the two guns, 11 men for the powder division, and 1 for the wheel, which I deem ample for the efficient working of her guns in action. That would leave 12 men (including those available in the engineer's department) to supply deficiencies at the guns caused by sickness or casualties. I propose to use a portion of the petty officers at the guns, and in naming that class, I thought that I would be enabled to obtain a better class of men for that purpose. It is believed that 17 men and 2 officers in the turret would be as many as could work there with advantage. A greater number would be in each others way & cause embarrassment.

The limited accommodations of the battery & the insufficiency of ventilation, renders it important that as few men as is consistent with her efficiency in action, should be put in her. In relation to master mates, one might be ordered, more would overcrowd her accommodations, and seem to be unnecessary.[11]

Worden selected Acting Master's Mate Louis N. Stodder and Acting Master John J. N. Webber to complete the officer complement. He also secured nine petty officers and several senior enlisted men to help provide leadership. Olivia's nephew Daniel Toffey was selected as captain's clerk. Worden also needed four engineers to manage the machinery. On 6 February he complained to Welles that "no Engineers, nor Asst. Surgeons have reported for duty in the U.S. Steamer *Monitor* yet."[12] Four engineers arrived two weeks later, led by First Assistant Engineer Isaac Newton Jr. with three others supporting his work.

Monitor was launched into the East River at Greenpoint on 30 January 1862 and was commissioned on 25 February. Worden now redoubled his efforts to muster a crew—and not just any men would do. The forty-five enlisted men who constituted *Monitor*'s complement were all volunteers. Since the ironclad was experimental and different from any other vessel in the Navy, Worden did not want to accept men arbitrarily assigned from receiving ships at the Brooklyn Navy Yard. Instead, he went on board *North Carolina* and *Sabine* to ask for volunteers. He needed firemen, coal heavers, and ordinary seamen to operate the vessel. The response was overwhelming. Many of the men he chose lacked experience, and few were seasoned sailors, but Worden was confident that he had assembled a crew that he could mold into a fighting team. The men began transferring to *Monitor* in early February and continued arriving until the day the ironclad sailed.

Worden needed to cross-train the enlistees to ensure that they could complete various additional tasks that might arise during emergencies or combat. It was a new experience for all because *Monitor* was a most unusual ship. Seaman Peter Truscott later called it "a little bit the strangest craft I had ever seen."[13] The ironclad featured more than forty of Ericsson's inventions, many of them new, and was like nothing else afloat. The officers and crew lived below the waterline and had to get used to using new contraptions such as pressurized heads. With just an eighteen-inch freeboard, *Monitor* was virtually awash with the sea. Many of the original volunteers deserted almost as soon as they stepped on board what they believed was an unseaworthy vessel. Master's Mate George Frederickson noted in *Monitor*'s log on 4 March 1862, for example, that "Norman McPherson and John Atkins deserted taking the ship's cutter and left for parts unknown."[14] Coal Heaver Thomas Feeney deserted seven days after he enlisted and on the very day he arrived on *Monitor*. Worden took these personnel losses in stride and continued to prepare his men for war.

As the crew settled into the ship and learned their duties, Worden rushed to get the ironclad through its trials and prepared for its voyage south. Although the vessel was still not ready, on 20 February Gideon Welles gave orders to Worden "to proceed with the U.S.S. *Monitor*, under your command, to Hampton Roads, Virginia."[15] Worden finalized preparations and set out for what proved to be a very short maiden voyage. On 27 February he advised Welles that "the U.S.S. *Monitor*, under my command, left the navy yard this morning to proceed to sea. In going down the East River she steered so badly that I deemed advisable not to proceed further with her."[16]

Monitor veered back and forth across the East River "like a drunken man on a side walk," William Keeler later wrote.[17] The ironclad finally crashed into a dock and was ignominiously towed back to the Brooklyn Navy Yard. Flag Officer Hiram Paulding, commandant of the Yard, suggested that *Monitor* be placed back into drydock to fix the steering problem with a new rudder. Worden sent Alban Stimers to work with Ericsson "to ascertain from him what he proposes to do, to remedy the defect in her steering apparatus."[18]

Ericsson and Stimers installed a series of pulleys between the tiller and the steering wheel drum to stabilize the steering. With the new mechanism installed, *Monitor* could turn about in less than five minutes. Worden was still not satisfied and insisted on trials off Sandy Hook. A review board of Flag Officer Francis H. Gregory, Chief Engineer Benjamin F. Garvin, and Naval Constructor Edward Hartt oversaw the trial. *Monitor* passed their inspection on 4 March.

Worden was not yet sure of his ship's sea-keeping qualities and could only estimate its fighting abilities. Nevertheless, on 4 March Paulding ordered Worden back out to sea. "When the weather permits, you will proceed with

Monitor under your command to Hampton Roads and on your arrival report to the senior officer there. . . . [W]ishing you a safe passage."[19] A powerful storm worked its way up the coast the same day Worden received his orders, and he decided to delay the departure. Despite Ericsson's claims to the contrary, he recognized that *Monitor* was not designed to be an oceangoing vessel, and he felt it best to wait for good weather.

Bound for Battle

The storm passed, and on the morning of 6 March Worden ordered *Monitor* to cast off from the Brooklyn Navy Yard quay, destination Hampton Roads. Since the engines made only seven knots instead of the specified nine knots, and Worden wanted to reach Hampton Roads "as speedily as possible whilst the fine weather lasts," he made arrangements to have the vessel towed to Virginia.[20]

Paulding had already secured the services of the tug *Thomas Freeborn* to tow the ironclad south but decided to contract a more powerful tug, *Seth Low*, instead. Once *Monitor* entered New York City's Lower Bay, Worden ordered the four-hundred-foot towline secured to *Seth Low*. The ironclad was joined by its escorts—the two steam-screw gunboats *Currituck* and *Sachem*—and by 4 p.m. the little squadron had passed Sandy Hook and turned south toward Hampton Roads.

During the first evening at sea, the officers congratulated one another on the excellent weather. Stimers noted there "has not been sufficient movement to disturb a wine glass setting on the table." Keeler remembered standing atop the turret with "the water smooth & everything seems favorable. . . . Not a sea has yet passed over our deck, it is as dry as when we left port." Once past the Delaware Capes, however, the sea turned violent. That morning Keeler found "much more motion to the vessel & could see the green water through my deck light."[21] Lieutenant Greene remembered that ten-foot waves "would strike the pilot-house and go over the turret in beautiful curves, and [the water] came through the narrow eye-holes in the pilot-house with such force as to knock the helmsman completely around from the wheel."[22]

Lieutenant Worden, Assistant Surgeon Daniel Logue, and numerous enlisted men became extremely seasick, and Greene had to assume command. With water leaking in everywhere, *Monitor* struggled to pass the Delaware

Capes from noon until after 7 p.m. The soaked blower belts slipped, so there was no air to keep the fires going. The pumps would not work without steam, and some on board feared the worst. Greene started a bucket brigade to calm the crew and had the men work hand pumps. With *Monitor* in danger of sinking, Greene signaled *Seth Low* to tow the vessel toward shore. Once in more protected waters, the engineering staff was able to make the necessary repairs. By the late afternoon of 7 March *Monitor* was able to continue down the coast. The calm seas that evening allowed some on board to rest.[23]

When *Monitor* passed Chincoteague Island, Virginia, Greene was startled awake by the "most infernal noise I ever heard in my life." The ironclad was passing over a shoal, and shallow water rushed through the anchor well and forced air through the hawse pipe. Water streamed across the wardroom table and into the berth deck. Greene thought the "noise resembled the death groans of twenty men, and was the most dismal, awful sound I have ever heard."[24] When a gale struck *Monitor* at midnight on 8 March, the crew feared they would never see the dawn. Worden, now recovered from his seasickness, and Greene took immediate action to save the ironclad. They organized another bucket brigade, redoubled efforts to work the hand pumps, and signaled *Seth Low* to move the ironclad closer to shore and away from the pounding seas.

Monitor finally reached Cape Charles, Virginia, late in the afternoon on 8 March, having survived two violent storms. As the ship entered the Chesapeake Bay, Worden could see smoke and gunfire in the distance and vessels streaming out of Hampton Roads. They were a day too late to stop the rampage of the Confederate ironclad ram CSS *Virginia* (Union sailors and Northern newspapers would continue to refer to this ironclad as *Merrimack* or *Merrimac*).

While *Monitor* was being towed down the Virginia coast, the Confederate warship had emerged from the Elizabeth River, crossed Hampton Roads, and attacked and sank two major Union warships, *Congress* and *Cumberland,* and two transports, *Arrango* and *Whilden*; captured the transport *Reindeer*; and damaged *Minnesota, St. Lawrence,* and *Zouave.* The stunning defeat rocked the Union high command. President Abraham Lincoln called it the greatest calamity since Bull Run. Secretary of War Edwin Stanton was frantic, fearing *Virginia* would destroy the entire U.S. Navy, attack every city on the East Coast, and then destroy Washington. Gideon Welles tried to allay his fears by reminding him that the Confederate ironclad could not go everywhere at once, and in any event could not move up the Potomac and attack Washington because its draft was far too deep. Furthermore, Welles reminded him, the Navy's newest ironclad, *Monitor*, was en route to Chesapeake Bay. When Stanton asked about *Monitor*'s armament and Welles replied, Stanton's "mingled look of incredulity and contempt cannot be described; and the tone of his voice, as he asked if my reliance on that craft with only two guns, is equally indescribable."[25] Nevertheless, Worden and *Monitor* seemed to be the Union's only hope for salvation.

As *Monitor* passed Cape Charles at about 5 p.m. on 8 March, the roadstead in the distance was aglow with the burning *Congress*, *Arrango*, and *Whilden*. Worden knew he was looking at the greatest Union naval defeat of the war. He ordered *Monitor* stripped of its sea rig in preparation for battle. The turret was "keyed up and in every way to be prepared for action." About midway between Cape Henry and Fort Monroe, Worden later wrote, "A pilot boat came alongside and gave us a pilot, from whom we learned of the advent of the *Merrimack*." Hearts sank as the pilot described the destruction of *Cumberland* and *Congress* and "the generally gloomy conditions of affairs in Hampton Roads."[26]

Worden anchored *Monitor* near *Roanoke* at about 9 p.m. and reported to Capt. John Marston, acting commander of the naval forces in Hampton Roads. Only then did he learn of new orders that had failed to reach him before he left New York: Welles wanted *Monitor* to proceed to Washington to protect the capital. Marston, with Worden's concurrence, rescinded that order, both men realizing that the best way to defend against a Confederate ironclad assault on Washington was to protect the wooden Union warships in Hampton Roads. Marston directed Worden to station *Monitor* near the grounded *Minnesota* to shield it from *Virginia*. Worden took a few moments to write to Olivia that "the *Merrimack* has caused sad work amongst our vessels." But, he added defiantly, "she can't hurt us." He closed this brief note as he prepared for his momentous battle invoking the divine and his family: "God bless you & the little ones. Yours ever & devotedly, Worden."[27]

Before he could do anything else, Worden needed to secure a pilot to guide *Monitor* safely through Hampton Roads' treacherous shoals.

Considering the damage wrought by the Confederate ironclad that day, few qualified pilots were willing to go on board the strange-looking *Monitor* and fight the seemingly unstoppable *Virginia* the next morning. After a two-hour search, Worden convinced Acting Master Samuel Howard of the bark *Amanda* to pilot *Monitor* through the shoals.

The death throes of *Congress* provided a spectacular conclusion to the events of 8 March as *Monitor* steamed over to *Minnesota* and anchored next to the grounded warship early the next morning. *Congress* had been burning since late afternoon, and the red-tongued flames dancing along the shrouds, masts, and stays cast an eerie glow across Hampton Roads. Greene was a witness when the frigate finally exploded. "Certainly a grander sight was never seen," he reported, "but it went right to the marrow of our bones."[28]

After *Monitor* was anchored, Worden went on board *Minnesota* to offer his assistance to its commander, forty-seven-year naval veteran Capt. Gershon Jacques Henry Van Brunt. Van Brunt replied that he expected to free his ship at the next high tide at 2 a.m. and had little faith in *Monitor*'s ability to stop the Confederate ram. If all else failed, he said, he would destroy his ship rather than allow it to be captured. Keeler concluded that the men of *Minnesota* thought the "idea of assistance or protection being offered to the huge thing by a little pigmy at her side seemed absolutely ridiculous."[29] *Minnesota*'s chief engineer, however, Thomas Rae, remembered that when he shouted down to the engine room, "The *Monitor* is alongside," the men below "gave a cheer that might have been heard in Richmond."[30] As Worden left *Minnesota*, he told Van Brunt, "I will stand by you to the last if I can help you." Despite Van Brunt's self-confidence, Worden knew that his ironclad was the only thing that could save the frigate.[31]

This Is the *Merrimac*

Monitor's crew had little opportunity to rest during the early morning of 9 March. At 2 a.m. Worden mustered his men to their stations. If *Minnesota* did indeed float free with the high tide, *Monitor* would need to move out of the way. But despite the efforts of *Minnesota*'s crew to free the frigate from the shoal, it remained stuck fast and seemed destined to await its fate. Worden, meanwhile, knew that whatever he chose to do that morning would prove

Monitor either a success or a failure. He was determined to do his utmost to save the day in Hampton Roads.

As he made preparations for *Monitor*'s expected engagement with *Virginia*, Worden detailed firemen Patrick Hannan, Wilhelm Durst, and John Driscoll at dawn "to screw the iron plates over the deck lights in the deck and to take down the blower pipes and smokestacks." Around 6 a.m. Worden ordered the men to a breakfast of "canned roast beef hardtack and coffee." It was the first food they had eaten in nearly two days. Then, also according to Driscoll, he gave a brief speech reminding the men that they had all volunteered and that "now having seen what *Merrimac* had done and from all appearances was now capable of doing and that the fate of *Cumberland* may soon be ours[,] that if anyone regretted the step he had taken he would put them on board *Roanoke*. He was answered by every man jumping to his feet and giving three cheers."[32]

In addition to going without food, many of *Monitor*'s crew had not slept in forty-eight hours. Undoubtedly, their nerves were on edge. Their ship had almost sunk twice on the way south, and they had seen the havoc wrought by the Confederate ironclad on the Union naval forces in Hampton Roads. They knew *Monitor* was an untried experimental vessel, and they had all heard the jeers of other Union sailors about their little ship's abilities. Still, the fact that they were enclosed inside impenetrable armor must have given them some confidence. Worden felt assured that his men would do their duty when their vessel joined battle with an enemy that seemed unstoppable. The experiment was about to be put to the test.

At daylight on 9 March the Confederate squadron prepared to finish the previous day's work. Although *Virginia* had suffered significant damage during its 8 March encounter with *Cumberland*, its acting commander, Lt. Catesby ap Roger Jones, believed that his vessel was in a satisfactory condition to continue the fight with the Union's wooden warships in Hampton Roads. Fog delayed the Confederate ships entering the Roads that morning, but by 7:45 a.m. the fog had cleared and Jones could see that *Minnesota* was still stranded on the shoal. At 8 a.m. Lt. Hunter Davidson's forward Brooke rifle sent the first shot of the day screaming through *Minnesota*'s rigging. Worden, Logue, and Keeler were watching the approach of the rebel ironclad when "a shell howled over our heads and crashed into the side of the

Minnesota." Keeler added, "Captain Worden ... came up & said more sternly than I had ever heard him speak before, 'Gentlemen, that is the *Merrimac*, you had better go below.'"[33]

Worden was the last to go back inside the ironclad. As he passed down through the turret, he saw the gun crew loading one of the XI-inch Dahlgrens and said, "Send them that with our compliments, my lads."[34] Worden took his station in the pilothouse with Quartermaster Peter Williams and pilot Samuel Howard and ordered the ironclad to steer directly toward *Virginia* and engage it as far away from *Minnesota* as possible.

At first, *Virginia* appeared not to notice *Monitor*. Van Brunt, watching from *Minnesota*, was astonished when Worden took *Monitor* "right alongside the *Merrimack*, and the contrast was that of a pygmy to a giant."[35] *Virginia*'s crew were prepared to make short work of the stranded Union frigate "when suddenly to our astonishment, a black object that looked like ... a barrel-head afloat with a cheese box on top of it" moved slowly out from under *Minnesota* and "boldly confronted us."[36]

Photo 7.1 Battle between *Virginia* and *Monitor*, painting by Thomas C. Skinner, circa 1935–50 *Mariners' Museum and Park 1935.0013.000001*

The two ironclads quickly took the measure of each other. As soon as his ship was in range, Worden stopped the engines and ordered Greene to begin firing. The first shot missed the Confederate ironclad; the second struck *Virginia*'s casemate but deflected off the iron shield and caused no damage. When the first Confederate shots slammed into *Monitor* the turret rang like a bell, but that shot too caused no damage. The men on both vessels now believed that their ships were impregnable. Greene remembered that a "look of confidence passed over the men's faces, and we believed the *Merrimack* would not repeat the work she had accomplished the day before."[37] During the first two hours of the engagement, however, neither ship's guns could damage the other vessel.

Worden planned to operate in concentric circles to approach his quarry. He knew his ship was faster and nimbler than the Confederate ram. He also recognized that *Virginia*'s deep draft limited where it could move in the channel, whereas *Monitor*'s eleven-foot draft gave his ship a decidedly larger range of movement. Nonetheless, the ensuing combat revealed several serious problems that limited *Monitor*'s offensive ability. The order to use fifteen-pound powder charges rather than the rated thirty pounds lessened the impact of *Monitor*'s solid shot. The fire control system was completely ineffective, and only Worden and the pilot in the pilothouse had an effective view of the battle. The lack of direct communication between the pilothouse and the rotating turret became a serious issue early in the engagement. A speaking tube had been installed to provide a constant link between the critical combat functions of command and fire control, and white marks were placed below the turret's stationary deck to indicate the vessel's direction. These marks, however, were quickly covered by gunpowder residue. The men inside the spinning clockwise-turning turret lost all sense of direction and could not respond to Worden's orders.[38]

The many problems caused by the separation of the command center and fire control were magnified when the speaking tube stopped functioning. Worden's solution was to use Keeler and his clerk, Daniel Toffey, to run messages between himself and Greene. "They performed their work with zeal and alacrity," Greene recounted, "but both being landsmen, our technical communication sometimes miscarried."[39] When the engine turning the turret malfunctioned, the gunners had to fire blind, hoping to hit the target.

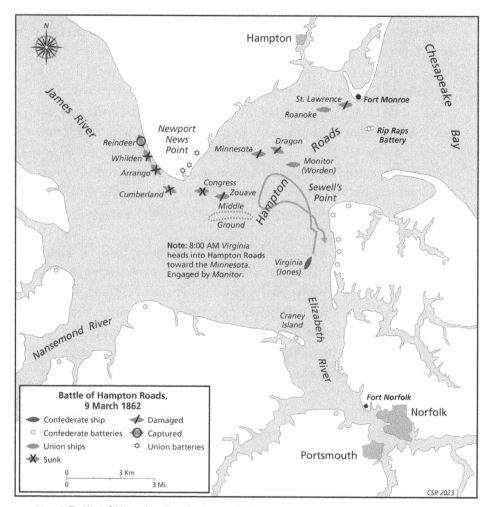

Map 2 Battle of Hampton Roads, 9 March 1862

After almost two hours of combat, Worden ordered *Monitor* to break off the action and steam onto a shoal where *Virginia* could not pursue it. The shot in the turret was exhausted and had to be resupplied. To accomplish this the turret had to be stationary so the 187-pound shot could be hoisted up through two scuttle holes, one in the deck and the other in the floor of the turret. It was a challenging and arduous task. Worden ordered Keeler to provide the powder division with a ration of spirits, then ventured out onto the deck to inspect the damage. He was pleased to note that while *Virginia*'s shot had dented the turret's iron plates, none were cracked, and no other damage was visible.

As *Monitor* was rearming, the rebel ram had steamed forward to destroy *Minnesota* but ran aground en route. Worden now had the opportunity to take his ship alongside the Confederate ironclad and pound it with shot. Because of *Monitor*'s inadequate fire control, *Virginia* suffered limited damage. Once *Virginia* freed itself from the shoal, Lieutenant Jones decided to ram the Union ironclad. As *Virginia* began its run at *Monitor*, Worden told Keeler to tell Greene to "give them both guns."[40] When Worden saw *Virginia* about to strike his ship, he ordered Quartermaster Peter Williams to veer the nimble ironclad off to starboard. *Virginia* thus hit only a glancing blow that inflicted minor damage to the smaller warship.

Monitor's move to starboard enabled Jones to turn again toward *Minnesota*. He fired on the screw steamer *Dragon*, exploding its boiler. Worden again moved his ironclad between the Confederate warship and the wooden frigate. With his shot having proved ineffective, he decided to ram the rebel ironclad and disable its propeller and rudder, neither of which was protected by armor. *Virginia* was riding high in the water after the day's large expenditures of coal, powder, and ammunition. A successful strike against its stern would leave the Confederate ironclad adrift and subject to capture. *Monitor* rushed toward *Virginia*'s fantail but missed because of a steering system failure.

As *Monitor* passed *Virginia*'s stern, Lt. John Taylor Wood fired his 7-inch Brooke rifle at *Monitor*'s pilothouse. Wood's shell blew off one of the wrought iron bars forming the command center just as Worden was peering through the observation slit. The explosion created a cloud of smoke and debris that blinded Worden. He fell back from the damaged slit exclaiming, "My eyes, I am blind."[41] Despite losing his sight, Worden sensed bright light and cool air pouring into the pilothouse and believed his command center had been destroyed. With remarkable presence of mind, he ordered Williams to turn *Monitor* to starboard, away from *Virginia*, and onto a shoal.

Keeler and Samuel Howard helped Worden out of the pilothouse, and Daniel Toffey was sent to the turret to get Lieutenant Greene. Greene immediately rushed forward. When he arrived, he found Worden holding onto the ladder below the pilothouse looking "a ghastly sight, with his eyes closed and blood apparently rushing from every pore in the upper part of his face."[42] Greene, along with Dr. Logue, William Keeler, and Wilhelm Durst, helped Worden to his cabin and laid him on a sofa as Logue began removing iron

Photo 7.2 Deck and turret of *Monitor* with shot damage, James River, Virginia, 9 July 1862, photo taken by James F. Gibson *Library of Congress digital ID stereo-1s02826*

particles from his commander's eyes. Worden told Greene he was critically wounded and directed the young lieutenant to take charge of the ironclad. When Greene asked Worden what he should do, Worden replied, "Gentlemen I leave it to you, do what you think best. I cannot see, but do not mind me. Save the *Minnesota* if you can."[43]

Meanwhile, Jones, having seen *Monitor* steam onto a shoal, again considered attacking the still-stranded *Minnesota*. But the tide was running out, so he took *Virginia* back to the Elizabeth River. As he saw *Virginia* steaming toward Norfolk, Greene exclaimed, "We [have] evidently finished the *Merrimac*."[44] The crew cheered vigorously, believing their little ship had saved the day for the Union. Greene followed Worden's instructions and anchored *Monitor* next to *Minnesota*. The first battle between iron ships of war was over, with both sides claiming victory. "Ericsson's Folly" had proven its worth, and Lt. John Lorimer Worden was about to become a national hero.

Although *Monitor* had successfully blocked *Virginia* from destroying the rest of the Union's wooden fleet in Hampton Roads, the battle revealed fatal flaws in its design. Worden had already discovered that his vessel was unable to steam in open seas because of its poor steering, limited freeboard, and weak engine power. He also now knew that *Monitor* had a limited field and a low rate of fire. Further, it had carried no small arms for defense against enemy boarders. Nevertheless, Worden and *Monitor* had captured the imagination of the nation for the perceived victory on 9 March 1862. Worden would retain and enhance his heroic status during the course of the war; the monitor design would not.

Photo 7.3 Lt. John L. Worden, 1862, by R. A. Lewis and J. C. Buttre *U.S. Naval Academy Special Collections and Archives 0035*

CHAPTER 8

RECOVERY AND RECOGNITION

In the aftermath of the battle, Dr. Logue began assessing the damage to his wounded captain's eyes. Worden's face was a swollen, bloody mess, and he was in considerable pain. Logue later reported that Worden's wounds were inflicted "in great measure from unburnt powder, by minute portion of iron from the broken iron bar of the Pilot House, driven into the texture about the eyes." Gunpowder and iron had been driven into Worden's eyelids and the skin over the temples and brow, doing serious damage to the mucous membrane that lined the eyelids and the front of the eyeballs. Fortunately, Worden's cornea and the interior of his eyes escaped serious injury. Logue noted that he made "no thorough attempt ... to remove ... the powder and iron that were embedded in these tissues." He used a "camel hair pencil and tepid water to remove all offensive particles possible. Cold water was constantly applied to Worden's eyes to assist in the healing process."[1]

"I've Only Done My Duty"

Lt. Henry A. Wise, assistant chief of the Navy Bureau of Ordnance, went on board *Monitor* to escort his injured friend to Fort Monroe. *Monitor*'s crew cheered wildly as Worden, his face covered with bandages, was led off the ship. The next day, 10 March, Wise took Worden via steamer to Baltimore, and then by train and carriage to Wise's home on H Street in Washington.[2]

Wise's daughter Charlotte was present when Worden arrived. Years later she vividly recalled Worden's arrival: "I remember, too, seeing the carriage drive up with this bandaged, bloodstained man—and saw him assisted upstairs by my father and two hospital stewards and put on to our nursery bed." Charlotte heard Worden "gasp out that he must go at once and report to the President." Her father insisted he stay where he was and then "ran down the stairs and hurried off to the White House."[3]

Arriving at the White House, just two blocks from his home, Wise interrupted a cabinet meeting to give President Lincoln his description of the fight between *Monitor* and *Virginia* as he had witnessed it from shore and told them Worden was there in Washington recovering from grievous wounds. When Wise finished, "President Lincoln got up and said, 'Well gentlemen I am going to see that fellar.'" Lincoln and Wise walked to Wise's house and entered Worden's room. "Jack, here is the President, he has come to see you," Wise said. Worden, lying in bed with his head swathed in bandages, reached for Lincoln's hand and said, "You have given me great honor, Mr. President, and I am only sorry that I can't see you." Lincoln, with tears in his eyes, respectfully replied, "No sir, you have done me and your country more honor, sir, than I can ever to do you, and I shall promote you."[4] In ten-year-old Charlotte's telling, "Capt. Worden was completely overcome" and responded to Lincoln, "I've only done my duty, sir." Lincoln sat on the edge of the bed and asked Worden to tell him the story of the battle.

Worden's version did not differ from those of others except for his conclusions. He acknowledged *Monitor*'s shot-proof capabilities but also explained its greatest weakness. Lincoln wasted no time passing that information on to Welles: "I have just seen Lieut Worden, who says the 'Monitor' could be boarded and captured very easily, first, after boarding, by wedging the turret, so that it would not turn, and then by pouring water in her & drowning her machinery. He is decidedly of Opinion that she should not go sky-larking up to Norfolk."[5] The small arms that *Monitor* needed were quickly issued, and orders not to expose the ironclad to close combat were reiterated.

According to Charlotte, after Lincoln left Wise's home, Worden was moved to her mother's bedroom, "where he lay eleven weeks, no one thinking he would ever pull through. There were no trained nurses then, and my mother, and later Mrs. Worden, took charge of him and slowly nursed him back to life."[6]

Photo 8.1 Lieutenant Worden at the Naval Observatory, 1862, photo taken by J. R. Gilliss. The women standing are believed to be Florence Washington Schley, an aunt of Lt. Winfield Scott Schley, USN, and whose name is on the back of the photo, and her sister Rose Maria Washington Aston. The older woman sitting next to Worden may be Olivia Worden. *Library of Congress John L. Worden Papers MSS 56051*

The conical shell of Lt. John Taylor Wood's 7-inch Brooke rifle could easily have killed Worden. If large fragments rather than sparks and gunpowder had entered the slit that Worden was peering through, he probably would have died. Civil War naval combat was brutal and deadly, with explosive shells, hot shot, bolts, and solid shot flying across a ship's deck. Even though most naval battles did not result in the high casualties of land engagements, heavy ordnance sent destructive projectiles that could cut a man in two. After the 15 May 1862 Battle of Drewry's Bluff, for example, William Keeler went on board the ironclad *Galena* to observe the damage caused by Confederate shot and shell. He saw "a slaughter house . . . of human beings. Here was a body with the head, one arm & part of Breast torn off by a bursting shell—another with the top of his head taken off the brains still steaming on the deck, partly across him lay one with both legs taken off at the hips & at a little distance was another completely disemboweled."[7] Thirteen men had been killed and eleven wounded. Worden survived *Virginia*'s shot and shell in part because of *Monitor*'s thick armor.

Expressions of Public Approval

As word of the battle at Hampton Roads spread, Worden began to receive accolades, awards, and honors. Three days after the battle, New York newspapers recognized "the genius and patriotism of Ericsson" and said that Worden, "whose zeal and efficiency betoken the highest skill and devotion, should receive prompt expression of the public approval." Congress obliged, and on 13 March a draft resolution of thanks was introduced and unanimously approved in the Senate and referred to the House Committee on Naval Affairs.[8]

Secretary Welles wrote to Worden that the Battle of Hampton Roads had "excited general admiration and received the applause of the entire country." He continued, "The President directs me, while earnestly and deeply sympathising with you in the injuries which you have sustained, but which it is believed are but temporary, to you thank you and your command for the heroism you have displayed and the great service you have rendered. . . . [T]he performance, power and capabilities of the *Monitor*, must effect a radical change in naval warfare."[9]

Other accolades arrived. When Worden learned of a resolution passed by the New York State Chamber of Commerce complimenting him and

Monitor's officers, he asked Wise to reply on his behalf: "Lieutenant Worden desires me to express his heartfelt appreciation for the honor conferred upon him, and to say that, in simply doing his duty with the brave men around onboard the *Monitor*, he feels nevertheless gratified that it has met with the approval of the Chamber of Commerce; and that should he recover from his injuries and his sight be restored, he hopes to do that duty again under similar circumstances."[10] Wise sent copies of the Chamber of Commerce resolution and his reply to Flag Officer Louis M. Goldsborough to be read to *Monitor*'s officers and crew.[11]

The citizens of Buffalo, New York, presented Worden with an expensive gold Tiffany snuffbox engraved with an image of the *Monitor-Merrimack* fight. The New York General Assembly passed a resolution ordering the manufacture and presentation of a sword to "that gallant son of the State of New York . . . as a slight testimonial of his bravery in the late naval engagement at Hampton Roads."[12] New York secretary of state Horatio Ballard informed Worden by letter on 16 December that the New York State Assembly would present him with a sword "emblazoned with the record of that glorious day [March 9] . . . as a memorial of your heroism and skill as commandant of the *Monitor*." Worden wrote in reply to Ballard, "To serve our country in any hour of peril has been my highest ambition. . . . [N]othing less than the aid of Heaven could have produced a result so gratifying."[13] The sword was created by Tiffany and Company and displayed in Tiffany's storefront for several days before it was given to Olivia.

Worden's eyes and face slowly healed. The 22 March *Brooklyn Eagle* reported that "Lieutenant Worden is improving. He slept well last night for the first time since his injury, and his friends are now confident that he will completely recover his eyesight." The paper also quoted a letter from one of Worden's friends: "Worden is getting on, and is regaining his strength; whether he will recover his sight or not, remains (by him) to be seen." Several of Worden's friends in New York, understanding that he might be obliged to retire from active service in the Navy, subscribed money toward the purchase of a farm and homestead for him and his family.[14]

On 25 March Wise's father-in-law, former secretary of state and former senator Edward Everett, published a four-page broadside in Boston on Worden's behalf detailing his services as *Monitor*'s commander and their

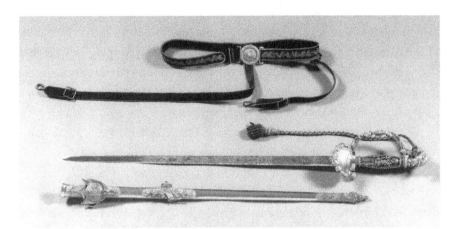

Photo 8.2 Presentation sword given to Lt. John L. Worden by the New York Assembly, 1862; donated to the U.S. Naval Academy by his son, Daniel T. Worden, 1912 *U.S. Naval Academy Museum, 1912.006.001*

worth to the nation ("millions of dollars"). Contributions had reached four thousand dollars by 15 May, but much more was needed to secure Worden's future. Everett published an updated broadside in July noting that there had been "many generous donors," but more contributions were needed because Worden "was unable to use his eyes for reading or writing; and it is feared that the sight of one of them is permanently injured."[15]

As Worden was recovering, *Monitor* underwent three command changes. Lt. Samuel Dana Greene, who had assumed command when Worden was wounded, was replaced on 10 March by Lt. Thomas O. Selfridge Jr. Some believed that Greene was too young for such a critical command, while others thought he should have taken a more aggressive approach by attacking *Virginia* before it left the roadstead.

Although Selfridge had been selected by Assistant Secretary of the Navy Gustavus Fox, it was the prerogative of Flag Officer Goldsborough, commander of the North Atlantic Blockading Squadron, to name *Monitor*'s new commander. Goldsborough wanted a more experienced officer and appointed Lt. William Jeffers, who was not popular with the crew. William Keeler described Jeffers as "a rigid disciplinarian, [with a] quick imperious temper & domineering disposition."[16] Fireman George Geer called Jeffers "a dam'd old hog."[17] Geer and other crewmembers wrote to Worden on 24 April expressing their hope to see him back in command and addressing him as "Our Dear and Honored Captain." "These few lines is from your own crew of the *Monitor* with there [*sic*] kindest Love to you[.] Hoping to God that they will soon have the pleasure of Welcoming you back to us again Soon. . . . [S]ince you have left we have had no pleasure on Board of the *Monitor*."[18] They signed it, "We remain until Death your affectionate Crew The *Monitor* Boys."

Country Gentleman magazine reported that Worden "will resume command of the *Monitor* as soon as he recovers from his injuries, which according to the latest accounts, he is expected to do very shortly." In fact, that was impossible because Jeffers had already been detailed as commander. Welles detached Worden, writing to him on 8 May, "I am compelled to consider you detached from the date Lt. Jeffers assumes command of the *Monitor*—you will thereby lose . . . sea pay—we can not pay two commanders for one vessel." Worden was ordered to Philadelphia to take command of the new ironclad *New Ironsides*. Barely a month later, on 10 June, Worden was detached from *New Ironsides* and placed on "awaiting orders" status.[19]

On the Road

After nearly two months of convalescence, Worden's eyesight was "now so much improved as [for him] to be out." His eyes still bandaged, he visited Congress on 6 May and shook hands with "nearly all of the Senators." Although he could not yet see out of his left eye, Navy surgeons did not believe his injury was permanent, and he was able to leave Washington on 10 May for Brooklyn. He attended a concert at the Academy of Music in Brooklyn to benefit the U.S. Sanitary Commission, where he was observed wearing a shade over his eyes, but the press reported that he looked "comparatively healthy, firm, and vigorous; and may be blessed in the course of Providence, with the opportunities of doing his country good service." When Worden returned to Quaker Hill, though, his neighbor Abby Jane Leach Landis thought he looked "sick and disfigured."[20]

Despite his activities in May, Worden suffered both mentally and physically during his recovery. The pain must have been intense. By his own account, he was "in bed in Washington about two months, during which period had erysipelas in the head, resulting from injury to it, and was much swollen. . . . Was able to go to New York near the last of May & was placed in charge of an occulest [*sic*] & and was under his treatment for some time & finally sent to Richfield Springs [north of Cooperstown, New York]."[21]

During his recuperation Worden traveled west via railroad "to see an aged mother, who I have not seen for several years, and who is now in great affliction." His younger brother Eugene Bucharnois Worden had died on 4 June in Kent County, Michigan, giving him still more incentive to visit the state. A joyous grand reception was held in Worden's honor on 9 July in Grand Rapids attended by men, women, and children "of all ages" as well as his mother and siblings. Thirty women and girls sang songs specially written to hail the "son of the sea, fresh from the battle's thunder."[22]

On 11 July the House of Representatives approved the proposed Senate joint resolution expressing the nation's thanks to Worden and his crew: "The thanks of Congress and of the American people are due, and are hereby tendered, to Lieutenant J. L. Worden, of the United States navy, and to the officers and men of the iron-clad gunboat *Monitor*, under his command, for the skill and gallantry exhibited by them in the late remarkable battle between the *Monitor* and the rebel iron-clad steamer *Merrimack*."[23] Section 2 of the resolution requested the president to communicate the text to Worden "and through him to the officer and men under his command." Welles subsequently advised Worden that he had been promoted to commander, effective 16 July.[24]

Eventually, Commander Worden granted himself some rest and returned to Quaker Hill. Brig. Gen. Lew Wallace, whose mother-in-law was a Quaker Hill native and kin to Olivia Worden, visited him there on 27 July. Wallace had recently fought in the 6–7 April Battle of Shiloh in Tennessee, where Worden's brother Maj. Frederick William Worden was in command of the Thirteenth Michigan Infantry "and [had] directed the affair with courage and coolness" during a "sharp brush at Shiloh."[25]

The peaceful days at Quaker Hill were soon over. The new *Passiac* class of monitors was under construction in Brooklyn, and Worden's knowledge and experience were required to oversee their production. If his recovery continued, he might even command one of them. He was back at the Brooklyn Navy Yard by mid-August to help strengthen the Union's new iron navy. His duties there would bring Worden additional accolades and fame through his devotion to duty and the nation.

CHAPTER 9

MEETING *RATTLESNAKE*

The general public's curiosity concerning Worden's next assignment ended on 14 August 1862, when, as a newly promoted commander, he was detailed for special duty as an assistant to Rear Adm. Francis Hoyt Gregory at the Brooklyn Navy Yard. Gregory was the superintendent of construction and fitting out of naval vessels in private yards. Worden was to help Gregory supervise the construction of a new class of ironclads. He was given this assignment not because of his knowledge of engine systems or ironclad construction techniques but because of his unique knowledge of the strengths and weaknesses of the monitor design. Worden had even more to offer than that. A twenty-five-year naval combat veteran, he had sailed the world's oceans battling fierce storms and his country's enemies. Sea experience aside, he offered tremendous value with his administrative skills as well as knowledge of logistics, navigation, staffing requirements, and general ironclad management. Commander Worden was the monitor man of the hour.

Monitor Fever

After *Monitor*'s success at Hampton Roads, "*Monitor* fever" swept the Union. Gideon Welles, Gustavus Vasa Fox, and some Union Navy leaders were convinced that a fleet of the new monitor-style warships could defeat anything the South could put up against them. Consequently, John Ericsson received a contract to build ten *Passaic*-class monitors. The design of the new class would correct many of the original *Monitor*'s flaws. The vessels would be longer than *Monitor*'s 179 feet and would weigh more—1,335 tons versus *Monitor*'s 987 tons—and carry crews of sixty-seven to eighty-eight men. The *Passaic*s would be 200 feet long, with a beam of 46 feet and a draft of 11 feet, 6 inches. They would be powered by a two-cylinder Ericsson vibrating-lever (trunk) engine with two Martin boilers turning a single-screw propeller that could produce 320 horsepower and make 7 knots. The *Passaic*-class vessels were heavily armored as well, with an 11-inch turret, 5-inch sides, 1-inch deck, and 8 inches for the pilothouse.[1]

The pilothouse design was novel. Acting Assistant Paymaster Samuel T. Browne described it as "standing upon the centre of the turret, and a miniature of it." "Twelve funnel-shaped eyeholes nearly five feet above the floor of the pilot-house . . . converged from . . . the large diameter inside, to an aperture an inch on the outside."[2] The improved pilothouse moved with the turret and was large enough to give the captain, pilot, and helmsman a good view of the events around them. This design also enhanced fire control and communications with other sections of the ship. Other improvements included a blower system that brought air into the vessel and a permanent smoke exhaust pipe.[3]

Assistant Secretary Fox specified that each *Passaic*-class vessel be armed with at least one XV-inch Dahlgren shell gun capable of taking on and defeating Confederate casemate ironclads. Fox had witnessed the XV-inch Rodman shell gun (nicknamed the "Lincoln gun") at Fort Monroe shortly after the ironclad engagement on 9 March 1862, and he challenged Capt. John A. Dahlgren, chief of the Navy's Bureau of Ordnance, to design a similar gun for the new *Passaic* class. A piece of ordnance this large posed problems in casting as well as placement within the confines of a turret.

Dahlgren had already developed and fabricated safe shell guns for the Navy capable of firing shot and shell, and he could cast and drill IX-inch, X-inch, and XI-inch versions. He realized that larger calibers than that could not be drilled out, so he decided to use the "core-barrel" casting process developed by West Point graduate Thomas Jackson Rodman. The gun was cast hollow and cooled inside by jets of cold water or air. Rodman envisioned the "casting as an outward succession of concentric rings that, in turn, would solidify and shrink. Each shrinkage would compress the cooler layers within, producing compression stresses to oppose firing pressers."[4] A specially modified version would have to be designed to fit within the confined space of a *Passaic*-class monitor.

The XV-inch Dahlgren would become the most powerful and effective smoothbore naval gun of the war. Dahlgren's tests proved that a shot from this huge gun could penetrate a 4.5-inch iron plate. The XV-inch gun weighed 42,000 pounds and could throw a 440-pound shell 2,100 yards. But it was huge. The barrel had to be shortened to fit inside a monitor turret. Even so, a ten-man crew was needed to load, fire, clean, and reload it. Consequently, it could be fired only every seven to eleven minutes.

Since the new XV-inch guns had limited availability, the second gun in the *Passaic*-class turrets would be an XI-inch Dahlgren. The use of XV-inch guns was problematic in other ways as well. The guns were mounted flush with the gun ports because the 26.5-inch-diameter muzzle was too large for the barrels to protrude out of the ports. The large volume of propellant gases released within the turret at each firing required the addition of a smoke box to capture the gases. The smoke box was built of iron plate and bolted to the turret's interior. It covered the port shutter and muzzle of the gun when not in battle conditions. The box was open at the top to allow the noxious fumes to escape through the turret's grated roof. A sliding iron plate with an opening for the gun would encircle and loosely enclose its narrow end while in battery and move up and down to allow for the full range of muzzle elevation. When the gun was run in for loading, the muzzle disengaged from the counterweighted sliding plate. Sectional handles for the gun tools could then be extended through the inner and outer smoke box openings and screwed together to achieve the full length required to service the gun.[5] Worden later recommended that this cumbersome device be removed and the gun port enlarged to accommodate a full-length XV-inch gun. The smoke box system prevented the gun crew from looking down the barrel to aim the gun, so they had to aim the XV-incher using the turret's XI-inch gun.[6]

On 8 October 1862 John Worden was detached from special duty at the Brooklyn Navy Yard and detailed to command *Montauk*, the second of the *Passaic*-class monitors. Like *Monitor*, it had been constructed at Greenpoint's Continental Iron Works. Delamater Iron Works in Manhattan built the engine. *Montauk* was launched at 10 a.m. on 9 October under the watchful eyes—now considered well enough for sea duty—of Commander Worden and was commissioned on 14 December.[7]

Worden meanwhile continued to receive laurels for his command of *Monitor*. On 8 December President Abraham Lincoln recommended to Congress that Commander Worden be promoted to captain for his heroic service at the Battle of Hampton Roads. Congress responded by passing a joint resolution tendering the thanks of Congress and promoting Worden to captain for his "highly distinguished conduct in conflict with the enemy, in the remarkable battle between the United States iron-clad steamer 'Monitor,' under his command, and the rebel iron-clad frigate 'Merrimack.' "[8]

The awards were fulfilling, but after *Montauk* arrived at the Brooklyn Navy Yard Worden focused on his current assignment. He had much to accomplish before heading south. The crew he had assembled, which included Paymaster Browne, were thrilled to serve under Worden, "whose gallant fight had restored a nation's confidence." Historians consider Browne's selection a happy choice as well because his vivid descriptions of *Montauk* in action add life to the log's sparse details. When he boarded *Montauk* at the Brooklyn Navy Yard, Browne thought the new design "in every point . . . much an improvement upon the *Monitor*." He added that he "watched the fitting out of this vessel in which we were to venture to sea, and by which we hoped to strike an effective blow to preserve the Union."[9]

Even before *Montauk* was commissioned, Worden received contradictory orders regarding where to take the new ironclad. On 29 December, Acting Rear Adm. Samuel Phillips Lee, commander of the North Atlantic Blockading Squadron at Hampton Roads, sent a confidential order to Worden telling him to proceed to Beaufort, North Carolina. Four days later, Secretary of the Navy Welles ordered *Montauk* to proceed to Hampton Roads, where Worden was to report to Lee for further instructions. Welles had two goals in mind for 1863.[10] Initially, he wanted to use the *Passaic* monitors to participate in a joint Army-Navy operation against Confederate blockade runners based in Wilmington, North Carolina. Welles wanted the ironclads to go through the Cape Fear River's Old Inlet to bombard the forts defending the river's entrance and, with Army units commanded by Gen. John G. Foster, capture Wilmington. But he dropped that idea when he learned that the new monitors' draft of eleven feet, six inches prevented them from entering the Cape Fear River. Once Welles was apprised of that, he began to focus on his other goal: the capture or destruction of that "evil bed of secession," Charleston, South Carolina.[11]

Southbound Again

On 23 December 1862 Worden took *Montauk* out of the Brooklyn Navy Yard to an anchorage off Sandy Hook, where lines were attached to *Connecticut*, a powerful Union sidewheeler capable of making ten knots, to tow *Montauk* south. *Montauk* left New York on Christmas Eve. Browne recalled that "there was no sea, but the short, 'choppy' waves, as we steamed into them, would overflow our deck."[12] The waves forced water into every crevice at the ship's bow. After seventeen hours careening through the heavy seas, *Montauk*'s bow was filled with water, but there were no forward pumps to remove it. Accordingly, *Connecticut* and *Montauk* anchored at Cape Henlopen Light near Lewes, Delaware, on 25 December. *Montauk*'s stern was riding higher now because the coal bunker had been reduced during the voyage, so Worden trimmed the vessel by having some crewmembers shift shot and ballast while others bailed out the ship. *Connecticut* and *Montauk* waited for better weather and put to sea again on 28 December and shaped a course to Hampton Roads.[13]

Montauk arrived off Fort Monroe at 11 a.m. on 29 December 1862. Several other Union warships were already present in Hampton Roads, including the ironclads *Passaic, Galena, New Ironsides,* and *Monitor*. Browne was pleased to see "the *Monitor*—to which our gray-eyed commander called our attention as we came in, and told us of its famous fight."[14] *Monitor*'s crew, many of whom had served under Worden during the 9 March 1862 engagement against *Virginia*, had hoped to see their former commander again, but that was not to be. *Monitor*, towed by *Rhode Island*, left Hampton Roads at 2 p.m. that afternoon, ran into heavy weather off Cape Hatteras, and sank.

Workers from the Gosport Navy Yard repaired *Montauk*'s leaks, and on 2 January 1863 the sidewheeler *James Alger* towed *Montauk* out of the Roads and set out for Beaufort, North Carolina. Worden reported that on "the passage from Hampton Roads the weather was exceptionally fine and the water smooth, except off Cape Hatteras, where I encountered a heavy swell from the northward and eastward, which caused the ship to roll considerably, taking water in large quantities on her deck."[15]

Paymaster Browne later wrote a colorful description of the storm—the tail end of the storm that sank *Monitor*:

> The seas swept across our decks like a deluge.... [I]t seemed we were having the latter and lesser half of the storm. Signals were exchanged from our turret and the paddle-boxes of *James Alger*. The ghastly light thrown by the signals out of the darkness upon the seething crests of the waves; the roaring of the sea as it dashed against the ship and turret and submerged the hull; a cold spray thrust by the wind against our faces... and we on this little tower... with not even the ship's deck, nine feet below us, in sight more than half the time... made it an experience never to be desired again.[16]

The *Passaic* class suffered from the same flaw as *Monitor*: the armored deck overhung the hull, allowing heavy seas to work in between the hull and deck. Browne remembered that "big seas came under our overhang as if they would rip it from its solid union with the hull, and with a shock that made the vessel tremble from stem to stern."[17]

The weather improved once *Montauk* passed Cape Hatteras, and the ironclad neared Beaufort at 7:30 a.m. on 4 January 1863. A pilot came on board to guide *Montauk* into Bogue Sound, and Worden cast off from *James Alger*. Unfortunately, the pilot took *Montauk* inside the channel marker, and the ironclad ran aground in ten and a half feet of water. Shot, shell, and ballast were removed to lighten the ship, and by 5 p.m., with high tide and the assistance of the paddler *Miami* and two Army tugs, *Montauk* was off the shoal. An hour later it was anchored off Fort Macon. A careful survey showed Worden that the grounding had not damaged the hull.[18]

Montauk remained in Beaufort until 17 January 1863, when *James Alger* towed the ironclad south to Port Royal Sound, South Carolina. Several other warships, including *Wabash*, *Vermont*, and *New Ironsides*, were present when *Montauk* arrived. Rear Adm. Samuel Francis Du Pont, commander of the South Atlantic Blockading Squadron, was collecting an ironclad fleet to implement Welles' plan to assault Charleston. Before attacking the cradle of secession, however, he wanted to test the endurance and firepower of the new monitors. Who better to do so than Commander Worden? Accordingly, Du Pont detailed Worden to take *Montauk* "down to Ossabaw to operate up the Ogeechee River and capture if he could the fort at Genesis Point under the cover of which ... the *Nashville* was lying ... and in case of success, the railroad [which] was also accessible."[19]

Montauk Tested

Worden's main target, Fort McAllister, was twelve miles south of Savannah at Genesis Point near the mouth of the Big Ogeechee River. The fort, built of marsh mud and sand by Georgia troops under the supervision of Confederate engineer Capt. John McCrady, was designed to guard the river against any Union advance and to protect the Big Ogeechee crossing of the Savannah and Florida Railroad to the west. Fort McAllister mounted eleven heavy seacoast guns, including a 10-inch seacoast mortar, an VIII-inch shell gun, a 10-inch Columbiad, a 42-pounder, and three 32-pounders. It also had twelve field pieces to guard the fort's land face and was protected by piles and torpedoes defending the channel.[20] Paymaster Browne was impressed by the "massive proportions of the fortification, its banks covered with rich green sod, and the muzzles of the guns just visible, pointing at us from heavily protected embrasures. Between the guns ... traverses extended back into the rear, effectively covering the guns from enfilading fire."[21]

Bad weather kept Worden in Port Royal Sound until 21 January, when *James Alger* was finally able to tow it out of the sound. When Worden reached Ossabaw Sound, Georgia, on 24 January, he assumed command of a small blockading flotilla that included the *Unadilla*-class screw-propeller wooden gunboats *Wissahickon* and *Seneca*. Each had a 114-man crew and carried one XI-inch Dahlgren and one 20-pounder rifle. The two other ships in his command were *Dana*, with two 32-pounders and one 20-pounder rifle, and the mortar schooner *C. P. Williams*, armed with one 13-inch seacoast mortar and two 32-pounders.[22] The squadron had already attempted three attacks against Fort McAllister, and all had failed. Du Pont believed that *Montauk* would make the difference. Worden was determined to fulfill that confidence.

Once in Ossabaw Sound, Browne noted, "our vessel was now entirely cleared for fighting trim. From stem to stern not a rope or chain, or a bolt, in

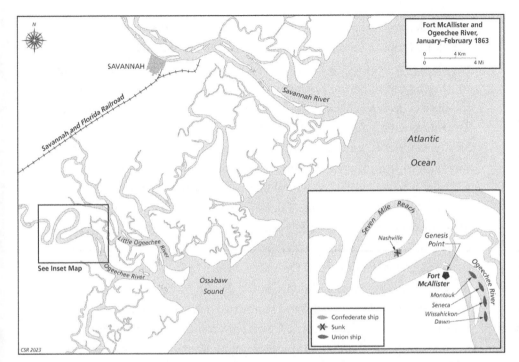

Map 3 Fort McAllister and Ogeechee River, January–February 1863

sight, nothing but the round turret and big smoke stack. Nothing remained to be done in case of sudden action but to close the battle hatches. . . . An armed watch was stationed on deck, and the battle rattle laid in one of the turret ports, ready for immediate use by the officer of the deck." Just as he had been on *Monitor,* Worden was concerned that *Montauk* was vulnerable to a boarding attempt by Confederates on a cutting-out expedition, so he provided his crew with small arms to repel attacks.

When the fog finally lifted on 26 January, *Montauk* and the flotilla moved up the Big Ogeechee, guided by a Georgia pilot named Murphy. Browne described the river as "narrow, and very crooked." Only later did Browne understand the danger of his situation: "A vessel of war of such type as the world had never before seen, vulnerable only in her hull below the water, steaming up a narrow, tortuous river, with the assurance that in its bed were torpedoes, the slightest touch to explode them, and containing powder sufficient to destroy a dozen vessels like our own—was a realization the full import of which we could not then comprehend."[23]

Worden anchored his force about a mile below the fort and sent Lt. Cdr. John Davis to reconnoiter the Confederate defenses. Davis was able to remove Confederate range markers and indicate an anchorage for *Montauk* to use when shelling the earthwork, but he could not get close enough to the obstructions to check them for torpedoes (as mines were then called). Torpedoes were a new Confederate weapon designed by Matthew Fontaine Maury, Gabriel Rains, and Hunter Davidson to protect the South's waterways against the advance of Union ships. The Confederate Navy organized a Torpedo Bureau and a Naval Submarine Battery Service to produce and manage these new tools of war. The torpedoes of the time were rather crude weapons made from wooden kegs coated with tar for waterproofing or tin/copper and filled with gunpowder ignited by a contact device or an electric current activated from shore.[24] On 12 December 1862, while participating in the Chickasaw Bayou Expedition clearing the river of torpedoes, the Union City-class casemate ironclad *Cairo* struck two electronically denoted torpedoes and sank in twelve minutes. Union ship commanders rightfully feared the new weapons. Worden was quite aware of *Montauk*'s thin one-inch iron hull and knew that his ship and the others in his small squadron needed to be aware of this very real danger.

Worden got his squadron under way at 7 a.m. on 27 January and took up the positions Davis had selected. The anchorage Davis had selected was around 300 yards from the pilings and about 1,500 yards from Fort McAllister. *Montauk* opened fire at 7:35 a.m. with two shots. The fort immediately replied, with its first shot striking the ironclad. A strong breeze kicked up at about 9 a.m., altering the flight of the ironclad's shot and shell. When *Montauk* turned with the changing tide, the smoke from the fort's guns blew back across the Union ships, also disrupting their aim. Worden noted at "11:55 a.m., our supply of shells being expended, and finding our cored shot did not affect the enemy, or at least we could not observe their effect with certainty, I ordered the firing to cease, tripped our anchor, and stood down river, and ordered the gunboats to discontinue the action."[25]

Once away from the fort, Worden surveyed *Montauk* for damage. His "vessel was hit fourteen times, to wit, four times on the turret, three times on side armor, four times on deck armor, once on smokestack, once in second cutter, and once on a spar lashed athwart our stern as a stern mooring for our boats."[26] Fort McAllister suffered only minor damage, and the garrison claimed to have achieved a great victory in repulsing the Union naval attack.

Many Union leaders had assumed that it would be a simple affair for *Montauk* to take the Confederate earthwork at Genesis Point, because ironclads had previously been very successful in overwhelming fixed fortifications such as Fort Henry and Island No. 10 in the Western Theater. While naval combat during the Civil War eventually proved the power of ironclads over land defenses, in the case of Fort McAllister, one monitor with only two shell guns did not possess the means to take the earthwork. The fort was situated on a point at the bend of a narrow river and was protected by obstructions and torpedoes. McAllister had to be destroyed before Union ships could proceed upriver, and Worden knew that this would not be easily achieved with his available resources. Nevertheless, as always, he was determined to do his utmost to fulfill his orders despite the odds against success.

The next day, 28 January, Worden met with a contraband river pilot, a freedman, who advised him about the position of the pilings below the fort and the location of torpedoes in the channel. Armed with this information, Worden could bring his ironclad closer to the fort. He took the man on board to serve as a pilot and servant. The log does not include the man's name, perhaps because he was not an official member of the crew. William Keeler, *Monitor*'s paymaster, wrote to his wife about his new servant, whom he referred to as "contraband." Although the man is mentioned in several of those letters, Keeler never gives his name. Keeler is known to have had deep antislavery sentiments, so this omission is a sad statement about existing prejudices during the Civil War era.[27]

Maj. Gen. Benjamin Franklin Butler's May 1861 "Contraband of War Decision" and Lincoln's January 1863 Emancipation Proclamation gave many newly freed people of African descent a way to support the Union war effort. While the U.S. Army refused Black enlistees until 1863, the Navy had maintained an open door for enlisted recruitment since the American Revolution. Men of color had long sought service in U.S. warships as a method of personal advancement. Approximately 10 to 15 percent of Union warship crews serving in Southern waters were African Americans. Escapees often volunteered their knowledge of local terrain to guide Union forces through the vast marshes and waterways along the southern Atlantic coast.

On 29 and 31 January 1863 the sidewheeler tug *Daffodil* replenished the flotilla's ammunition, and on 30 January Worden sent Lt. Cdr. William Gibson with *Seneca* up the Big Ogeechee to survey Fort McAllister. Gibson also took a look up the Little Ogeechee to ascertain the whereabouts of CSS *Nashville*. He reported back to Worden that the minor damage to McAllister's earthworks had been repaired and that *Nashville* remained in its same location.[28]

Worden called his gunboat officers together in the early evening on 31 January to arrange the next day's plan of action, and at 4 a.m. the flotilla got under way with *Montauk* in the lead. The ironclad anchored six hundred yards below the Confederate battery on the riverbank, as close to the shoal as it could get, and opened fire on Fort McAllister. The thick mist over the marsh combined with the smoke from the fort's guns obstructed the view, and, Worden reported, "We could neither see their position nor the effect of our own shells."[29] The Confederates opened fire as soon as they realized that the Union flotilla had arrived, but they too were hindered by the poor visibility, and the fire from both forces slackened.

Montauk's turret took a hit just before 8 a.m. An hour later, the tide began falling. A sounding reported the depth as about fourteen feet, and Worden knew it would continue to drop another five feet. With *Montauk*'s draft of 11 feet, 6 inches, Worden had no choice but to move his vessel downriver into deeper water, increasing the range to the fort to 1,400 feet. *Montauk* continued its bombardment nevertheless, but the cannonade was only tearing up the earthen parapets and traverses and not damaging the Confederate artillery. Having concluded that he could not inflict significant damage, Worden broke off the action at 11:53 a.m.

Fort McAllister had suffered more damage than Worden realized. The fort's commander, Col. Robert H. Anderson, reported that the "enemy fired steadily and with remarkable precision. At times their fire was terrible."[30] The bombardment had focused on the VIII-inch Columbiad and destroyed its parapet. A shell from *Montauk* hit one of the fort's 32-pounders, knocking off its trunnion and blowing the brains out of the gun commander, Maj. John B. Gallie. He was the only Confederate casualty.

The Confederates' fire had been accurate as well. Worden reported that forty-eight shots and shells had struck *Montauk*: "sixteen times on the turret, three times on the pilothouse, seven times on the smokestack, seven times on the side armor and had two flagstaffs shot away." Browne noted the Confederate guns made "scores of indentations on our turret and pilothouse; broke off some of the bolts and drove them inside—two of them, had passed within three inches of my head."[31]

After *Monitor*'s battle with *Virginia*, the monitors' pilothouse had been redesigned to enhance visibility and communications during combat, but Worden would later recommend that mantelettes (nut guards) and more armor be added to future pilothouses to protect those inside. He knew the dangers of an exposed pilothouse firsthand. Despite the constant reminder of his wounded eyes, Worden nevertheless continued to show fortitude, bravery, and determination by standing firm in *Montauk*'s pilothouse during its engagements.

Worden ordered *Montauk*'s chief engineer, Second Assistant Engineer Thomas A. Stephens, to compile a report detailing conditions on board the ironclad during the two engagements. After the 27 January attack, Stephens noted that the temperatures within the engine room had averaged about 103 degrees during the battle. Following the 1 February battle, he was critical of the vessel's operations and construction. His conclusions about *Montauk*'s material and workmanship were damning: "Having examined the broken bolts and injured plates of iron . . . that the broken bolts from the pilothouse are of inferior quality of iron, showing in large fractured crystals, and are cold short. . . . [T]hey have been improperly fitted, either for strength or safety."[32]

Stephens' damage survey also found that all of the "bolts fit loosely, depending on the heads and nuts, which are screwed up rigidly, causing them to part by concussion of the plates outside and endangering the lives of those inside. . . . The deck iron plates are fractured in several places, as well as those of the outside armor." Worden forwarded this report, along with his own, to Admiral Du Pont as a contribution to the admiral's experiment to ascertain how the *Passaic*-class monitors could withstand shot. Clearly, this new class had numerous flaws. Nevertheless, Du Pont assembled his ships to make a fifth attempt on Fort McAllister. Worden's command moved up the Big Ogeechee and anchored below the fort on 27 February.[33] Captain Worden was determined to use *Montauk* to inflict the greatest possible damage upon the Confederates.

Photo 9.1 Worden stands on the deck of *Montauk* with Fort McAllister in the background
The Mariners' Museum 1934.1044.000001

Rattlesnake Is Doomed

The paddlewheel privateer *Nashville* sitting upriver beyond Fort McAllister was another target of interest. *Nashville* had been one of the Confederacy's first commerce raiders and had long evaded capture by the Union Navy. Commerce raiding was an important part of Confederate secretary of the navy Stephen Mallory's approach to winning the war at sea. Mallory wanted to strike at Union shipping on the high seas and disrupt the North's economy by destroying its merchant marine. He believed that a fleet of fast, lightly armed commerce raiders striking heavily laden merchant vessels would weaken the North's resolve to wage war. The Union Navy was forced to take ships away from the blockade to track down and destroy the raiders. *Nashville* was one of the first raiders sent to strike at Northern shipping. The paddle-wheelers' notoriety was greatly enhanced by later raiders such as CSS *Alabama*.

In November 1861, while en route from Charleston to Southampton, England, *Nashville* captured and burned the Union merchant ship *Harvey Birch* in the English Channel. After *Nashville* reached Southampton, a Royal Navy warship recognized its Confederate flag and, under the British Act of Neutrality, enabled it to escape the Union blockader *Tuscarora*. During the return trip to Beaufort, North Carolina, *Nashville* captured and destroyed the merchant vessel *Robert Gilfillan*. *Nashville* was then sold to Fraser, Trenholm and Company and served as a blockade runner under the name *Thomas L. Wragg*. After two successful runs, *Wragg* was trapped near Savannah. A group of investors acquired the ship to serve as a privateer and renamed it *Rattlesnake*, although it continued to be known as *Nashville* in the North.[34] The raider was a constant menace, and Du Pont was determined to destroy it. He wrote to Gideon Welles that *Nashville* was "proverbially fast, and doubtless rivaled the *Alabama* or *Oreto* [CSS *Florida*] in their depredation on our commerce. I have never lost sight of the great importance of keeping her in or destroying her if I could."[35]

The task of destroying *Nashville* fell on the shoulders of Capt. John Lorimer Worden. Although he had other missions to perform in the Big Ogeechee, he leapt at the opportunity to take out the Confederate privateer. Paymaster Browne once again recorded a vivid picture of the events. *Nashville* had been sitting "under the guns of Fort Allister, intending to take advantage of the spring tides prevailing then and seize the first opportunity to slip to sea. But we had been waiting for this moment. She reminded me of a caged rat seeking a hole for escape and finding none."[36]

Wissahickon's lookout was the first to spot *Nashville* coming down the Big Ogeechee. Stephens, *Montauk*'s senior engineer, recounted, "At 4:08 p.m., while at dinner, the rebel steamer was reported in sight. All hands were called to quarters at once."[37] Worden sent *Seneca* upriver to investigate, and *Seneca* reported that *Nashville* had run aground in the Seven-Mile Reach section of the river. Since it was so late in the day, Worden decided to move against the ship and the fort the next morning.

Early the next morning, *Montauk*, followed by *Seneca*, *Wissahickon*, and *Dawn*, moved to their designated positions below the fort. Worden thought that by "moving up close to the obstructions in the river as I was able, although under heavy fire from the battery, to approach *Nashville*, still aground within a distance of 1,200 yards."[38] *New York Herald* correspondent Bradley Osbon reported that *Nashville* "lay, hard and fast aground, the hasty unloading and sturdy labors of the little tug, which had been going on through the night, having failed to relieve her. She was a fair mark and knew that she was doomed."[39] Browne noted that those in *Montauk*'s pilothouse could "see the whole steamer. . . . She is newly painted, and is the same light drab colors as our own vessels of war. Her masts and spars look well, her rigging is taut, and her figurehead newly gilded."[40]

At 7:07 a.m. Worden fired on the privateer with the XV- and XI-inch Dahlgrens to establish the range. The fifth shot from *Montauk*'s XV-inch shell gun struck *Nashville* at 7:58. Browne recorded every shot the fort fired against *Montauk* and every shot the ironclad fired at the rebel ship, noting that they could see the fifth shot from *Montauk*'s XV-inch Dahlgren and "follow it distinctly with our eyes, and it penetrates the rebel's deck near the foremast." Browne saw that the shot "has done its work and we can see a column of whitish-gray smoke from her fore-hatch, and in five minutes more tongues of flames leap out with the smoke, high into the air."[41]

Under heavy fire from Fort McAllister, Worden sent fourteen shots at *Nashville*. Browne continued to detail the impact of *Montauk*'s gunnery: "Another shell smashes through the paddle-box, and explodes at the base of the smoke-stack, which comes tumbling down." The last shot was fired at 8:03 a.m., "and as the smoke clears away from our last shot, we can see the flames bursting out around her paddle-boxes, issuing in great sheets from the fore-hatch, creeping up the foremast rigging, and gaining aft."[42] Worden moved *Montauk* a short distance away and watched the privateer burn. At 9:20 a large pivot gun forward of the foremast dramatically exploded, and

Photo 9.2 *Rattlesnake* [*Nashville*] burning after being shelled by *Montauk*. Fort McAllister is in the right-center background. *Naval History and Heritage Command NH 59286*

at 9:55 *Nashville*'s magazine erupted, leaving the Confederate privateer a smoking ruin. Worden had used his shot-proof ship and the most modern ordnance technology the Navy owned to prove the power of iron over wood. Wooden paddlewheel steamers had virtually no chance to defeat a monitor in ship-to-ship duels.

Once he was certain that *Nashville* was doomed, Worden took his flotilla down the river and out of range of the fort's guns. At 9:35, there was "a violent, sudden and seemingly double explosion" on *Montauk*.[43] At first Worden thought that a shell had entered the engine room, and he feared the boilers might explode and send deadly steam throughout the ironclad. *Montauk* began to take on water. The bilge pumps countered the inflow for a while, but when the water rose six inches in the engine room, Worden ordered the bilge injection pump started and called for a bucket line and handpumps to be readied. On learning that a torpedo exploding beneath the ship had caused the damage, Worden ordered the pilot, Murphy, to beach the vessel on an even keel in the marsh mud to form a temporary seal. The next news Worden learned was even worse. The explosion had fractured the hull, creating a quarter-inch opening to the outside. Permanent repairs being impossible, a temporary fix was made using oakum before high tide lifted *Montauk* off the mud bank. The engines were started at 3 p.m., and the wounded ironclad steamed down to Ossabaw Sound.

En route to the sound, *Montauk* passed the *Passaic*-class monitor *Nahant*, which was commanded by Worden's good friend Cdr. John Downes. Ship's boy Alvah Hunter recalled that as the two ships steamed by each other, Worden exhibited a "boy-like enthusiasm . . . [that] was very manifest as he called across the narrow space between the two vessels. . . . Worden fairly danced up and down with enthusiasm as he told of the jolly-good-time he had enjoyed."[44]

Montauk returned to Port Royal and spent the entire month of March 1863 in naval workshops. Engineer Stephens provided Worden with a report on the torpedo damage and other issues on board the ironclad, adding, "I feel bound to complain in the name of and for all engaged in the engine department of these vessels the indifference, negligence, manifested in the construction of the machinery and hull by builders to the lives and well-being of those necessarily engaged below hatches in the engine room."[45] In his opinion, mechanical flaws caused by poor design, materials, and workmanship had amplified the torpedo's effects. He blamed shoddy workmanship in Northern shipyards due to "unreasoning avarice, if that be an excuse." Worden was no engineer, and his lack of specialized mechanical skills may have caused him to overlook problems with *Montauk*'s engines and fittings, but he agreed with Stephens. When he forwarded Stephens' report to Du Pont he noted, "This is, in my opinion . . . so serious a flaw that I beg leave to urge that a remedy may be applied if possible."[46]

When Du Pont reported *Nashville*'s destruction to Secretary Welles, he credited the "quick perception and rapid execution of Commander Worden, who has thus added to his already brilliant services."[47] Worden once again received national press coverage. He was proud that *Montauk* had achieved "the final disposition of a vessel which had long been in the minds of the public as a troublesome pest" because of his determined and decisive actions.[48] He was proud also that his quick thinking helped to save his ship after it struck the torpedo. Few other ironclad commanders would have been able to do that under such circumstances. Yet again, Worden was quick to note that he was just "doing his duty."

CHAPTER 10

INTO THE RING OF FIRE

The destruction of *Nashville* on 27 February 1863 was welcome news in the war-weary North. Nevertheless, when the battle smoke cleared, a dismayed Worden had an ominous report to present to the South Atlantic Blockade Squadron's commander, Rear Adm. Samuel Francis Du Pont. While his flotilla had sunk the notorious *Nashville*, *Montauk* had been unable to achieve its other goals of reducing Fort McAllister and destroying the nearby Savannah and Florida Railroad bridge. These were key strategic objects whose loss could have hastened the war's conclusion. One monitor, Worden said, with its limited firepower, was simply not up to these tasks.

Improving Monitor Designs

Worden's experience working on the *Passaic*-class monitors as an assistant to Rear Adm. Francis Hoyt Gregory, combined with his command of *Montauk*, helped him identify significant flaws in the *Passaics*. He had told Rear Admiral Du Pont after the Fort McAllister action that *Montauk*'s slow rate of fire (one shot every seven to ten minutes) could not match the firepower from Confederates' land-based heavy guns. *Passaic*-class monitors needed more effective guns and ordnance and better aiming if they were to crush the opposition. The XV-inch 440-pound solid shots and 330-pound shells could penetrate soft marsh mud and sand, but they did not seriously damage Fort McAllister's hardened mud walls. Worden recommended replacing the XI-inch Dahlgren with a 100- or 150-pounder Parrott rifle, which he believed would prove more effective at damaging the Confederates' earthen and masonry forts. He also pointed out that ships alone could not defeat fixed fortifications. Their guns could damage forts, but infantry was needed to secure their capture.

During its operations up the Big Ogeechee River, *Montauk* had been hammered by Fort McAllister's heavy shot. While monitor turrets had adequate iron protection to withstand such fire, the vessels had other armor deficiencies. The link between the turret and its pivoting machinery, for example, could easily be jammed by solid shot, so an iron ring should be added to protect this vulnerable spot. The pilothouse was extremely exposed to enemy gunners and needed additional armor equal to the turret's. Likewise, the deck armor was only one inch of iron plate and was subject to significant damage from plunging shot. The thin hull armor (one-inch iron plate) made the *Passaic* monitors vulnerable to Confederate torpedoes, as Worden had learned the hard way when *Montauk* struck a torpedo in the Big Ogeechee River after destroying *Nashville*. The torpedo explosion made him aware that if a boiler burst, there was no effective escape plan to protect crewmembers from scalding. In addition, once bolts and nuts holding the turret's iron plate together were damaged, a turret's overall resistance to shot was weakened. Worden concluded by stating that *Passaic*-class monitors were too slow, a fact that lessened their steering qualities, especially in strong currents. Worden also forwarded the report of *Montauk*'s engineer, Thomas Stephens, concerning mechanical flaws and other evidence of poor workmanship.[1]

Du Pont forwarded Worden's report of his experiences at Fort McAllister to his superiors along with his own conclusions:

> My own previous impressions of these vessels, frequently expressed to Assistant Secretary Fox, have been confirmed, viz: that whatever degree of impenetrability they might have, there was no corresponding quality of aggression or destructiveness against forts, the slowness of fire giving full time for the gunners in the Fort to take shelter in the bombard proofs. ... This experiment also convinces me of another impression, firmly held and often expressed, that in all such operations, to secure success, troops are necessary.[2]

Now convinced that the monitors' slow rate of fire, slow speed (seven knots), poor steering qualities, unreliable engines, and limited fire power rendered them unfit to attack the harbor defenses of Charleston, Du Pont tried to persuade his superiors. Unfortunately for the admiral, Welles and Fox refused to be swayed from their belief that monitors were perfectly designed to assault forts.[3]

Despite all the problems and faults Du Pont and Worden pointed out, the monitor-building program continued at a rapid pace. Eventually, fifty-one monitors, unmodified from their original design, were laid down. Du Pont lamented to Fox, "But, oh! The errors of details, which could have been corrected if these men of genius could be induced to pay attention to the people who are to use their tests & inventions."[4]

While many politicians were convinced that the ironclads were super-weapons and the key to victory, those who served in them knew better. Nevertheless, it was politicians and those with a financial stake in the venture who dictated what type and how many new ironclads the Navy would construct. At the beginning of the war, the U.S. Navy had rushed to meet its new commitments to enforce the blockade and capture Southern ports. The urgency to use new technology to achieve victory enriched many, and politicians saw the monitor program as a way for private yards and foundries to flourish during the war. Many entrepreneurs took advantage of this situation and used their wealth and political connections to reap financial rewards.

John Ericsson's ironclad and subsequent monitor classes were built because of the wealth and political influence of his partners: Cornelius Scranton Bushnell, John Augustus Griswold, and John Flack Winslow. Bushnell's friendship with Gideon Welles provided him with access to President Abraham Lincoln. Winslow, a good friend of Secretary of State William H. Seward, told Ericsson on 2 January 1862 that if *Monitor* proved successful, he could guarantee twenty more ironclads would be built. Griswold continued to be a major financial backer and political supporter of Ericsson's new monitor classes. Griswold was elected to Congress in 1863 and served on the House Committee for the Conduct of Naval Affairs. Because of these connections, Ericsson did not have to lobby for new ironclad contracts. They fell into his lap.[5]

CHAPTER 10

Like a Cul-de-Sac

Du Pont's report was exactly what Welles and Fox did not want to hear. Fox in particular was determined to punish Charleston, the home of the rebellion. Maj. Gen. John G. Foster believed Charleston could be easily captured if the Navy supported Army actions to capture Morris and James Islands. Fox rejected this notion out of hand. He wanted the Navy to receive complete credit. "I feel my duties are twofold," Fox wrote to Du Pont. "First, to beat our Southern friends; second, to beat the army."[6] Consequently, Du Pont had no other option but to attack Charleston. Taking the city would be no easy task.

The Confederate fortifications surrounding Charleston were indeed comprehensive. Gen. P. G. T. Beauregard had begun developing defensive fortifications immediately after the Confederates took Fort Sumter in April 1861.

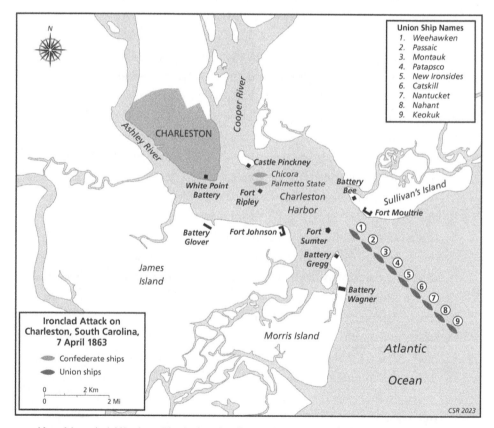

Map 4 Ironclad Attack on Charleston, South Carolina, 7 April 1863

When Beauregard was called away for other duties, Maj. Gen. John C. Pemberton and Brig. Gen. Roswell S. Ripley continued expanding the defenses until Beauregard returned in September 1862 as commander of the Department of South Carolina, Georgia, and Florida.

Beauregard knew that the Union fleet in Port Royal Sound would attack Charleston in spring 1863, and he made all the arrangements he considered necessary to repel them. Three rings of fortifications protected Charleston. The outer ring consisted of Battery Wagner and Battery Gregg on Morris Island, Fort Sumter on an artificial island in the middle of the harbor's entrance, and Fort Moultrie with supporting batteries on Sullivan's Island. The main shipping channel passed between Fort Sumter and Fort Moultrie, and the Confederates had placed obstructions and torpedoes to block any attempts to bypass the forts.

The floating barricade initially was railroad iron with chained logs anchored at intervals. Strong tides destroyed much of the original barrier, so two rows of netting were strung across the broken wooden boom. Fifteen-foot rope tentacles were added to the netting to entangle propellers. Floating barrels that Union spies thought might be torpedoes supported the rope obstructions.[7] Fort Johnson and Battery Glover were on James Island, Fort Ripley and Castle Pinckney were in the harbor, and White Point Battery was at the city's south end. These defenses were further protected by the ironclads CSS *Chicora* and CSS *Palmetto State*. The inner ring consisted of batteries on the Ashley and Cooper Rivers built to guard against land assault.[8]

Charleston's harbor was a cul-de-sac. Once past the outer ring and into the inner harbor, the Union ships would be surrounded by menacing batteries. The outer ring alone had more than 130 heavy guns. Fort Sumter mounted 76 cannons, including 10-inch Columbiads, 7-inch Brooke rifles, and 10-inch mortars. The guns of Battery Bee (on Sullivan's Island), Fort Moultrie, and Fort Sumter were focused on a red buoy, Confederate No. 3, 1,200 yards from the obstructions. The Confederates had placed their most powerful seacoast guns in position to fire on the invading ships to create a two-thousand-yard "wall of fire to reach the obstructions."[9] Beauregard believed that no ship—iron or wooden—could pass through the ring of fire and survive; the gauntlet was simply impassable. The Confederates were prepared to have this cauldron of fire tested at any time.

Worden, meanwhile, brought the torpedo-damaged *Montauk* back to Port Royal Sound in early March, and Chief Engineer Alban Stimers and his team gave it a close examination. Stimers recommended beaching the vessel and applying an iron patch to repair the torpedo damage properly, which he estimated would take ten days. The Port Royal Sound Naval Station was prepared to make the repair. The station, which had grown dramatically during the war, provided coal and other supplies and a safe anchorage to the South Atlantic Blockading Squadron. The station also operated two temporary monitor maintenance and repair workshops known as the Port Royal Working Parties. The workshop had skilled workers, specialized tools, supplies, and spare parts to effect major modifications, overhauls, and repairs.[10]

Once the repairs were completed, *Montauk* joined Du Pont's other ironclads for the attempt to capture Charleston. Du Pont had no confidence in the operation's success, but he had to follow Fox's plan. Passing the outer ring of the Confederate fortifications would be challenging enough. His goal was to make the attempt and keep his ships from disaster while doing so. He planned for his squadron to remain in motion to upset the enemy's aim and to fire at Fort Sumter's barbette batteries, whose plunging fire was the most dangerous threat to a monitor's thin deck armor.[11]

Du Pont was particularly concerned about the obstructions and torpedoes positioned between Fort Sumter and Sullivan's Island. John Ericsson, who in the eyes of Welles and Fox could do no wrong at this point, designed an antitorpedo raft to resolve Du Pont's fears. The "devil's raft" would be affixed to a monitor's bow with chains and fitted with grapples to remove torpedoes impeding the monitor's course. The raft, which weighed seventy tons, also carried a torpedo to blow a hole through obstructions. Many ironclad commanders feared the raft might flip over and damage their own ships. Only Capt. John Rodgers of *Weehawken* was willing to try the strange contraption—but only without the torpedo.[12]

Into the Ring

Du Pont's squadron of ironclads assembled off Edisto Island on 1 April 1863 and then moved north to the outer Charleston Bar, arriving four days later. Commo. Thomas Turner, commanding *New Ironsides*, had concerns about how his untested ironclad would perform during the attack. *New Ironsides'*

Photo 10.1 *Grand Attack of the Ironclads on Charleston*, 7 April 1863, painting by W. T. Crane, circa 1884 *Library of Congress Digital ID 58726*

15.8-foot draft would give it only a few feet of clearance in Charleston's main channel; its unarmored bow and stern were vulnerable to rifled shot; and it was somewhat unmanageable in shallow water. Further, Turner believed his big ironclad would be the focus of Confederate cannon fire. Turner would have preferred to keep his vessel out of the fight altogether, but Du Pont knew that public opinion demanded the ship's inclusion in the attack.[13]

Captain Rodgers' *Weehawken*, fitted with the torpedo raft, led the assault. It was followed by *Passaic* (Capt. Percival Drayton), *Montauk* (Capt. John L. Worden), and *Patapsco* (Cdr. David Ammen). Next came *New Ironsides* (Commo. Thomas Turner), Du Pont's flagship, carrying the fleet captain, Capt. Christopher Raymond Perry Rodgers. The flagship was followed by *Catskill* (Cdr. George M. Rodgers), *Nantucket* (Cdr. Donald M. Fairfax), and *Nahant* (Cdr. John Downes). The final vessel in line was the tower ironclad *Keokuk* (Cdr. Alexander C. Rhind).[14]

On Saturday, 4 April, Du Pont issued his attack orders:

> The Squadron will pass up the main ship channel without returning the fire of the batteries on Morris Island unless signal should be made to commence action. The ships will open fire on Fort Sumter when within easy range, and will take up a position to the northward and westward of that fortification, engaging its left or northeast face at a distance of

from 600 to 800 yards, firing low and aiming at the center embrasure. The commanding officers will instruct their officers and men to carefully avoid wasting shot and will enjoin upon them the necessity of precision, rather than the rapidity of fire. Each ship will be prepared to render every assistance possible to the vessels that may require it. . . . After the reduction of Fort Sumter, it is probable that the next point of attack will be the batteries on Morris Island. The order of battle will be line ahead. . . . [A] squadron of reserve . . . will be formed outside the bar and near the entrance buoy, consisting of . . . *Canandaigua, Housatonic, Huron, Unadilla, Wissahickon* will be held in readiness to support the ironclads when they attack the batteries on Morris Island.[15]

The squadron assembled off the harbor's entrance the next day. While most of the fleet anchored off the Charleston Bar, Du Pont sent *Keokuk*, supported by *Patapsco* and *Catskill*, to a buoy near the bar to keep the Confederates from moving the marker buoys. The rest of Du Pont's command crossed the bar on April 6 and was prepared to begin the assault, but the pilots refused to proceed because a thick haze masked the critical landmarks they needed for navigation.[16]

On the morning of 7 April, a light breeze blew the haze away, and Du Pont ordered his vessels to get under way at 11 a.m. to take advantage of the slack tide. The ships would be fighting on an ebb tide, which Du Pont believed would float any disabled ironclad away from the Confederate forts. Du Pont knew that he faced a determined and powerful enemy, and he recognized that he would need to improvise as the battle developed. He did not intend to force the attack at the cost of any of his ships. Any ironclad that incurred too much damage was to retreat, and the admiral gave no orders for his ships to pass through the obstructions.

The start was inauspicious. As *Weehawken* led the column toward Fort Sumter, its anchor became fouled in the grapples on the antitorpedo raft at its bow. After a delay of almost two hours, the ships were once again under way. At 12:15 p.m. the ironclads came under fire from Fort Sumter and all the batteries on Sullivan and Morris Islands. *Weehawken* was in trouble from the beginning of the cannonade. The raft slowed the ironclad's speed to 3.5 knots, making it difficult to steer. This slow pace hindered the following ships, and their captains had difficulty maintaining the battle line. The ironclads passed by buoys they recognized as range markers for the Confederate gunners. Some ship commanders thought the buoys marked the location of torpedoes as well.

When *Weehawken* reached the obstructions, Rodgers veered to port because the obstructions appeared "so formidable, that, upon deliberate judgment, I thought it might not be right to entangle the vessel in obstructions which I did not think we could have passed through, and in which we should have been caught."[17] Rodgers turned *Weehawken* seaward to prevent the outgoing tide from forcing it into the obstructions. The torpedoes he feared became reality when an explosion "lifted the vessel a little." Although the torpedo did not damage the ship, *Weehawken* took fifty-three hits from more than a hundred guns during its forty minutes in the fire zone. Heavy shot struck and broke the side armor. Another shot made a hole in the deck, which caused a leak. Bolts were broken, and the turret was temporarily jammed.

Passaic, following in *Weehawken*'s wake, was struck thirty-five times. Its turret was jammed twice, all the iron plates on the upper edge of the turret were broken, and a Brooke bolt badly dented the pilothouse. The XI-inch gun was disabled for more than an hour, and Captain Drayton was able to fire it only four times; the XV-inch got off nine shots.

Worden's *Montauk* avoided major damage during its exchange of fire with the Confederate forts. At 2:10 p.m. Fort Moultrie opened fire on *Montauk*; Fort Sumter followed ten minutes later. Worden moved *Montauk* seven hundred yards away from Fort Sumter and began to bombard the fort's northeastern face, keeping up a deliberate pace of fire. *Montauk* fired seventeen XI-inch solid shot and XV-inch core shot at the fort, but other problems limited the vessel's effectiveness. Worden later described the events: "The flood tide moved the ironclads towards some formidable looking obstructions (which I deemed it highly important to avoid), and the ships turned their head toward the flood and I followed in their wake. I turned toward the fort again, got within about 700 yards of it, and delivered my fire as long as I was able to hold that position; but the tide drifted us, and other vessels being close around me, I again turned to avoid fouling them, still delivering my fire as opportunity occurred."[18] *Montauk* broke off the action after receiving signals from the flagship. By 5:40 p.m. the battle was over and *Montauk* was anchored two and a quarter miles below Fort Sumter. The ironclad had been struck fourteen times by Confederate shot but suffered minimal damage. Three shots struck the turret upper deck plating and smokestack. One of the ship's cutters was lost. One shot hit the pilothouse (with Worden inside) and severely damaged it by loosening several bolts and forcing in the iron plate. The executive officer, Lt. Cdr. Charles Haddock Cushman, noted in the ship's log that the ironclad had been struck twenty-two times. Dents from shell fragments may account for the difference.[19]

Patapsco, following *Montauk*, lost headway and failed to answer its helm. Situated only 1,200 yards from Fort Sumter and 600 yards from Fort Moultrie, *Patapsco* made a good target and was hit forty-seven times. The flagship, *New Ironsides*, next in line, became unmanageable in the shallow water and strong current. The current almost swept *New Ironsides* ashore, and it would not answer its helm. It had already collided with the monitors *Catskill* and *Nahant*, and Turner had to anchor the huge ironclad to avoid running aground. Du Pont signaled the rest of the fleet to disregard the flagship's motions. The temporary anchorage was directly over a 3,000-pound electronic torpedo, which failed to ignite either because wagon wheels on shore had broken the copper wires or the wires were too long for the current to create a spark. *New Ironsides* fired only one broadside at Fort Sumter and was blanketed by fifty shots and shells.

After colliding with the flagship, *Catskill* passed *New Ironsides* and got within six hundred yards of Fort Sumter. Cdr. George W. Rodgers was able to dismount a barbette gun with *Catskill*'s guns, but his own vessel was hit twenty times. One shot created a hole through the deck, and *Catskill* began to ship water. Had the river been rougher the monitor might have sunk. *Nantucket*, which came next, was struck fifty-one times. Its XV-inch gunport and the turret were both jammed. *Nahant*, the last monitor in the attack, collided with *New Ironsides* as it steamed past. *Nahant* took thirty-six hits and suffered the most damage and casualties of all the monitors. An eighty-pound section of armor broke away from the pilothouse, mortally wounding the helmsman, Quartermaster Edward Cobb, while flying bolt heads injured six others.[20]

Keokuk, the final Union ironclad to enter the fray, was not a monitor but a tower ironclad mounting one pivot-mounted XI-inch Dahlgren in each of its two casemates. *Keokuk* moved ahead of the crippled *Nahunt* to within six hundred yards of Fort Sumter and received the brunt of the Confederates' fire: ninety rounds, almost twenty below or at the water line. It limped away from the Charleston forts barely afloat. Despite the crew's efforts to save it, *Keokuk* sank the next day.

Assessing the Damage

After Du Pont called off the action, the battered Union ironclads moved out of range of the Confederate batteries. Du Pont was prepared to press the attack again the next day, but after conferring with each of the monitor captains he knew the attempt would be futile. Worden told Du Pont that the Union warships had withstood a "concentrated and terrific fire" for about fifty minutes during the day's action and advised him, "After testing the weight of the enemy's fire, and observing the obstructions, I am led to believe that Charleston cannot be taken by the Naval force now present, and that had the attack been continued it would have not failed to result in disaster."[21]

Acting Assistant Paymaster Samuel T. Browne served with Worden in the pilothouse throughout the one-sided battle and was impressed that Worden "had commanded his vessel in a noble manner despite the firestorm that exploded around our ship." In turn, Worden lauded Browne for volunteering to "act as a signal officer and made himself familiar with the new code of signals adopted, was with me ... and by his quickness of sight and of apprehension was material service to me, particularly in view of my much-impaired eyesight."[22]

Browne concurred with Worden about the infeasibility of renewing the attack on the Confederate forts, later explaining that he was "confident the force of iron-clads then available would have been insufficient for that purpose, and it would have been mad folly to have sent wooden vessels into that cul-de-sac whose sides bristled with few hundred guns, and the waters of whose harbor were filled with every variety of torpedoes; I have held the opinion ... that even if the ironclads had penetrated the harbor, and escaped the network of torpedoes, that with four hundred guns hammering them to pieces would have only been a question of hours."[23]

The Confederates had achieved a stunning victory and in the process uncovered the weaknesses of the feared monitors. With their limited volume of fire, monitors could not single-handedly overwhelm fixed land-based batteries. The monitors were able to send only 139 shots against the forts, while the Confederates countered with 2,209 Brooke bolts, shells, and solid shot. Du Pont had ordered his captains to concentrate their fire against the barbette guns because their plunging shot could penetrate the monitors' relatively thin deck armor. Both *Weehawken* and *Catskill* were holed through their decks, damage that could have sunk either ship in heavier seas. The "improved" pilothouse was not only a good target for Confederate shells, it also did not provide adequate views for steering and fire control. Worden noted that he had "experienced serious embarrassment in maneuvering ... in the narrow and uncertain channel, with the limited means of observation afforded from the pilothouse under the rapid and concentrated fire from the forts ... and neither a compass nor buoys to guide."[24]

Gustavus Fox had been a firm believer in the monitor design ever since witnessing the fight between *Monitor* and *Virginia*. Fox had pushed Admiral Du Pont to attack Charleston with his ironclads as soon as the *Passaic* class was operational, but it was Du Pont, who did not share Fox's enthusiasm for monitors, who was criticized for not forcing his squadron to enter Charleston Harbor. After he read Worden's report, however, Fox, who had served on *Cyane* with Worden in the early 1840s, began to understand why monitors alone could not capture Charleston.

The two sides viewed the engagement differently. Charleston's citizens had long anticipated a Union naval attack. When the attack came, the *Yorkville Enquirer* reported, "At last, the long period of doubt and delay is at an end; and this godly city, girded with the fiery circle of its batteries, stands confronted with the most formidable Armada that the hands of man have ever put afloat.... The scene at that hour, as viewed from the Battery promenade, was truly grand."[25] The *Enquirer* called it "a curious coincidence of war that the commanders, Gens. Beauregard, Ripley, Col. Rhett, Lt. Col. Yates, and nearly all the garrison of Fort Sumter, were the same men who were the chief actors in the bloodless reduction of Fort Sumter in April 1861, and who have now repelled a formidable attack upon this famous fortress, while in their keeping."

In Union-controlled Port Royal, South Carolina, the *New South* expressed a different opinion:

We have every cause to congratulate the Department and Country upon the results of the initial or experimental attack upon Fort Sumter by the iron-clad squadron. While those who absurdly believe that the grim defenders of Charleston would fly affrighted from the first fire of our Monitors, have been inevitably disappointed, the results of this experiment furnish solid grounds, not merely for hope, but for conviction, that the rebel stronghold cannot eventually, nor for any length of time, resist the agencies now employed for its subjugation.[26]

After the ironclad attack failed, both North and South recognized that new efforts using combined arms would have to be employed to destroy Fort Sumter and conquer Charleston.

Farewell to *Montauk*

John Worden would not be present to relish Charleston's capture in 1865. On 13 April 1863 he was detached from *Montauk* due to illness. He had been on active sea service since December 1862. His ship had been torpedoed, bombarded by heavy guns, and had twice nearly sunk. The arduous service took a heavy toll on Worden's health. Admiral Du Pont, "being painfully struck by the condition of your health . . . and your own statements in reference to it," ordered Worden to leave Port Royal to report in person or in writing to the Secretary of the Navy.[27]

On 14 April Worden bid farewell to the crew of *Montauk*. The ship's log noted that in a "brief and feeling speech," he thanked the officers and men for "their readiness in carrying out his orders at all times, for their coolness when under the enemies [*sic*] fire, and also for their general good conduct." After taking a final leave of all, Worden stepped into the blockade frigate *Wabash*'s boat and proceeded—amid three hearty cheers from the crew—toward the Army steamer *Ben De Ford* to take passage to New York.[28]

The Civil War continued without him on the front lines, but many of his relatives remained in peril. Only two days after Worden took his final leave of *Montauk*'s crew, Acting Rear Adm. David Dixon Porter made his dramatic nighttime run past Vicksburg. The feat was a national news event, and Worden, back in Brooklyn, must have been concerned. His younger brother Isaac Gilbert Worden had been appointed acting assistant paymaster in early

April and assigned to the river ironclad *Carondelet*, one of the six *Cairo*-class ironclad river gunboats that steamed past Vicksburg with Porter's flagship, *Benton*. He had no need for concern. Isaac did not report to *Carondelet* until 9 May, although he witnessed other action on the ironclad the following year. In the meantime, another brother, Frederick William, a lieutenant colonel with the Thirteenth Michigan Infantry Regiment, had seen action at Shiloh, Corinth, and Stone's River but was released on disability in February 1863. John Lorimer Worden Jr. was a first-year cadet at the Military Academy in 1863 but left and joined the Thirteenth New York Heavy Artillery Regiment as a second lieutenant in 1864. Later that year he served as an aide-de-camp to Brig. Gen. Charles Kinnaird Graham, former construction engineer at the Brooklyn Navy Yard, who commanded the Army of the James Naval Brigade. Worden's first cousin, James Henry Worden, a prewar whaler, enlisted in 1861 and served as a quarter gunner on the West Gulf Blockading Squadron ship *Morning Light* until the entire crew was taken prisoner in Texas in January 1863. James' brother William Worden also enlisted in 1861. He saw considerable action as a private with the Thirteenth New York Infantry at Second Manassas, Fredericksburg, Chancellorsville, and other engagements in between, including five days as a prisoner of war after Second Manassas followed by four months in the parole camp at Annapolis.[29] Capt. John L. Worden, however, returned to a safe post at the Brooklyn Navy Yard.

CHAPTER 11

THE EXPERT

Worden returned to Brooklyn on 20 April 1863 and was back at the Brooklyn Navy Yard the next day, still in poor health but as always following orders. The local press reported that he "was received by every demonstration of pleasure, from all the officer the premises crowding around and congratulating him on his brilliant engagement before Charleston."[1] Worden was the ironclad man of the hour. His fellow officers and the public praised him for his valor in two of the greatest ironclad battles of the war and the destruction of CSS *Nashville*. But another such command was not in the cards. Worden was the Navy's most seasoned monitor officer, and his expertise was needed to oversee the completion of the new monitors being constructed in New York and Jersey City, New Jersey.

Building Better Monitors

On 22 April Worden reported to Washington to receive his new assignment from Secretary Welles. He was detailed once again to serve as special assistant to Rear Adm. Francis Hoyt Gregory. Worden took the lead in applying his specialized knowledge to correct many of the monitor flaws he had observed as *Montauk*'s commander. With each new monitor class, he hoped for more effective firepower, better armor, improved steering, and greater seakeeping qualities. As Gregory waited for Worden to return from Washington and assume his post, he forwarded Worden's captain commission to him with his congratulations "for your well-deserved reward for the great service you have rendered your Country.... I hope your health has improved by the genial influences of home and country air and you will soon be able to assume [your new] position."[2]

On 11 June 1863 Worden was called before a court of inquiry examining the actions of Chief Engineer Alban Stimers. Stimers, who had served in *Monitor* with Worden, had observed the 7 April engagement from the wooden gunboat *Unadilla*. His duty during the attack on Charleston was to study the performance of the monitors and assist in their maintenance before and after the battle. Following the engagement, he had publicly asserted that Rear Adm. Samuel F. Du Pont's 7 April assault had been "feeble" and should have been renewed. He claimed that the ironclad captains wanted to renew the attack and that any damage the vessels had suffered in the initial attack was easily repaired. Du Pont insisted on holding a court of inquiry to dispute Stimers' claims and his "language unbecoming an officer of the U.S. Navy."

The proceedings were held in Brooklyn, and only two men testified: Capt. Percival Drayton of *Passaic* and Capt. John Worden of *Montauk*. Worden testified that none of the ironclad captains had thought it wise to renew the attack, because the ships were in no condition to do so, although he could have brought *Montauk* back into action if so ordered. The other commanders, he said, considered "their vessels ... very considerably damaged." Some would have gone into battle with damaged or disabled guns. Even after repairs, he added, once the bolts securing the armor had been broken, the ironclads would not have been able to resist shot as before the battle. He made his opinion very clear:

> I am and was of the opinion that a renewal of the attack on the 8th would have been likely to have resulted in a very serious disaster to the ironclads. After feeling the weight of the enemy's fire on the 7th of April last, and looking at the obstructions, which were of a very formidable character, I thought, if we had attempted to break through the obstructions and gotten the propellers of the ships involved with network which we were all well advised was there, and which we stood a good chance of doing, they would have become unmanageable, and, in all probability,

so injured by torpedoes that they would have sunken in the harbor, or have fallen into the enemy's hands; and I did not think the risk of such a disaster was justifiable under the circumstances. The rebel iron-clads were lying behind their obstructions, and any vessel of our forces that been disabled would have been exposed to them, and I have no doubt they were lying there for that purpose.[3]

Worden did not believe Du Pont had any prejudices against monitors, merely that he recognized the firepower limitations of this type of vessel, as Worden did himself. Despite Worden's and other monitor captains' confidence in Du Pont, Assistant Secretary Fox and Secretary of the Navy Welles could not tolerate the defeat at Charleston and replaced Du Pont with Rear Adm. John A. Dahlgren as commander of the South Atlantic Blockading Squadron.

Worden returned to Brooklyn a famous man noted for his intelligence, kindness, and generosity. He was continuously courted by citizens who believed him to be a true naval hero. In August 1863 the Union League of Philadelphia, wishing "to pay tribute ... of gratitude," voted to present a gold medal to him. Worden was delighted to receive an invitation to travel with a Russian admiral and officers to Niagara Falls but received the invitation too late to attend. He served on the Grand Reception Committee for the Long Island Sanitary Fair held at the Brooklyn Academy of Music. A "white medallion portrait of Captain Worden of the *Monitor* fame" in the Gallery of Fine Arts was predicted to "attract deserved attention."[4]

Worden's fame even put him in a sort of popularity contest in New York City, a raffle for a sword that was to be presented to the naval hero who received the most votes. Worden received 2 votes, but Rear Admiral Farragut received 119 votes and was given the blade and its scabbard.[5]

Worden was detailed to serve as an observer or witness at a court of inquiry concerning Capt. Charles Wilkes, whom the Secretary of the Navy had censured for allowing CSS *Alabama* to escape in the West Indies. While he was in Washington for that, Worden visited the Armory Square Hospital where Amanda Akin, a distant relative of Olivia's from Quaker Hill, volunteered. She later wrote, "Captain John Lorimer Worden (husband of our old friend and neighbor) spent an Hour with me. He is attending Admiral [*sic*]

Wilkes court-martial and will remain some time."[6] On that same trip, Worden and Rear Admiral Stringham called on Gideon Welles to recommend that Worden's old friend Henry Wise be appointed chief of the Ordnance Bureau.[7]

Worden's life was not all invitations and accolades. He was kept busy at the Brooklyn Navy Yard. Among his duties was oversight of the production of John Ericsson's two final monitors. Both were huge, ocean-going vessels. The first to be constructed was the single-turreted *Dictator*, 312 feet long, built by C. H. Delamater Iron Works. The second seagoing armor-clad was *Puritan*, built at Continental Iron Works and the largest of Ericsson's monitors with a length of 340 feet, beam of 50 feet, and draft of 20 feet. Ericsson's original design called for two turrets, but only one turret was mounted.[8] On 22 June 1864 Worden and several other Brooklyn Navy Yard officers were in attendance during the attempted launch of *Puritan*. The enormous ironclad failed to move down the ways; it would not be launched until 2 July. *Puritan* was rebuilt after 1874 as a "new navy monitor" and was not commissioned until 1896.[9]

Captain Worden was on board the *Canonicus*-class monitor *Mahopac* when its engines and guns were tested on 20 August 1864. *Mahopac* had been built at an independent yard, Zeno Secor and Company of Jersey City, New Jersey, and Worden was there to ensure that it had been properly constructed.[10] Apparently the vessel's galley was adequate, because the *New York Times* reported that "an excellent collation was served up in the mess-room."[11]

Worden joined other officers on board the new torpedo boat *Stromboli* when it first steamed up the North River from the Secor Yard in Jersey City on a test of its engines and torpedo mechanisms. The voyage was not announced ahead of time, "as it is desired that the invention shall be kept a secret for a time," but the *New York Times* blared out the news. So much for secrecy during the Civil War. *Stromboli* was later renamed *Spuyten Duyvil* and fought during the 24 January 1865 Battle of Trent's Reach on the James River below Richmond.[12]

Because the federal government was investing heavily in new ironclads, the U.S. Senate reviewed all of Worden's official reports. "Monitor fever" was still rampant in the Navy, with some believing that additional ocean-going and light draft monitors were required to ensure victory. More specialized designs were invented as the war continued.

When Assistant Secretary Fox said that monitors of six-foot draft were needed for operations in the upper reaches of Southern rivers, Ericsson agreed to design—without pay—a shallow-draft monitor, the *Casco* class.[13] Ericsson then turned over his preliminary concepts for the *Casco*-class ironclads to Alban Stimers. When Stimers took over the *Casco* project, neither Ericsson nor Benjamin Franklin Isherwood, the Navy's engineer in chief, supervised his progress or modifications. Stimers, who was very ambitious, made major modifications to the engine system and used larger boilers that he had patented. Ericsson was infuriated by these modifications and refused to solve the design problems that cropped up as a result.[14]

The first *Casco*-class light draft monitor, *Chimo*, was launched on 5 May 1864 and had a draft of five feet eight inches without a turret. A frustrated Rear Admiral Gregory wrote to the chief of the Bureau of Construction and Repair, John Lenthall, that it "will be impossible for her to float."[15] Naval Constructor William L. Hanscom estimated that a full load of coal and ammunition would place the ship three inches below the water.[16] Stimers was removed from the project, and construction was suspended until the Navy decided how to use the design. Worden was present for the launch of another *Casco*-class monitor—*Modoc*—on 21 March 1865. *Modoc* was laid up as soon as it was completed.[17]

During the time he was witnessing the efforts to find some use of the *Casco* class, Worden wrote a two-page letter to President Lincoln introducing an old friend, William Crawford Bibb. Worden told Lincoln that Bibb was a "leading & influential citizen of Montgomery" who "did me various kind & friendly acts" during his time in prison there in 1861 and asked for "kind consideration at your hands."[18] Bibb, son of former senator George M. Bibb of Kentucky, met with Lincoln at the White House on 12 April and presented Worden's letter of introduction. Bibb later wrote that "as he read, I noticed a change from rather sad to a more pleasing expression of [Lincoln's] face, and at its close he extended his hand, and again expressed his pleasure at seeing me."[19] A few days later, Lincoln was dead.

Worden was among the "distinguished gentlemen," including representatives of the British, French, and Russian navies, on board the torpedo steamer *Naubuc* when it sailed from the Brooklyn Navy Yard on 22 June 1865 and anchored below Governor's Island to test its submarine and buoyant percussion shells, "with terrible effect." *Naubuc* was one of the five *Casco*-class vessels completed without turrets. These entirely exposed "torpedo vessels" were armed with one XI-inch Dahlgren gun where the turret would have been located and carried a spar torpedo apparatus at the bow. *Naubuc* was commissioned on 17 March 1865 and decommissioned three months later.[20]

The Confederates had a similar idea. They developed fast, lightly armored, cigar-shaped steam torpedo boats to attack blockaders, counting on speed and the element of surprise to sink much larger Union warships with their spar torpedo. Despite the marginal successes of CSS *David* damaging *New Ironsides* and CSS *Squib* injuring *Minnesota*, spar torpedo boats did not turn the tide in favor of the Confederacy. On the Union side, Lt. William Cushing destroyed the Confederate ram *Albemarle* on 28 October 1864 with a spar torpedo mounted on *Picket Boat No. 1*. The Navy decided to transform the failed *Casco* class into torpedo boats, but the *Casco* spar torpedo boats were doomed from the start because of their lack of speed and seaworthiness.[21]

Testing *Idaho*

Capt. John Worden was detached to command the steam-screw sloop *Idaho* on 31 January 1866. His son John Lorimer Worden Jr. joined him as captain's clerk soon afterward. Former volunteer army 2nd Lt. John Lorimer Worden Jr. returned a sworn oath of office to his father on 5 February 1866. His Navy service was brief, however, and ended when Captain Worden was detached from *Idaho* in late May. The younger Worden had meanwhile secured a Regular Army commission. He reported for duty as a second lieutenant with the First U.S. Infantry Regiment on 3 June 1866 and went on to serve in New Orleans during Reconstruction.[22]

Worden was familiar with *Idaho* because he attended its launching at the Brooklyn Navy Yard on 8 October 1864.[23] The hull, designed and constructed by Henry Steers, featured a unique iron trussing system, and the engines were built by Paul Forbes at Morgan Iron Works in Manhattan using the "Dickerson Plan." After commissioning, the sloop was taken out on "a cruise of three or four hundred miles along the coast" to determine "the merits of the engines."[24] Worden secured a crew for the cruise, and several engineers were detailed to temporary duty on the ship. They included chief engineers from the Board of Naval Experts Henry H. Steward and Edward D. Robie. Forbes, the contractor, sent eighteen engineers to operate the machinery.

The development of the steam Navy was a contentious process as engineers sought to use new technology to build the most efficient and powerful engines. The Navy's chief engineer, Benjamin Franklin Isherwood, designed most of the Union Navy engines during the war, but he was often criticized for his engineering concepts. Some politicians and naval officers complained that Isherwood's engines "were excessively heavy, inefficient, uneconomical, underpowered, and based on unsound engineering principles."[25] His detractors endeavored to find a civilian replacement, and many looked to New York lawyer Edward N. Dickerson. Articulate, brilliant, and well connected, Dickerson was the national expert on patent law and was employed by inventors like Samuel Colt and Cyrus McCormick. Dickerson's hobby was steam engineering, and he convinced Senator Stephen Russell Mallory to grant him a contract to build the engines for a new ship, *Pensacola*, in 1858. His design employed the short-cut-off valve theory, which called for smaller boilers to power four cylinders with large cubic capacity. *Pensacola*'s engines were heavier, more complex, produced less steam power, and used more coal than those of other steam ships. Frank Marion Bennett, a Navy passed assistant engineer, noted that "the design of the engine abounded in amateurish and weighty mechanical redundancies."[26]

Pensacola was built at Warrington Navy Yard in Pensacola and then sailed to the Washington Navy Yard for engine installation. Once commissioned, *Pensacola* made only 8.8 knots and used 25 percent more coal than the other *Hartford*-class sloops. Rear Adm. David Glasgow Farragut wrote to Assistant Secretary Fox in 1862 that the Dickerson engines were "perfectly worthless."[27] The sloop served as a floating battery on the Mississippi River until ordered to the Brooklyn Navy Yard in 1864 for a replacement engine.

Idaho left the Brooklyn Navy Yard on 9 April 1866 and proceeded to a point off the Battery to make a series of trial trips. The *New York Herald* predicted on 13 April that "*Idaho* is a model ship, and on her sea trials . . . she will no doubt attain a rate of speed that will astonish American engineers."[28] Despite the media's optimism, the engine system was flawed from its conception and failed to meet Navy requirements. The hull design by Henry Steers

Photo 11.1 *Pensacola* at an unidentified anchorage, 1861–65 *Library of Congress Digital ID 3b32818*

was said to be "flawless, but her motive power is complicated, and her consumption of fuel larger than that accorded to vessels of her class, either by our own or European nations."[29]

One of the major problems confronting Civil War–era shipbuilders was how to combine two motive powers—sail and steam—in one seagoing vessel. During the early days of steam, ocean-going warships generated power using both sail and steam. Sails were more economical at sea, but steam was far better for ships to operate in harbors and rivers and during battle. For example, the steam-screw frigate *Merrimack*'s engines were troublesome from the beginning. Eventually they were condemned in 1860. The engines of its sister ship, *Minnesota*, worked well from the beginning and throughout the war. This was a period of experimentation, and many new concepts were flawed from conception while others were merely adequate. The integration of new concepts brought new designs, which resulted in steam-only ships by the 1880s.

Idaho had numerous mechanical problems. It could make only 8.27 knots instead of the contracted speed of 15 knots, and it used an uneconomical 7.6 pounds of coal per horsepower. Worden's report detailing the poor performance of the vessel's power plant prompted the Navy to reject the ship.

Photo 11.2 *Idaho* in its original steam screw configuration laid up at the New York Navy Yard, 1866 *Naval History and Heritage Command NH 85971*

Although *Idaho* was judged a failure, Paul Forbes forced a resolution through Congress to pay him for the ship. It was the last time a Dickerson engine system was used. A Navy board that surveyed the ship noted that its machinery "occupies much of the space in the vessel that should have been appropriated for other purposes."[30] *Idaho* was converted into a fully rigged storeship and was recorded making eighteen knots over a two-hour span. It was severely damaged in a typhoon off Yokohama on 21 September 1869 and later sold.[31]

Pacific Bound Again

Worden was detached from *Idaho* on 23 May and ordered on 10 June to report to Rear Admiral Gregory "without delay for special duty"—which turned out to be ironclad construction again.[32] But just under two months later, on 6 August, Worden was ordered to command *Pensacola*, a recommissioned screw steamer with a complement of 366 officers and crew.

Pensacola was slated to become the North Pacific Squadron's flagship once Worden had sailed it around Cape Horn to California. The sloop's original Dickerson engines had been removed and replaced by machinery designed by Benjamin Isherwood and intended for the failed *Contoocook*-class cruiser *Wanaloset*. Worden tested the engines during dock trials on 22–24 August.[33] *Pensacola* had its sea trials from 30 August to 1 September and then returned to the Brooklyn Navy Yard. Worden advised the Yard's commandant, Rear Adm. Charles H. Bell, that he had conducted additional tests in New York Bay with engineers from the Board of Engineers. The sloop of war maintained an average speed of 9.3 knots, and the engines worked smoothly with "evidence of reliability and endurance." But, he added prophetically, "I beg to call to attention to the fact the nearness of the smokestack to the mainmast. And its great height will render the use of the main mast difficult at all times, and the main topsail when under steam. In making the long passage to the Pacific and in cruising under sail . . . [it] will be a serious disadvantage and will lessen her efficiency as a sailing cruiser."[34]

Worden knew one of the officers assigned to *Pensacola* quite well. Acting Volunteer Lt. Samuel Howard had been at Worden's side throughout the 9 March 1862 Battle of Hampton Roads as *Monitor*'s volunteer acting master and pilot and had helped Worden to his cabin after he was wounded.[35]

Writing from his cabin on *Pensacola* on 6 September, Worden revealed his feelings about Reconstruction. He declined an invitation from his old Brooklyn Navy Yard colleague Brig. Gen. Charles Kinnaird Graham to attend the Soldiers and Sailors Convention in Cleveland, Ohio. He added his assurance, however, that

> the policy of sustaining the administration meets my hearty approval and nothing would give me greater pleasure than uniting with my old companions at arms in this effort. . . . During the rebellion my whole heart and soul were enlisted in the effort towards its suppression; and now that it is oppressed, I feel it a pleasant duty to extend to our repentant Southern brethren the right hand of fellowship. Generous magnanimity toward a fallen foe is characteristic of brave men, and their principle is eminently shown in the sentiments so warmly and frequently expressed lately by the brave men who participated in subduing the rebellion.[36]

It is apparent from this statement that Worden agreed with Lincoln's desired outcome of reconciliation rather than retribution. Not everyone did.

Less than a year later, concerned that President Andrew Johnson's policies toward the rebellious states were too lenient, Congress overrode his veto of the Reconstruction Act of 1867. Military supervision in the South was seen as the best method to ensure the citizenship and voting rights of formerly enslaved people and the mechanisms for former Confederate states to be reintegrated into American civil society.

Union Navy and Army veterans, grudgingly or not, recognized the valor of African American sailors and soldiers during the war and the justice of equitable treatment for those freed from the bonds of slavery. Reconstruction had two elements: political and social. Political reconstruction was partly resolved, a least at the federal level, and in spirit if not in practice, with the Thirteenth, Fourteenth, and Fifteenth Amendments to the U.S. Constitution. All military personnel were bound by oath to defend the Constitution, and thus the three new amendments. But sectional differences and prejudices would have been reflected in the personal opinions of armed forces personnel, which in turn affected their thoughts about social reconstruction. The U.S. Army's supervision of Reconstruction in the South confronted some of the recalcitrance of unreconstructed Southern officials. Worden's son John Lorimer Jr. was a second lieutenant and later a first lieutenant with the First U.S. Infantry in New Orleans from 1866 to 1869 and would have told his father about the problems of Reconstruction in that area. Worden's own later statements as Naval Academy superintendent about racism and equity for African Americans speak well for him (see chapter 12).[37]

As Worden made final preparations for his voyage to the Pacific, the *New York Herald* noted that *Pensacola* was considered "a splendid specimen of naval architecture and pronounced to be the model vessel of the United States Navy."[38] Worden did not entirely agree with these sentiments. When *Pensacola* reached Rio de Janeiro on 8 November 1866, he advised Gideon Welles that the sloop rolled uneasily. He also reported that the mainsail could not be used at all due to the funnel's placement and size, and much of the ironwork was inferior in both materials and workmanship. *Pensacola* was becalmed during this part of the voyage, and Worden had to use steam to get out of "the Equatorial Calms." On the plus side, he noted that the engine performed "very satisfactory and reliably; no stoppage of it having occurred for any purpose."[39]

Eager to leave Rio as soon as possible after coaling, provisioning, and caulking were completed, Worden decided to wait for the ironwork and funnel improvements until he reached Callao, Peru, on the other side of the continent.[40] Just before leaving port, *Pensacola* swung at anchor at flood tide, and its stern struck the *Kansas*-class gunboat *Nipsic*. The damage was not enough to delay the ship's departure on 25 November.[41]

The voyage into the South Atlantic was difficult. On 30 November the ship was running before the wind in drizzling rain. The thirty-first began with stormy weather and lightning, and *Pensacola* ran into heavy squalls. The ship pitched and rolled badly in the heavy swells generated by the storms, which pushed it off course. On 3 December, the ship braved gales throughout the day. When the wind shifted, *Pensacola* was pushed back and Worden had to direct the ship north by west on the port tack. By midnight the gale was increasing and the seas were running high. As the storm increased from the southwest, *Pensacola*, losing sails and rigging, was forced to operate under steam. The deck officer reported the sloop was "laboring heavily, rolling and pitching deeply."[42] Finally the wind abated, and Worden set course toward the mouth of the Rio de la Plata. Using sail and steam, *Pensacola* entered Montevideo harbor on 8 December.[43]

Worden wrote to Rear Adm. Sylvanus W. Godon, commander of the South Atlantic Squadron, explaining why his ship needed significant repairs before he could proceed. Especially important was reducing the height of the smokestack to allow safe use of the mainsail. Worden deemed this reduction "absolutely essential before leaving this port" because he expected to meet "boisterous weather" during the passage to the Pacific.[44] Godon immediately approved the repairs, and *Pensacola* began refitting on 10 December. This included caulking, sail repair, and restoring the magazine. By Christmas Day 1866 the repairs were finished and Worden shaped a course for Valparaíso.

Pensacola entered the Strait of Magellan on 7 January and reached the South Pacific five days later. After a rough passage, the ship arrived in Valparaíso on 21 January and immediately began refitting. Four days later, Worden, plagued by kidney and gallbladder problems, wrote Gideon Welles, "I have the honor to request that I may be detached from this ship, and authorized to return to the United States. I ask this because I am not in a condition of health to enable me to stand the wear and tear of active sea service."⁴⁵ The relief he asked for was long in coming.

Meanwhile, as at other ports, Worden and *Pensacola* received local dignitaries. The U.S. ambassador to Chile, Maj. Gen. Judson Kilpatrick, visited several times with the American consul Ambrose Clark and several ladies. Chilean commodore J. Williams Robelledo made an official visit. Worden always had to take the local political situation into account in his interactions with visitors. Chile's Chincha Islands War (1864–66) with Spain had recently ended. Spain had seized the guano-rich islands, and a Spanish squadron had bombarded a defenseless Valparaíso in March 1866 but was repulsed at Callao and withdrew in May. The U.S. government opposed Spain's actions, and U.S. naval forces in the South Pacific had monitored the war. When Worden arrived in Valparaíso, Rear Admiral J. Randolph Tucker of the Peruvian Navy led a parade of warships out to meet him: the ram *Independencia*, the monitor *Huáscar,* and the corvettes *La Union* and *La America*, escorted by the Chilean corvette *Esmeraldo*. Worden was quite familiar with Tucker. He had been the commander of the Confederate James River Squadron and had fought against *Monitor* during the Battle of Hampton Roads. The two former enemies did not meet in Valparaíso.⁴⁶

Pensacola stayed in Chilean waters until 13 February, when it left for Callao, arriving ten days later. Rear Admiral Dahlgren, the new commander of the South Pacific Squadron, U.S. minister Alvin P. Hovey, and other American and Peruvian dignitaries visited Worden in Callao on his ship. *Pensacola* received an upgrade to its battery when *Powhatan* transferred a 100-pounder Parrott gun for use as a pivot gun.⁴⁷

Pensacola left Callao on 4 March 1867 and arrived at Mare Island Navy Yard at Vallejo, California, on 6 April. Shortly afterward Worden received a request from the San Francisco Board of Supervisors asking him to set a date "to receive the citizens of San Francisco." Worden was agreeable, but first he wanted to find his brother James Barenloe Worden, whom he had not heard from "in many years." News reports of his quest quickly brought a location, and Worden set out for El Dorado County, where James had gone to seek his fortune in gold mining and later established a store, married, and raised a family. Having reunited with his brother, Worden returned to San Francisco for a grand reception in his honor held at City Hall on 25 April. He was introduced by an "old friend" and former officer from Mare Island, Cdr. Selim E. Woodworth. Both men had served with the Pacific Squadron during the Mexican-American War, on some of the same ships but not at the same time, and their paths would cross again in Germany in 1868. In his introduction, Woodworth praised Worden with "high appreciation for [his] gallant and distinguished service." The press reported that Worden responded that the "difficulty of meeting that kindness appropriately was greater to him than that of meeting the enemy in battle." Characteristically, he added that he found it "difficult to give utterance to the feelings that I experience at your kindness and consideration" because his "sphere of duty has been poorly calculated to make me an orator." Later that summer, the Board of Supervisors adopted a resolution naming a city street after Worden.[48]

Photo 11.3 Capt. John L. Worden (*front, center*) on the deck of *Pensacola* at Mare Island Navy Yard, 8 May 1867. Other officers may include Cdr. Paul Shirley, *Pensacola*'s subsequent captain; Lt. Cdr. Henry L. Howison; Lt. Cdr. Albert Kautz; Lt. Cdr. John G. Mitchell; and Acting Volunteer Lt. Samuel Howard. *Naval History and Heritage Command NHF-133, Rear Adm. W. W. Phelps Collection*

Return to the East

Following a change-of-command ceremony on 8 May, Worden was finally detached from *Pensacola*; he departed San Francisco ten days later. He traveled by ship to Panama, crossed the isthmus to Aspinwall, and reported his arrival in New York on 11 June. Later that summer he visited his mother, sisters, and brothers in Michigan. Family matters were also on his mind when his son, now 1st Lt. John Lorimer Worden Jr., a company commander with the First U.S. Infantry Regiment in New Orleans, fell ill with yellow fever. Worden wrote to Adjutant General of the Army Edward Davis Townsend asking that his son "be allowed to go home for a few weeks for his mother's care." The request was granted, and young Worden recovered and later returned to duty. Captain and Mrs. Worden were staying in Washington at the time. Worden visited Philadelphia in November, where he was "the recipient of marked attentions," but reticent as always, he "excused himself from making any extended remarks."[49]

Worden was more voluble in his written praise of the officers and crew he served with on *Monitor*. He knew that the story of their legendary service together in 1862 had become skewed. On 5 January 1868 he sent a twelve-page letter to Secretary of the Navy Welles that was intended to document his version of the battle for the official record. Worden was frank about *Monitor*'s deficiencies and the damage that Atlantic storms and *Virginia* had done to it in Hampton Roads. He was full of praise for the crew, the officers, and especially Samuel Dana Greene and a few others. He wanted to "remedy a wrong" concerning "ungenerous illusions" about Greene and "to do justice to the gallant and excellent officer" concerning his actions as *Monitor*'s executive officer on 9 March 1862 after Worden was wounded. Greene had assumed command and returned to continue the fight, demonstrating his "good judgment and sound discretion [which] forbade" him from pursuing the rebel ironclad as it withdrew. Four years later, Worden would take his determination to reward his crew directly to Congress with the hope of securing prize money for having taken action that led to the destruction of *Virginia* (see chapter 13).[50]

Worden, now residing again in Brooklyn, was ordered to the Washington Navy Yard to appear on 19 May for examination for promotion to commodore. The medical examiners found that his left eye was "slightly impaired" but determined that he was "physically qualified to perform the duties of a Commodore." The board unanimously approved his promotion on 21 May. The president approved the promotion on 27 May, and the Senate confirmed it on 5 June. Worden had been ranked tenth among the Navy's thirty-five active-list captains, and the promotion advanced him over four more senior captains to become the twenty-fifth and most junior among the Navy's commodores.[51]

On 23 May Worden requested a one-year leave of absence, to begin 15 June 1868, with permission to go abroad. At age fifty, with a long history of fragile health exacerbated by incarceration, wounds and other injuries, and illnesses, he was ready for an extended period of recuperation. He was so confident that his request would be approved that he wrote the same day to President Andrew Johnson asking him to direct the Navy Department to issue a letter of credit so he could draw his pay while in Europe. He told Johnson that he knew that the Navy had a new rule that disallowed letters of credit, and he did "not object to the rule or its application" to him; he merely asked that the rule be "relaxed," as had been done for others. He stated his belief that Welles would grant the indulgence because of his "kindly disposition" toward him, but the president's "superior authority" was first required. He also noted that "many friends" had told him that he was "entitled to the consideration asked for" and had assured him that it would be granted. The many friends were wrong. President Johnson forwarded the letter to Welles, who denied the letter of credit request. Welles approved the leave of absence for six months, not the year Worden had asked for, but did grant Worden permission to request an extension along with permission to go abroad. The press reported that Worden's leave was because of ill health resulting from the wounds he received at Hampton Roads. News reports also revealed that he planned to spend time in German spas, perhaps "several years."[52]

European Sojourn

The voyage to Europe provided the opportunity for a grand reunion with Henry Wise, who had recently resigned from the Navy because of poor health. The two left New York City together on the North German Lloyds steamer *America* on 11 June, bound for Bremen via Southampton. Press reports indicated that they traveled with family, which meant they were accompanied by Olivia Worden and daughters Grace and Olivia, and Charlotte Wise and perhaps Wise's teenage children, Charlotte, Katherine, and Edward. A London newspaper noted that Wise also traveled with servants.[53]

The *Sun* reported in September that Worden was "now in Dresden, having been in Europe on leave of absence since June 1868." The *Brooklyn Eagle* added that he was one of the American "lions in Dresden." As the capital of Saxony, Dresden was a cosmopolitan city with numerous guesthouses and cultural amenities. Essential for the ailing Worden, Dresden also offered soothing mineral baths.[54]

During his time in Dresden, Worden sat for a formal portrait by Philipp Albert Gliemann, a well-known portrait and genre artist. Several copies were made of the painting. Selim Woodworth, whom Worden had met in San Francisco in 1867, was staying in Dresden with his wife, Lissette Marie Flohr Woodworth, at the time, and they acquired one of the copies. After he returned to the United States in 1869, Worden wrote to Lissette to thank her for her "kindness throughout our whole stay in Dresden, and particularly so for the aid and comfort you gave us in our parting hours." He invited Lisette to visit him and Olivia in Annapolis when she returned to the United States and informed her that his son Daniel had sent her a draft for 440 North German Thalers to settle debts she and others had paid on his behalf in Dresden. The Woodworths' copy of the Gliemann portrait was later bequeathed to the Naval Academy by their son, William McMichael Woodworth. It has been displayed in various locations at the Naval Academy since 1912 and in its museum since 1988. At least one other copy of the Gliemann portrait exists. It was offered in auction sales in the early 2020s but was withdrawn for lack of sufficient bids. Two of Woodworth's sons entered the Naval Academy during and just after Worden's superintendency: Selim E. Jr. entered in 1872, graduated in 1877, and had a Navy career; Frederick Augustus entered the Academy in 1875 but was dismissed for hazing in 1876.[55]

Eighteen sixty-nine began with troubling news for the Wordens. Henry Wise, then staying in Rome, asked the Navy Department for a yearlong extension of his retired-status leave so he could continue to recover his health at the German baths. But no recovery was possible. He was seriously ill with kidney disease resulting from a severe contusion to the kidney incurred when his foot was caught in the train tackle of a IX-inch gun being

Photo 11.4 Philipp A. Gliemann's portrait of Commodore Worden at Dresden, 1869; bequeathed to the U.S. Naval Academy by William McMichael Woodworth in 1912 *U.S. Naval Academy Museum 1912.003.0002*

test-fired at the Washington Navy Yard in 1857.[56] He died on 2 April 1869. Wise's remains were sent back to the United States, and he was buried on 21 June 1869 at Mount Auburn Cemetery in Cambridge, Massachusetts, in the same plot as his father-in-law, Senator Edward Everett. The *New York Times* reported the "impressive funeral solemnities" several days later and mentioned Wise's care for the wounded Worden after the Battle of Hampton Roads.[57]

The Navy Department extended Worden's leave twice while he was in Europe. The first extension was for an additional six months, starting 25 December 1868, and the second was for another year, beginning on 15 June 1869. By this time, he was said to be "in greatly improved health" and ready to return home. The Wordens were in Paris at the Hotel Hollande on 3 November when Worden was one of the "principal guests" at an evening reception at the new residence of Elihu Benjamin Washburne, the American minister to Paris.[58] When the Wordens returned to Washington, Secretary of the Navy George Robeson officially notified Commodore Worden that he was to report by 1 December to become superintendent of the U.S. Naval Academy.[59] The lion of his own generation was now going to oversee the education of his successors.

CHAPTER 12

TRAINING THE NAVY'S FUTURE LEADERS

John Worden was the seventh superintendent of the U.S. Naval Academy. He served from 1 December 1869 to 21 September 1874, the second longest tenure in the Academy's history, and only five days shy of the longest.[1] The assignment placed him in a top leadership position overseeing the education of hundreds of young men aspiring to become naval officers. His previous assignments had made him a mature and well-rounded officer. He himself had been a midshipman and a passed midshipman for twelve years in the 1830s and early 1840s, a time when there was no Naval Academy and training was on board sailing ships at sea, service that was perhaps less relevant to the increasingly steam-powered Navy of the 1870s. He had served at the Naval Observatory in the mid-1840s and learned the skills needed for patient scientific observation. Worden had served on California's Pacific coast as a sailing master and seen action during the Mexican-American War as a lieutenant. The 1850s took him to Europe, where he observed the Navy in its role as a roving diplomatic corps. The decade also presented him with two more assignments at the Naval Observatory and practical administrative experiences in ship construction and maintenance at the Brooklyn Navy Yard. The Civil War brought him fame, increasingly dangerous commands, and physical disabilities. His wounds and chronic illnesses notwithstanding, after his respite in Europe he stood ready for more work. The middies of the early 1870s might have considered him an "old salt," but he was also a widely revered national hero and an inspiration to his youthful charges.

Worden's first involvement with the Academy was his May 1865 appointment to its Board of Visitors. It was a critical time for the Academy because the Navy Department was under pressure from Rhode Island authorities to keep it in Newport, where it had relocated during the Civil War. The wartime Board of Visitors had even recommended abolishing the Academy and establishing seven separate training schools. But Secretary of the Navy Gideon Welles held firm in his decision to return the Academy to Annapolis when the war was over.[2]

Rear Adm. David Dixon Porter succeeded the wartime superintendent, Commo. George S. Blake, in October 1865. Porter was a reformer who believed the Academy had the potential to become a national institution rivaling the Military Academy at West Point. He obtained increased appropriations, expanded Academy property, revised the curriculum, replaced numerous civilian professors with war-experienced naval officers, initiated an honor code, emphasized education over training, and encouraged athletics and social activities. He was a hard act to follow.[3]

Steady Progress

Historians have disagreed regarding Worden's contributions to the Academy, some seeing him as a conservative and others as a progressive influence. Modern historians tend to call Worden's approach conservative. Jack Sweetman, for example, said that "Worden saw his task to be that of keeping the Academy steadily on the course Porter had plotted" and "made no significant changes in its organization or curriculum." His "mind-set remained that of the days of wooden ships and iron men." And indeed, Worden emphasized frequent hands-on drills on board the practice ships, and summer cruises at sea took on greater importance.[4]

Leland Lovette called Worden "one of the rare characters of the old Navy—every inch a sailor. When good work was done, he carried out his old shipboard practice of passing out warm and sincere praise; but for breaches

Photo 12.1 The Board of Visitors at the U.S. Naval Academy, 1873. Seated in front, from left: Rear Adm. Charles H. Davis, the board's president; Rear Adm. John L. Worden, superintendent; and Alvah Sabin, board member. Behind them are other board members, professors, and family. *Naval History and Heritage Command NH 53396*

of discipline, he usually gave the offenders hell. He was slow to wrath, but a very stormy figure when angry."[5]

Worden's contemporaries were more generous. English professor James Russell Soley, writing in 1876, viewed Worden's tenure as "one of steady progress" and noted that he made many improvements to the Academy buildings and grounds.[6] Thomas G. Ford, a former English professor and assistant librarian, wrote, "The Navy Department could not have made a better choice than . . . John L. Worden as a reward for great service in battle." He suggested that Worden's demeanor and cheery manner were such "as to win at once the good will of everybody." But the Academy was "a new and untried sphere of duty" for Worden and required the "rarest qualification for success." Ford believed that Worden had the necessary qualities, noting that "by the exercise of good judgment and firmness, coupled with the due regard for the opinions of experienced men in the departments of instruction and discipline . . . [he] succeeded in lifting the institution to a higher plane of efficiency than it ever before occupied."[7]

Worden's staff aide, Lt. Cdr. George Dewey, said that he was "a positive character, in keeping with the determined way that he fought, not only the *Monitor* in the famous action against the *Merrimac[k]*, but also the other ships intrusted [sic] to his command during the war. In common with many of the older officers, he was not yet convinced that the academic schooling at Annapolis was a wiser system in giving officers a groundwork than the old-fashioned system of apprenticeship on board ship while actually cruising."[8]

Modern Languages Department chair Lt. Cdr. Winfield Scott Schley had fond memories of his two "pleasant years" with Worden. The time "was agreeable," Schley wrote, because it associated him with "that distinguished officer who had won undying fame" at the Battle of Hampton Roads.[9] Worden's old comrade in arms Cdr. Samuel Dana Greene, now chair of the Astronomy, Navigation, and Surveying Department, gave Worden "judicious advice." When Worden or the commandant was absent, Greene was sometimes detailed to serve as senior officer in charge.[10]

As the war-weary nation looked toward rebuilding its infrastructure and was less interested in naval affairs, Worden was faced with budget cuts. His officers experienced slow professional advancement, and the Navy became a less attractive profession. Congress legislated in 1870 that midshipmen would "henceforth be styled cadet midshipmen." Only upon successfully passing the graduation examination would they become midshipmen. Then they would wait for a vacancy before promotion to ensign.[11]

Worden recognized that Navy line officers did not necessarily make the best department heads, and he wanted the best-qualified faculty to teach the Academy's students. The Board of Visitors agreed and recommended engaging the "best talent in the country" for department chairs and making the positions permanent and well paid. Traditionalists opposed Worden's recommendation to develop postgraduate studies for junior officers returning from sea duty; that concept was not realized until the Naval War College was established in 1884.[12] However, building on a program begun in 1865, a new student category of cadet engineer was established. The first cadet engineers arrived in 1871 for a two-year steam engineering program. In 1873 Worden recommended expanding the program to a third year and acquiring up-to-date equipment for practical instruction. The program was later expanded to four years.[13]

Determined to develop a more professional naval officer corps, Worden issued numerous disciplinary orders for the cadets. He let it be known that insubordination and disobeying orders particularly "pained and disappointed" him, as did cheating in recitations and examinations, which threatened "the very existence of the Institution itself." Anyone who was "deliberately false and deceptive" was considered unworthy of a Navy commission. Like Porter, Worden fostered an honor code and emphasized personal responsibility. Naval officers must always cultivate "a spirit of strict integrity and careful attention to duty."[14]

The Hazing Scandal

The most persistent disciplinary problem Worden had to confront was hazing. The practice had been relatively benign until it reached physically injurious levels in the fall of 1870 and led to a "battle royal" in the cadet quarters between plebes and their third-classmen hazers. Outnumbered by the plebes, the third-classmen agreed to cease their hazing. This affair did not attract press coverage.[15]

The situation reversed in 1871, when the plebes of 1870 became the hazers of 1871 and inflicted cruel punishments on the newcomers. Some were dunked under fire hydrants; others were forced to run a gauntlet between rows of third classmen who kicked and punched them; still others were stripped "almost to nudity" and made to drill or to pose as statues. An Annapolis newspaper called the abuse "outrageous and disgraceful" and exclaimed that the perpetrators "deserve a greater punishment than mere dismissal." Worden ordered an immediate stop to the hazing and threatened to recommend dismissal for anyone who persisted. He angrily issued another order less than a week later when he found that the hazing continued in "open defiance" to his previous "stringent order." He quarantined fifteen upper classmen pending the Secretary of the Navy's decision on their fate. Soon after Worden's second order, the third-year class sent Worden a pledge to stop hazing and "by our example to do our utmost to abolish the practice."[16]

This episode gained national coverage in newspaper reports that embarrassed Worden, the Academy, and the Navy Department. Secretary of the

Navy Robeson signed an order on 14 October calling hazing "coarse, cruel, and oppressive" and said the department was determined to root out "the recently exhibited tendency to treat the incoming Cadets with violence and inhumanity." Robeson backed Worden, who had "warned them of the consequences" should this "system of oppression" continue. Five cadets were dismissed outright, others were restricted for the rest of the academic year, and two others guilty of lesser offenses were denied summer leave. The press hailed the expulsions "as a wholesome sign of the times" and noted that they "will serve to remind students everywhere that they are not above civil law."[17]

Worden and the Navy Department were aware that public opinion as expressed in newspapers was running strongly against the Annapolis staff. Those who tolerated hazing "without an earnest attempt to bring the offenders to justice, ought to be impeached or dismissed with ignominy," and if "the Annapolis outrage" could not be contained, the Academy "had better be abolished altogether." At Worden's request, Robeson issued another order on 16 November acknowledging that the initial order had "failed to entirely remove the evil against which the order was directed." After this episode, Worden personally investigated violations and recommended expulsion for six more offenders; seven others were charged with lesser offenses. The Baltimore *Sun* reported that these actions seemed "to have met with general approval . . . [and] the scandalous practice has entirely ceased."[18]

Such was not really the case. Hazing resumed in October 1872, just after Worden had issued a warning against it and threatened "speedy punishment." Fourteen third-class members were punished with restrictions and demerits. Worden declared, "I will make it my duty, as far as my power extends, to purge the School and Naval Service of such unworthy members" who engaged in hazing. His warning apparently had the desired effect for sixteen months.[19]

Hazing reemerged in February 1874. While an investigation was under way, the third class met and, instead of condemning hazing, sent a resolution to Worden supporting the attackers. Worden called the resolution "gross insubordination" and recommended dismissal for the ringleader and confinement to the Yard for the rest of the academic year, daily double drill, and forfeiture of summer leave for nineteen other instigators. Robeson again agreed with Worden's recommendations, noting that class organizations, meetings, or actions not approved by the superintendent were "incompatible with naval discipline and must be suppressed."[20]

Up until this time, only the Secretary of the Navy could order dismissal from the Academy. Worden sought a solution from Congress that would broaden his authority. On 4 May 1874 the House of Representatives introduced a resolution aimed at ending hazing at the Academy, on board practice ships, and "at any other time or place." It made those dismissed for hazing ineligible for reappointment to the Academy or any naval service. Worden testified before the House Committee on Naval Affairs that he had done everything in his power to prevent hazing, including expulsions, but the hazers had been reappointed by members of Congress. He also complained about preferences shown to the sons of generals and admirals in obtaining appointments and reappointments against his recommendations. "An Act to Prevent Hazing at the Naval Academy" became law on 23 June 1874. Worden now had the authority to order courts-martial for hazing and to dismiss guilty offenders. Moreover, those dismissed were "forever ineligible to re-appointment." The law was too late to be of any help to Worden, however, because his tenure at the Academy ended on 21 September. And despite the law, hazing plagued the Academy for decades to come. In 1885 the Navy Department asked the attorney general for a clarification of the intent of the 1874 law. The opinion published later that year quoted extensively from Worden's 1871 and 1872 orders.[21]

The First Black Midshipmen

During his time at the Academy Worden faced another controversial social issue: the ill treatment of the Academy's first Black midshipmen. How they came to be appointed and the details of their treatment at the Academy are well covered in the book *Breaking the Color Barrier*.[22] This account concentrates on Worden's response.

The Naval Academy and the local African American population had a long history of working together amicably. Black women worked as domestics in officers' quarters, and Black men were employed as barbers, laborers, mechanics, stewards, and waiters. Sixty-two of the 179 sailors assigned to the Academy were African Americans. But there had never been a Black midshipman.

That Black midshipmen were admitted at all was a reflection of the times. Reconstruction was under way, and constitutional amendments had been passed to integrate African Americans into the mainstream. The Army was ahead of the Navy in this regard. The first Black cadet was admitted to the U.S. Military Academy in 1870. Although that man did not finish, a Black cadet graduated from West Point in 1877, the year Reconstruction ended. The Naval Academy did not graduate a Black midshipman until 1949. Like White society in general, most Navy officers did not acknowledge Blacks' social equality and were reluctant to accept African Americans into their officer corps.

Two Black cadet midshipmen from South Carolina briefly attended the Academy during Worden's tenure: sixteen-year-old James Henry Conyers in 1872–73 and eighteen-year-old Alonzo Clifton McClennan in 1873–74. A Richmond newspaper reported that Conyers "was received very kindly by Commodore Worden" and claimed that "his reception by the cadets has been kind and courteous." The Annapolis press, however, said Conyers' arrival caused "much excitement" and predicted that he "will not fare so well."[23]

Worden told Conyers "that if he treated the other cadet midshipmen 'with politeness,' the 'same would be shown to him.'" Conyers evidently was surprised and gratified by the kindness Worden and other officers showed to him, and some cadet midshipmen did indeed treat him well. But eventually Conyers "collided head-on with the Academy's institutional racism."[24] When he received word of Conyers' appointment, Worden had informed Secretary Robeson that the young man was "duly qualified for admission" and diplomatically asked for instructions. Robeson replied that "any breach of etiquette or discipline" toward Conyers should be "rigidly punished." But seamanship instructor Lt. Cdr. Robley Evans recalled that the Academy "was in an uproar at once," and Conyers was a victim of hazing from the outset. All first-year cadet midshipmen underwent hazing, but Conyers' treatment was particularly severe and overtly racist. The situation was reported in the national press and reverberated politically in Washington.[25]

As soon as Worden learned of what he called an "unprovoked and cowardly attack" on Conyers, he ordered a "thorough & minute investigation into this gross breech of discipline." Acting Secretary of the Navy Rear Adm. Augustus Ludlow Case advised Worden that the incident "has gone through the press of the country like wildfire" and the department was "beset by reporters and others for the facts of the case." Case ordered him to keep the department "fully and daily advised of any attempt to haze, or infringe upon the rights of Mr. Conyers."[26] Worden replied that he had not found evidence of an "organized combination to persecute" Conyers or any instances of depriving him of his legal rights. However, Worden did not attempt to deny the racism rampant in the Academy. "That [Conyers] is disagreeable to many, on account of his race and color, there seems to be no doubt, and while we may confess, that this arises from a most unwarrantable prejudice, it cannot be denied that, it is the growth of more than a century, and is not limited to any section of our country, nor to any class of people, but is wide spread and embraces all conditions of men."[27]

Still, Worden continued, he hoped "that the new element introduced into the Academy, might be so controlled as to prevent any serious discord." He did not conceal his disappointment at Conyers' treatment but added, "It seems to me scarcely surprising that it [Conyers' presence] has produced more or less irritation among youths whose impulses are not always controlled by sober reason." Worden understood his responsibility. "There is no question," he said, "that it is the duty of the authorities to protect Midshipman Conyers, in common with all others, in his rights, and to save him, as far as possible from annoyances, nor is there the slightest hesitancy on their part in performing this duty."

Furthermore, Worden added, the Fifteenth Amendment required that violations of regulations should be punished "without making any distinction on account of 'race, creed, or previous condition.'" He viewed Conyers' treatment as hazing and recommended expulsion for two of his attackers and confinement to the Yard for seven others. Robeson's resulting order condemned racist attitudes at the Academy and declared the attack on Conyers "a deliberate violation of . . . repeated injunctions" and an "unprovoked . . . seemingly concerted persecution" of a cadet who was "equally entitled to official protection." National law had abolished "all political distinction of race," and naval authorities had "at once and unmistakably made known to all at the Academy, that no imposition or indignity upon this Cadet, on account of his race, would be permitted from anyone." Quotes from Robeson's order were carried in newspapers nationally.[28]

Conyers' reactions to the ongoing abuse gained him numerous demerits. When he failed his year-end exams, the Academic Board recommended he be dropped from the Academy. Fearing political repercussions, Robeson allowed him to stay, and Worden sent him home for the summer to study. When he returned in the fall, he failed his exams again and was allowed to resign.[29]

Black cadet Alonzo Clifton McClennan arrived just as Conyers' Academy career was ending. But he was demoralized by Conyers' departure and struggled academically because he was less prepared than most other plebes. Shunned and insulted, McClennan responded with belligerence that earned him numerous demerits and extra duty as punishment. He fell further behind in his studies, was found deficient in the semiannual exams in January 1874, and was subject to dismissal.[30] Around this time, McClennan was also found guilty of lying and was recommended for dismissal. He appealed to the department, and Robeson overruled the Academy's recommendation and allowed him to remain. Then he got into a fight in the dining hall and was confined nightly on the practice ship *Santee*. Although Worden had felt sympathy for Conyers, he had none for McClennan and urged his dismissal. During his confinement McClennan was befriended by two civilian professors who arranged his admission to another college. With this prospect in hand, McClennan willingly resigned on 11 March 1874.[31]

Historian Robert Schneller said that Worden "attempted to level the playing field" for the Black cadets. Although he did not tolerate their physical mistreatment, he had not come to accept social equality as a right that came with equal professional opportunity. When Black midshipmen "responded to the discrimination with defiance instead of deference," then and later, "superintendents recommended their dismissal." Worden "considered the offense and not the victim in determining punishments for Conyers' and McClennan's tormenters." He provided counseling, ordered investigations, and tried to eliminate racially motivated attacks on the Black cadet midshipmen.[32]

For many decades to come, however, most White midshipmen were not willing to consider future naval service alongside Black fellow officers, and much less under the direction of a Black commander. Neither the Navy nor American society was open to this kind of acceptance.

The Japanese Arrive

Social inequality was not restricted to Black Americans. Although many Americans were antagonistic toward the Chinese laborers who flooded the country in mid-century, they were more accepting of temporary visitors from Japan, a nation that had recently embarked on reform, military modernization, and Westernization. The U.S. government and American private sector perceived it to be in the national interest to support Japan's modernization, and in 1868 Congress authorized the Navy to receive Japanese candidates at the Naval Academy.[33]

Eight Japanese cadets enrolled at the Academy during Worden's tenure. The first two—Matsumura Junzō and Sataro Ise—entered on 8 December 1869, just a week after Worden took over as superintendent. They were "advancing finely" in June 1871 and sailed on that summer's practice cruise. Worden reported on their progress in January 1872, noting Matsumura's good record and expressing confidence that he would graduate in 1873; he deemed Sataro's conduct and general bearing excellent and reported of both that their "amiability and strict regard for regulations has been worthy of all praise." He observed that they attended morning prayer and Sunday services and said their "seeming interest and respectful deportment ... [were] not at all behind that of their nominally Christian fellow students."[34]

Next to arrive were Katsu Koroku, an admiral's son, and Kunitomo Jiro, who had been preparing himself in America a year in advance for the entrance examination. Worden later praised Katsu's summer cruise performance and said his academic record was "commendable." He excused Kunitomo from studying French so he could concentrate on seamanship and gunnery.[35] Worden later reported that Kunitomo wanted to be baptized. While Worden believed Kunitomo's desire was sincere, he deemed it an act of courtesy to Japan and his duty to the Navy Department to submit the question for a decision before Kunitomo took "so important a step whilst at this institution." No record of Kunitomo's baptism has been found, but he was confirmed, taking the name John, on 20 May 1874 by Bishop William Pinkney at St. Anne's Episcopal Church in Annapolis. Kunitomo also signed a pledge that he would abstain from drinking intoxicating beverages while at the Academy. Although Worden is not known to have been a temperance man himself, this must have pleased him, because throughout his Academy tenure he sought similar pledges, as well as abstinence from tobacco products, from all underclassmen.

Azuma Takahiko (a member of the imperial family), Nanbu Hidemaro, Machida Keizero, and Arima Kantaro were admitted between 1872 and 1874. Three of the eight Japanese cadets who entered during Worden's time completed their four years and went on to successful naval careers. Matsumura became a vice admiral in the Imperial Japanese Navy and commandant of Japan's Naval Academy, Katsu became a navy commander, and Kunitomo reached the rank of captain.[36]

Keeping the Yard in Order

In addition to hazing and racism, Worden dealt with troublesome issues ranging from political intrigues to a lawsuit over the expansion of the Academy's campus. The Central Committee of the Maryland Republican Party protested directly to President Ulysses Grant in 1870 that only 5 of the Academy's approximately 120 civilian mechanics and laborers were Republicans. The rest were either Democrats or "persons utterly hostile" to the Grant administration. The party had appointed a committee of ten local Republicans "to urge the removal of the present force now employed" and "to name a number of Republicans to take their places." Grant forwarded the resolution to Robeson, who referred it to Worden for action "for the good of the country and the best interests of the service." Worden replied with a list of forty-five civilians, most of whom had been employed at the Academy since before the war and had accompanied the Academy to Newport in 1861. He noted they all had declared their loyalty to the Union and "stood by" Superintendent Blake as preparations were made to defend federal property against a feared secessionist attack. Political affiliations were not mentioned. The Republicans tried again in 1871 to remove "dissenting mechanics, laborers, &c." The matter was again referred to Worden, "who declined to give it any notice, beyond a refusal to put off or put on any man for political proclivities."[37]

Worden dealt with another political problem after the 7 November 1871 Maryland elections. Annapolis' Black voters largely supported the Republican ticket and were prematurely celebrating victory before returns from outlying parts of Anne Arundel County dampened their enthusiasm. Black voters in rural areas, presumably under the sway of conservative White landowners, had voted the Democratic ticket, and Democratic candidates swept most local and statewide contests. Tension was high in the Black community as a result. When a Black Democratic voter ventured onto the Academy grounds on 9 November, a group of Black Republican employees reportedly threw "bricks and other missiles at him." The man complained directly to Worden, who "delivered a scathing rebuke to the colored gentlemen and informed them that if such miserable conduct were again indulged in, he would dismiss the entire lot of them." The editor of the *Maryland Republic*, a staunch Democrat, supported the approach taken by Worden, who would "not permit... any low and disgusting practices, and [is] one who cannot be tampered with by narrow-minded and filthy politicians."[38]

Worden's abilities were next tested by the expansion of the Naval Academy's campus. At Worden's request in 1872, Navy surgeon general James Croxall Palmer personally inspected the midshipmen's New Quarters and mess-rooms. Although they had been completed only three years earlier in 1869, Palmer found "dangerous causes of disease" in water closets, laundry, and kitchen. He recommended constructing a new four-story attachment to the rear of New Quarters to house these functions, although the Academy would require additional land to accommodate it.[39]

Worden oversaw the expansion in 1873–74 through fourteen separate grant, purchase, and condemnation procedures of a predominantly low-income four-acre adjoining neighborhood known as Lockwoodville, which Academy professor Henry Hayes Lockwood once owned. The state of Maryland and the city of Annapolis passed legislation in 1867 and 1874, respectively, facilitating U.S. government acquisition of adjacent properties.

Problems arose when workers began to grade land and build a brick wall that blocked access to a waterfront parcel owned by the Annapolis and Elk Ridge Railroad Company. The county circuit court issued an injunction against Worden, Greene, and others to stop the work. The matter was settled out of court, and the parcel went to settlement. Some of the land Worden acquired in 1873–74 became the Academy's parade ground, which was officially designated Worden Field in 1910.[40]

New Tenants

In October 1873 the Navy's chief signal officer, Commo. Foxhall Alexander Parker Jr., and his staff were transferred from Washington to Annapolis. Robeson informed Worden that the department believed "greater facilities would be found" in Annapolis for conducting experiments in signaling and asked him to make suitable arrangements. The Signal Office was fully operational by December, and Parker and an assistant began running nautical light experiments.[41] The addition was a good supplement to the Academy's activities.

Worden was much less pleased by the next proposal. The House of Representatives passed a resolution in February 1874 suggesting the removal of the Naval Asylum for naval retirees from Philadelphia to Annapolis. Worden was quick to respond with his opinion. He told Robeson that Annapolis was no more suitable than Philadelphia and that "a more desirable place ... ought to be selected." Annapolis was a "particularly unfortunate" location because of the prevalence of "somewhat serious" malarial diseases. Further, the Academy was out of sight of passing vessels on Chesapeake Bay and "therefore, to a sailor's eye, practically an inland situation"; and beyond boating, bathing, and fishing, there were "no means of occupation or recreation suited to the tastes and habits of old sailors." Retirees, he declared, should be placed "within sight of the ocean wave," and moving to Annapolis "would have no beneficial result, either on the health, comfort, or happiness of the old sailor." The department accepted Worden's argument, Navy medical officers agreed, and the Naval Asylum remained in Philadelphia until it closed in 1976.[42]

Founding the U.S. Naval Institute

On 9 October 1873, at 7:40 p.m., Rear Adm. John L. Worden called to order the inaugural meeting of the U.S. Naval Institute. The Navy was in the postwar doldrums. Shrinking congressional appropriations, an aging fleet that included wooden sailing ships and obsolete monitors, and diminishing support for the officer corps in training conspired to inhibit modernization. But at the Navy's premier educational institution, a desire emerged to promote the service's future development and create a brain trust to discuss it.

The meeting was attended by Commodore Parker, Commandant of Cadets Cdr. Edward Terry, Cdr. Samuel Dana Greene, and eleven others who discussed how to establish a "society of Officers of the Navy for the purpose of discussing matters of professional interest." The initial concept is believed to have come from Parker, who was appointed to chair a committee "to determine what steps were necessary to further the objects of the association." Terry was tasked to communicate the new concept to bureau chiefs and naval yard commandants and ask for their advice.[43]

Three months later, at the 8 January 1874 meeting, Worden was entered into the official record as USNI Member No. 1. When the Institute members met in May 1874 they listened to Parker's paper on the Battle of Hampton Roads. Parker praised the "gallant" Worden for having "steadily steered" *Monitor* within a few yards of *Virginia* before he "coolly waited until his battery was reported 'ready for action.' " He praised Greene for sighting *Monitor*'s guns, placing "a shot full and fair in the roof of the *Merrimac[k]*," and returning *Monitor* to action after Worden was wounded, concluding that *Virginia*'s captain, Roger Catesby ap Jones, "would . . . never have retired from the fight while a hope remained to him of winning it."[44]

Less than two months after the Institute's founding, Worden served on a court of inquiry concerning the sinking of *Virginius*, a former Confederate blockade runner now sailing under the American flag. The Spanish navy had apprehended *Virginius* off the coast of Cuba on 30 October 1873 carrying munitions and supplies for Cuban insurrectionists. The Spanish authorities in Havana treated the vessel's American, British, and Cuban passengers and crew as pirates, and 53 of the 156 men on board were summarily executed. Americans clamored for war, and President Grant issued an ultimatum to Spain to release the surviving prisoners and ordered the Navy to mobilize its monitor fleet. The aging, largely out-of-service fleet was embarrassingly unprepared for war. Fortunately, diplomacy led to a peaceful solution, with Spain releasing the prisoners, paying an indemnity, and turning *Virginius* over to the United States. *Virginius* was under tow to New York with a Navy prize crew when it foundered off Cape Hatteras on 26 December 1873. The incident made Worden and his Naval Institute colleagues painfully aware of the Navy's obsolete ships and lack of preparedness for war. Thereafter, the Institute's *Proceedings* became a forum for much-needed discussions of naval policy and naval modernization.[45]

Life on and off the Yard

Now that Worden was ensconced at the Academy, he and Olivia were at last able to lead a busy social life in style. A letter from Worden to their friend Lissette Woodworth reveals some personal details of these social activities. He had been at the Academy only six weeks, he told her, and "events have crowded on me in rapid succession." He had been "constantly occupied" by his new official duties, and hours that could be spared from Navy duty were "appropriated to the organizing of my household." Of the superintendent's residence he said, "We . . . [h]ave a large & roomy house, well furnished & provided, where we propose to see & entertain our friends."[46]

Worden also told Lissette that initially Olivia had not been well, and he found it "necessary . . . to relieve her as much as possible." Later in the letter, he said that his wife was "getting now much better & is able to run our establishment creditably." Just a few days earlier, he told Lissette, he and Olivia had hosted "very satisfactorily" the Secretary of the Navy, a senator and his family, and the Russian minister, all of whom had come to Annapolis for the

Photo 12.2 Family of Commo. John L. Worden in front of the superintendent's residence, U.S. Naval Academy, 1873 *U.S. Naval Academy Special Collections and Archives 0151*

annual winter ball. Such activities, he wrote with uncharacteristic openness, "transformed me into quite a dignified 'cuss.' A hard role to assume, but one in which I hope to perfect myself by practice so as to meet your approval when you come."

Worden was surely well practiced by May 1871 when he and Olivia hosted President and Mrs. Ulysses S. Grant and their fifteen-year-old daughter, Ellen ("Nellie"). The group watched the annual drill competition and color parade in front of the superintendent's residence. For the first time, the event included a "color girl" who presented the champion's flag to the commander of the best-drilled company. Worden's eighteen-year-old daughter Grace served as the first "color girl," a role she played again in 1874. Unfortunately, it was a very hot day, and Grant suffered a severe headache and had to go inside to receive medical assistance. President and Mrs. Grant were given an early dinner before they returned to Washington. Nellie remained overnight to attend a hop held in her honor and presumably lodged with the Wordens and enjoyed the company of their daughters, Grace and Olivia ("Lilly").[47]

In January 1873 the Wordens again hosted the Grants at the Academy's annual ball. Secretary Robeson, Admiral Porter, Rear Admiral Case, and other officers from Washington also attended. The ball lasted through the night, and the Grants did not return to Washington until ten o'clock the next morning. Grant signed Worden's promotion to rear admiral the following month, effective back to 20 November 1872. On 4 March Worden led his middies to Washington for their first-ever inaugural parade appearance at the start of Grant's second term.[48]

Graduation was a highlight of Worden's Academy experiences. He and his wife and daughters, along with the Secretary of the Navy, the Board of Visitors, and other dignitaries, sat front and center in the chapel for the commencement ceremonies. Afterward the graduates and the rest of the battalion marched to the armory for a dress parade and presentation of diplomas. Each diploma was handed to Worden, who called out the graduate's name and passed the diploma to the Secretary for presentation. When all the diplomas had been handed out, Worden officially dismissed the graduates.[49]

The June 1871 graduation was of particular interest for the Wordens because it included John Tracy Edson, whose sister, Anna Maria, had married John Lorimer Worden Jr. just two months earlier in Albany, New York.

Another 1871 graduate was Perrin Busbee, who would marry Olivia Steele Worden in 1879. Worden wrote sadly to Secretary Robeson in February 1872, "My son's wife is dying and I feel it is necessary to go to him, at Albany, N.Y." He arrived too late to see Anna Maria, who had died during childbirth along with her baby the morning of Worden's letter to Robeson. The double loss of a daughter-in-law and grandchild was an overwhelming source of grief. But more grief was to come a year later. Distraught over the death of his wife and child, young Lieutenant Worden committed suicide in his quarters at Madison Barracks, Sackets Harbor, New York, on the morning of 4 May 1873. Admiral Worden hurried to nearby Watertown to claim Johnny's body and accompany it to Pawling, New York, for burial in a recently purchased family lot.[50]

John and Olivia spent their summer of bereavement with their remaining son and his wife, Daniel and Anna Worden, and their twenty-two-month-old daughter Harriet at Mamaroneck, on Long Island Sound. If Admiral Worden was disappointed not to have his name carried on with the loss of Johnny, he must have been pleased when Daniel and Anna named their son born on 9 August 1873 John Lorimer Worden.[51]

But life and official duties went on. As had always been the case, Worden did not like giving public speeches. When called on to speak at the annual meeting of the Society of the Army of the Tennessee held in Toledo, Ohio, in October 1873, he spoke with humility and humor: "I was not educated to make speeches. The only oratory I have been accustomed to indulge in has been 'Quarterdeck' oratory, which is mostly generally carried on through what is called a speaking trumpet, and if any of you should happen to have such an instrument, perhaps I might give you a specimen."[52]

Worden had been personally invited to the event by Army General in Chief William Tecumseh Sherman and was the only naval officer present. He was in prestigious company. The other attendees included President Grant, Secretary of the Army William W. Belnap, and many other generals and senior officers who had served in the Army of the Tennessee. At the next evening's banquet, when called upon to respond to a toast to the Navy, he said he had "too little confidence in my powers of language to attempt to do it justice." Instead, he referred his audience "to the history of the country, on every page of which its eulogy is written," and praised the contribution of Porter's 1863 run past Vicksburg, noting with a hint of bragging that the

Navy "contributed largely to the success achieved by the bravery and endurance of the armies of the West."[53]

As might be expected of a humble man, Worden refused the Naval Academy officers' offer to hold a "grand ball" in his honor at the end of his tenure. The local press reported he "declined for private reasons" but noted that he would leave with "the good wishes of many of our private citizens and all who have been connected with the Academy during his administration." He did allow his officers to host a dinner in his honor. It was held in the new mess hall and included "the most choice dishes." Toasts were offered, and "the festivities continued until a late hour of the night."[54]

As he prepared to leave the Academy, Worden was already anticipating his next assignment: command of the Navy's European Squadron. Just before he left Annapolis for a summer holiday, he received an invitation to meet Tsar Alexander III and to spend the night at Peterhof Palace.[55] The invitation presaged the busy diplomatic life ahead as commander in chief of U.S. naval forces in Europe.

CHAPTER 13

COMMANDING THE EUROPEAN SQUADRON

The Annapolis press lamented Worden's departure but noted he was going "into more active life in the service by taking command of the European Squadron."[1] This overseas command was the pinnacle of Worden's naval career. The scientific officer who had fought in battles, supervised the construction and testing of warships, and overseen the education and training of a new generation of naval officers now commanded a major naval force in foreign waters. As such, he became an itinerant goodwill ambassador, collector of intelligence, and war-front observer, the veritable face of the U.S. government.

Europe had been in upheaval since the 1848 revolutions. Russia had been defeated in the Crimean War of 1854–56. Austria lost its war against France and the Kingdom of Piedmont-Sardinia in 1859. Then came revolutionary activities that led to Italian unification in 1861, the Austro-Prussian War of 1866, the Franco-Prussian War of 1870–71, and the establishment of the German Empire in 1871. The opening of the Suez Canal in 1869 created a strategic sea link with Asia. Britain, France, and Germany were rapidly industrializing, modernizing their armies, building ironclad fleets, and expanding their colonial empires in Africa and Asia. In 1872 Germany engineered an alliance with the emperors of Austria-Hungary and Russia aimed at neutralizing unrest in the Balkans and offsetting the influence of France. The Ottoman Empire was frequently unsettled. The United States needed to be ever watchful, and the European Squadron played an important role in intelligence gathering and diplomacy.

Petitioning Congress

Just before departing for Europe, Worden attended to old business. Prior to his sojourn in Germany in 1868 he had written a glowing account of the role of *Monitor*'s crew, especially Samuel Dana Greene, during the Battle of Hampton Roads. He took a new tack when he sent a memorial to Congress on 20 November 1874. Other Union Navy crews had been awarded prize money for Confederate ships captured or destroyed and valuable goods they had seized. His own brother, Acting Paymaster Isaac Worden, was included in the bounties awarded to the crew of *Carondelet* for the cotton seized during the ironclad's Mississippi and Red River campaigns.[2]

Worden was seeking the prize money that he reasoned was rightfully due to *Monitor*'s officers and crew for having defeated *Virginia*. *Monitor* had in effect destroyed the Confederate ram and prevented its escape after Union forces occupied Norfolk. *Monitor*'s action saved millions of dollars in potential property damage and kept one or more cities from bombardment. He also noted the political value of the victory, which made "it highly improbable that foreign powers would interfere in our domestic affairs" during the remainder of the Civil War. Worden thanked Congress for its earlier gratitude to *Monitor*'s officers and crew and for approving his promotion. Now he requested that the men be granted *Virginia*'s estimated value, which he did not state.[3] Worden's memorial was submitted to the Senate and House of Representatives on 7 December and 9 December, respectively, and each referred it to their naval affairs committees. Worden testified before the House committee on 15 December and the Senate committee on 18 December 1868. The matter was tabled until 1881 (see chapter 14).

Back in 1865, Worden also had inquired about prize money for the crew of *Montauk* for its destruction of the rebel blockade runner *Nashville* on the Ogeechee River in February 1863. He suggested that his consort vessels—*Dawn*, *Seneca*, and *Wissahickon*—might also be included with *Montauk* in the bounty. Three years later, on 8 January 1868, the Treasury Department authorized a payment of $19,361.80, to be shared among the officers and crews of the four ships. Rear Adm. Samuel F. Du Pont received the largest portion: $968.20. Worden's share was the second highest at $492.10 (worth nearly $11,000 in 2024), about 14 percent of his annual salary in 1863. The lowest payout was $120.00 to *Montauk's* first-class boy.[4]

Bound for Europe

On 18 January 1875 John and Olivia Worden and their daughters Grace and Olivia embarked at Norfolk, Virginia, on *Powhatan*. Also on board was Ens. Perrin Busbee—young Olivia's future husband. Busbee had been assigned to serve on Worden's flagship *Franklin* and would soon join the admiral's staff. *Powhatan* arrived in Lisbon on 29 January, and on 3 February Worden transferred his flag to *Franklin*, commanded by Capt. Samuel R. Franklin, relieving Rear Adm. Augustus Ludlow Case.[5]

Worden's first port visit as commander in chief of U.S. European naval forces was Tangier, where he called on the Moroccan leadership. This was followed by Gibraltar, where he reviewed the British ironclad squadron, and then Villefranche-sur-Mer, France, the port city of Nice, the headquarters of

Photo 13.1 *Franklin*, flagship of the European Squadron, in European waters, circa 1874–76 Naval History and Heritage Command NH 92051

the European Squadron. *Franklin* joined two other squadron ships there—*Congress*, commanded by Capt. Alexander C. Rhind, and *Juniata*, commanded by Cdr. Samuel Dana Greene. Worden exchanged visits with officers on Russian ironclads and met a Russian admiral and a Prussian general. The U.S. consul and French civil and military officials also visited *Franklin* to meet *Monitor*'s old commander. After two months at Villefranche, *Franklin* sailed for La Spezia, Italy, where a third squadron ship, *Alaska*, commanded by Capt. Samuel P. Carter, was undergoing boiler repairs.[6] The Wordens disembarked at La Spezia to visit John's cousin in Florence, James Lorimer Graham, an expatriate poet, writer, acquaintance of internationally famous literati, and, since 1869, U.S. consul. They spent five days with Graham and his wife, Josephine.[7]

After returning to Villefranche, Worden prepared to take his family and squadron on a major diplomatic trip to five nations. Accompanied by *Alaska* and *Juniata*, *Franklin* sailed out of the Mediterranean and up the Atlantic coast to the Baltic Sea. Between 8 June and 1 August 1875 they made port calls and inland visits to Hamburg, Kiel, Berlin, Potsdam, Stockholm, Kronstadt, St. Petersburg, Copenhagen, and various points in between. The Americans exchanged numerous ship-to-ship visits and at Kronstadt participated—in a position of honor—in a forty-seven-vessel Russo-Swedish naval review. Worden and his staff officers met Bismarck and Germany's crown prince, Russia's tsar and a grand duke, and the kings of Sweden and Denmark. They also met U.S. and foreign diplomats, government leaders, and high-ranking naval and army officers wherever they traveled. During the Sweden visit, the local press highlighted the achievements of Swedish-born John Ericsson. King Oscar II praised Worden for his "eminent services," which, he said, were "well known and admired in my country—in all countries, indeed, where good conduct and heroism are appreciated." Following the Baltic cruise, the ships headed to Southampton, England, with finally a respite in London for Worden and his family.[8]

A Speck of War

Two days after arriving at Southampton on 9 August, Worden received an urgent telegram from the Navy Department. *Hartford*, which had just transited the Suez Canal from Asia, had been ordered to divert to Tripoli. U.S.

consul Michel Vidal and his wife reportedly had been insulted by Ottoman sailors, and American newspapers were demanding action. Under the title "A Speck of War," the *New Orleans Republican* said the incident was "of sufficient importance to cause the ordering of the United States steamship *Hartford*... to Tripoli to investigate the case and demand the punishment of the insulting parties." Worden had been "ordered to acquaint himself with the result" of *Hartford*'s visit and, if necessary, to send sufficient vessels "to strike terror to the Tripolitan heart." Allusions to the Barbary Wars of 1801–15 were made. One account said the Tripolitans "may have forgotten that little episode in their history," but U.S. Navy officers "have not, and if it is necessary to throw a shell or two into Tripoli, to remind the inhabitants our consul must be respected, they will doubtless do it with the greatest of pleasure."[9]

Worden took "prompt and decisive" action.[10] He was concerned that *Hartford* might not have received Washington's order to divert, and as the Navy commander in chief closest to the scene, but still quite distant, he used the advanced technology available to him and sent a telegram. He directed *Congress*, then at Corfu under the new command of Capt. Earl English, to proceed immediately to Tripoli. *Franklin* was still at Portsmouth and not ready for sea because of a disabled rudder, so Worden sent *Alaska* and *Juniata* ahead with orders to wait at Lisbon for further instructions. *Congress* reached Tripoli on 17 August, followed by *Hartford* on 21 August. Captain English reported that upon arrival, *Hartford* anchored "so as to bring her battery to bear on the fortifications."[11]

Although the U.S. press may have exaggerated the importance of the incident, Vidal had just cause to be upset. He had filed a formal complaint on 5 August with Mustapha, the pasha of Tripoli, noting that an Ottoman sailor had "surreptitiously entered [his] house" where his wife, three daughters, a nurse, and women servants were present. Vidal confronted the sailor, who fled, and chased after him until he encountered the sailor and two Ottoman officers. Vidal got into an argument with them, grabbed one of the officers by the collar, and, according to his own account, "gave him a shake or two" before returning home. This confrontation was followed by the arrival of a gang of sailors who made a menacing appearance outside Vidal's seaside villa. Vidal demanded that Mustapha court-martial the offenders, but the pasha countered that Vidal had struck the sailor, torn the officer's collar, and acted "in a very unbecoming manner." Mustapha demanded reparations, which began a round of antagonistic letters.[12] The matter was at an impasse when *Congress* and *Hartford* arrived.

Captain English, favoring diplomacy over war, advised Vidal to accept Mustapha's terms and meet him "in a liberal spirit of conciliation, and do not press a fallen foe to the wall." Two American warships in Tripoli's harbor and a prod from Constantinople to concede produced the desired effect. The charges against Vidal were withdrawn, the pasha apologized, and the sailor and others were punished.[13]

Worden managed this affair from afar while keeping in frequent contact with Captain English, who provided detailed reports and transcriptions of the Vidal-Mustapha correspondence. Worden's full report to the Navy Department included twenty-eight documents.[14]

Rumors of Piracy and Abduction

Piracy had been declining in the Mediterranean in the 1870s, but there still were periodic threats to merchant shipping. Concerned about reports of piracy on Spain's Mediterranean coast, U.S. minister to Madrid Caleb Cushing asked Worden in September 1875 to investigate, and Worden obliged. He made inquiries during a port stop at Barcelona and later reported that the piracy rumors were "greatly exaggerated." Nevertheless, obeying subsequent department orders, he sent *Alaska* to protect merchant shipping by cruising the Spanish coast.[15]

Worden had to deal with a real crisis in Turkey in early May 1876. A mob had murdered the French and German consuls at Salonica and attacked other foreign consuls over the alleged abduction of a Muslim girl by the U.S. consular agent, Pericles Hadji Lazzaro. Although Lazzaro had not even been present in Salonica at the time, his life was threatened and other Americans were worried. The Turkish government had been slow to respond to the deadly disturbances, so the U.S. minister at Constantinople, Horace Maynard, sent Worden a "delay not" plea. Worden, then at Villefranche, ordered *Franklin* immediately to sea. When he arrived at Salonica on 24 May he found Ottoman, French, and Russian warships at anchor and discovered that the local authorities had already executed six perpetrators, put others on trial, and court-martialed the local pasha and police chief. Worden was anxious to get to Constantinople to confer with Maynard, but just before departing he learned that a coup had deposed the reigning Ottoman sultan. He reached Constantinople by mail steamer on 2 June and spent four days conferring with Maynard and gathering intelligence on the new regime and the state of unease among American missionaries and Christian residents. He rejoined *Franklin* at Smyrna and proceeded to Beirut to consult with the local pasha and foreign emissaries. The crisis dissipated as the new Ottoman government took control. Worden was back in Villefranche by 4 July for a grand shipboard American Centennial celebration.[16]

The Mutiny Hoax

American newspaper readers were startled by ominous reports concerning Worden's flagship in early September 1876. Headlines such as "A Bloody End to a Mutiny" told of a supposed uprising on *Franklin* while the ship was moored at Leghorn, Italy. These stories were quickly followed, however, by "Looks Like a Hoax" and "The Story of a Baseless Canard."[17]

The story originated in Torino's *Gazzetta Piemontese* on 29 August. The article was based on a brief note from a correspondent in Nice saying that the vessel's "captain of arms" and several sailors had been killed by mutineers. The article claimed that the revolt ended when two Italian warships in the harbor threatened to fire on *Franklin*. The Paris newspaper *Le Figaro* "confirmed" the mutiny rumor on 9 September, adding that *Franklin*'s commander—"to save the lives of his threatened officers"—ordered a "battery-powered machine gun" fired at the mutineers, killing nine of them before order was restored. The report alleged that the idea of a rebellion "had prevailed among the crew" for a long time and that "death threats had been made." *Franklin* arrived back in Villefranche on 10 September unscathed, but the 11 September *Figaro* insisted that the authors of the story still had "every reason to believe that the details we have given . . . are absolutely correct." The *Gazzetta Piemontese* repeated the gist of *Le Figaro*'s original article, adding comments from Italian sailors, but ending, "We have reason to believe that the account of the revolt is not entirely accurate."[18]

When *Franklin*'s captain, Samuel R. Franklin, learned of *Le Figaro*'s reports, he wrote to the newspaper "declaring that this news is false" and that "there was not the slightest unrest on board." The editors insisted that they "were right to accept without reservation" the report from their correspondent in Nice, although they admitted that "the good faith of our correspondent was obviously surprising."[19] Worden's flag lieutenant, John C. Soley, engaged in further damage control. He telegraphed the Associated Press agent in London saying "that there is no truth in, or foundation for" the mutiny story and asked that the report be contradicted. American newspapers and the London *Times* obliged. The *Philadelphia Inquirer* said the story had "created a painful sensation not only among the friends of the officers on board, but throughout the country." Criticism of the false story and *Le Figaro* continued for weeks.[20]

In fact, a few elements of the story were accurate. *Franklin* did have a 50-inch Gatling gun among its armament at the time of the alleged incident that was used in live-fire training while at sea, and there had been discontent on *Franklin* when it arrived at Leghorn on 15 July.[21] Besides numerous cases of sailors returning intoxicated from liberty, bringing liquor on board, and engaging in "riotous conduct on shore," there were several instances of disrespect and insolence toward officers and assaults on some of *Franklin*'s guards. Nevertheless, the situation did not escalate into mutiny. Between 24 and 30 July several groups of Italian naval officers, civil officials, and the public visited the ship. On the evening of 1 August the crew gave a theatrical performance and on 11 August held a dress parade.[22]

How the mutiny story came about is unclear. Entries made in *Franklin*'s log just before the initial *Gazzetta Piemontese* report recorded a case of desertion as well as instances of unruly conduct and insolence toward superiors, all likely incubators for discontented talk because of the punishments received. But nowhere in *Franklin*'s log is there mention of a mutiny or violence.

Thirteen courts-martial were held on board *Franklin* and *Marion*, a recommissioned ship recently added to the squadron, during the Leghorn stay. Unfortunately, just four case files survive, and only two involved *Franklin* crewmembers. Ordinary Seaman Charles Stuart pleaded guilty to using insubordinate and offensive language and conduct against an acting Marine corporal, repeatedly striking him, refusing to obey his lawful order, and resisting lawful authority on 14 July. He was sentenced to confinement on *Franklin* until he was sent back to the United States, there to be confined for eighteen months and then dishonorably discharged. A second ordinary seaman, Alfred Almond, was found guilty of striking the paymaster's yeoman on 3 August during a captain's mast investigation of an earlier onshore altercation between them. Almond was sentenced to thirty days' confinement on bread and water, with full rations every third day, and forfeiture of two months' pay. The proceedings mention neither a Gatling gun nor any loss of life.[23]

Worden transferred his flag to *Marion* on 14 September, and *Franklin* left Villefranche to return home. At Vigo, Spain, *Franklin* took on board the notorious embezzler and escaped prisoner "Boss Tweed" (William M. Tweed) to return him to prison in New York. Tweed reportedly was given Worden's former cabin and placed under Marine guard.[24]

The Expert Reprised

Worden brought the expertise he had gained testing ships and engines at the Brooklyn Navy Yard to bear on the European Squadron's readiness. He made frequent complaints to the Navy Department about faulty engines and the need for constant maintenance and timely repair. His Naval Academy experience also came into play, as evidenced by his directives for squadron-wide training and shipboard education of cadet engineers.

Worden's ability to deploy his squadron was constrained by the nature of his ships—sailing ships transitioning to steam power—and their failure-prone engines. He issued standing orders to his ships' commanders to have their chief engineers thoroughly examine the engines and boilers and report any needed repairs. Such repairs were to be started "without delay and prosecuted with zeal and industry." He expected the ships under his command to be "kept at all times ready for such duty as the exigencies of the public service may require."[25]

Worden's flagships during this time offer good examples of the problems he faced in being able to deploy when needed. Following the 1875 Baltic cruise, *Franklin*'s rudder had to be replaced. The following spring, its engines and boilers needed overhauling. The ship was detained at Villefranche for repair when Worden needed to be in Turkey to protect American citizens and interests threatened by increasing instability there. He told the Navy Department, "It appears, in my judgment, very desirable that the United States Naval Force on this station should be increased with the least possible delay to a strength to meet the requirements of the service it may be called upon to do, for which in its present state it is utterly inadequate."[26]

In the same report he regretted that it was not in his power "to make a more effective display of available force" with more than the one ship—*Marion*—he had in the area. The department's endorsement of the report reads, "No answer required we have no ships available at present." Although *Franklin* had been in commission only since 1867 and was recommissioned in 1873, by the time it returned to the United States in 1876 it was suitable only for service as a receiving ship.

Worden's temporary flagship, *Marion*, was an elderly third-rate screw steamer with engine problems. It was at Genoa undergoing repair in October 1876 when Worden told the department that if he had to proceed to Turkey in person, he had no ship "in any way suitable for such purpose: none which will not serve, rather to diminish than to augment the respect of an Eastern people for the flag of command which is borne by so inconsiderable a vessel alone in the presence of ships of other nations."[27]

In response to Worden's plea for a new flagship, the department sent *Trenton*, a new wooden-hulled steam frigate. When *Trenton* finally arrived, Worden reported that he had wanted "to sail at once" but a broken engine part had "rendered [the ship] useless"; furthermore, the ship badly needed recaulking. He advised the department how "dangerous such delay might be under circumstances of most common occurrence." The squadron was unable to pursue its standing mission. While *Trenton* was being repaired Worden exercised the squadron's crews in tactical boat drills before sending the other vessels off to the emerging Russo-Turkish war front. Abandon-ship drills revealed another problem: *Trenton* did not have enough boats to carry the entire crew, and eighty men had been left behind. Worden also found that some of the boats were old and needed repairs that should have been made before *Trenton* left home. One boat was "so weak and rotten that she broke in two in being hoisted, while two others are to be surveyed as unfit for service."[28]

Worden also had repair issues with his other ships. When he sent *Alaska* to cruise the Spanish coast in November 1875, he feared that the "unreliable condition of [its] boilers" might lead to a "total breakdown" in a storm. In fact, *Alaska*'s boilers had been repaired just seven months earlier and would need repair again in 1876. *Juniata*'s engines were disabled at Lisbon and again at Hamburg in 1875, and its boilers required repair. Leaks in *Congress*' boiler necessitated repairs at Gibraltar, again at Malta, and yet again at Trieste between June and August 1875. When the recently commissioned screw sloop of war *Vandalia*'s cylinder head fractured in June 1877, the ship had to be withdrawn from Constantinople at a critical time during the Russo-Turkish War.[29]

Always aware of his responsibilities, Worden also insisted on his men receiving the education they needed to fulfill their duties. In an early order, he said it was "most important" that Navy boys receive "systematic and careful instruction in the branches of common school education." He wanted the junior enlisted men to learn their duties well while gaining knowledge to move to higher ratings. He reminded his officers about the "beneficial results" of training and insisted that they needed to "seriously comply ... not only with the letter but the spirit and intention" of Navy regulations in this regard. Moreover, this was still a sailing Navy. He directed that all boys should go aloft to learn how to send light yards and masts up and down and set, reef, and furl sails. They were to be instructed on making knots, splices, hitches, ends, and mats; in seizing, pointing, worming, and serving; in working wire rope; in heaving the lead; and steering the ship. He expected them to spend time every day except Saturday and Sunday learning about the compass, deck log, rigging, and purchases, whether at sea or in port. He had learned to operate a sailing ship, and so would they.[30]

Worden directed that cadet engineers be "afforded every facility for professional instruction and improvement" in new technologies. He insisted that cadets give special attention to their lessons about engines and fire rooms and required them to keep journals and to work on their mechanical drawing proficiency. When they were ashore at ports that had large machine and construction establishments, cadets were expected to visit them and take notes. He required chief engineers to make quarterly reports on cadets' proficiency, professional aptitude, and deportment. Naval forces under Worden's command would be well prepared for whatever their country required of them.[31]

Another Battle Won

On 26 February 1877 the department directed Worden to relocate the European Squadron's headquarters from Nice to Lisbon and to transfer public stores from Villefranche to the new Portuguese station. He was directed to proceed immediately to Lisbon to make necessary arrangements.

The Navy Department was in flux at the time. Congress was in a postwar budget-cutting mood and demanded a reduction of personnel. Nor were legislators certain that Secretary of the Navy Robeson was doing a good job. Robeson's management of the Navy Department was under investigation by the House Committee on Naval Affairs, and he was even threatened with impeachment. Robeson was replaced as secretary by Richard W. Thompson when Rutherford B. Hayes was inaugurated on 3 March 1877.[32]

Worden received Robeson's order on 13 March, but with *Marion* and *Vandalia* in the eastern Mediterranean, he was without a ship to make the move. He wrote from Nice on 15 March that "as soon as practicable after the return of these ships" he would "proceed to carry out the Department's orders." *Marion* returned to Villefranche on 16 March, but instead of proceeding to Lisbon, Worden sent the department a twelve-page reclama explaining why he objected to being ordered to transfer his headquarters "without ... previous intimation to me of so important a movement."

He acknowledged that the department's instructions were "definite and ... issued as a result of a decision already arrived at," but he insisted that he should first have been consulted: "It does not lie beyond the province of my duty as Commander in Chief to present my views." The European Squadron was the mobile representative of the U.S. government in European and North African waters. What the squadron learned was reported to the department and then shared with Washington policymakers. The hero of Hampton Roads was the public face of America in the troubled Mediterranean, and Worden pointed out that his ships had a critical mission in the eastern Mediterranean: to protect American citizens "from the violence of its turbulent population."[33]

He went on to explain that Villefranche had a more beneficial climate and better sanitary conditions and public hospitals than Lisbon. The French government provided a commodious storehouse with a deep waterfront rent-free. The port was fully supplied and convenient for ships bound for Italy, Sicily, and the Grecian islands. Lisbon was 1,000 miles west of Villefranche and 2,500 miles from the eastern Mediterranean. Further, it was on a river with rapid currents that made ship navigation difficult and was subject to incessant rain. Worden cited his personal experience that the anchorage was "not only difficult but often a matter of danger." Lisbon was "a Port no Commander would seek as a healthful or convenient harbor." There was no wharf, and channel navigation lights were aground at low tides, "causing often great delays and inconveniences." If the relocation took place, storehouses would have to be rented "at perhaps a high price." When he had been at Lisbon previously, stores were not readily available and had to be purchased at high cost on the open market. Worden cryptically added that "social and moral influences must also be considered." In other words, his sailors would behave better in France than in Portugal.

As his final word on the transfer, Worden stated that he had important business to conduct as soon as *Trenton* arrived. He needed to make a cruise to Turkey, Syria, the North African coast, Tunis, and Tripoli, where it was "very desirable that we should show our Flag... in some considerable force." He ended his lengthy missive by asking for a telegraphed response.

Not satisfied to use only his own ammunition to fight this battle, Worden solicited support from his French ally. Two days later after sending his reclama to Washington, Worden forwarded copies of letters between himself and Villefranche's mayor, who expressed "deep chagrin" that the "firm ally of France" had decided to remove the public storehouse to Lisbon and asked Worden to intervene and get the decision either delayed or revoked. Worden also reported that the U.S. chargé d'affaires in Lisbon had not received official instructions regarding the transfer and that he would need the consent of the Portuguese government to make the move. Worden's bluntness had the desired effect. On 6 April he was informed by telegram that the relocation order was revoked. He responded, "I beg leave to say that the Department's decision was received by me with great satisfaction."[34] Another battle was won.

Showing Leniency

Although Worden usually agreed with the court-martial sentences issued during his European command, he was not above demonstrating leniency when he thought it was deserved. One case involved a second-class boy who had used abusive, profane, and threatening language toward his superior officer. Because of the boy's "youth and inexperience," Worden reduced the stiff sentence from three years' confinement and dishonorable discharge to one year of confinement. In another case, Worden had the sentence of twelve months' confinement and forfeiture of $120 for a Marine private who assaulted a petty officer read to the assembled crew so it "may still have its effect as a warning," then, because of the prisoner's "excellent conduct heretofore," remitted the sentence altogether. He reduced the sentence of a landsman (an inexperienced sailor) found guilty of having liquor on *Franklin*'s berth deck from solitary confinement in double irons on bread and water for thirty days to confinement in single irons. Conversely, when a landsman was sentenced to three months' confinement in double irons, with one of the months in solitary, for refusing to obey an order and using disrespectful and abusive language toward his superior officer, Worden let it be known that he did not regard the sentence "as adequate punishment for the very grave offenses" and let it stand.[35] The same sense of honor and respect for authority Worden sought to instill when disciplining his charges at the Naval Academy held true in Europe, perhaps even more so because Navy men were expected to be a reflection of America overseas.

On the War Front

The Russo-Turkish War broke out on 24 April 1877. Worden, then at Villefranche, received a Navy Department dispatch a day later about the imminence of war, but *Trenton* was not yet ready for sea. He previously had dispatched *Vandalia* to Constantinople, *Marion* to Smyrna, and the screw gunboat *Alliance* to the coast of Syria. He and *Trenton* were stuck in Villefranche while repairs continued. Meanwhile, he reported the arrival of British and French warships at the port and received the Prince of Wales, the future King Edward VII, on board *Trenton*.[36]

Foreign correspondents and military attachés kept the U.S. government abreast of events at the front. One such rapporteur was U.S. Army 1st Lt. Francis Vinton Greene, the attaché to St. Petersburg and younger brother of Cdr. Samuel Dana Greene. But Greene did not arrive in Russia until 18 July and was then embedded with the Russian army in Bulgaria, so the Navy was America's quick response and intelligence force. Worden arrived at Smyrna on 15 May and planned to remain there as "the most convenient point" from which to move quickly to protect American interests. *Trenton* could not proceed to Constantinople because an international agreement restricted the class and armament of ships passing through the Dardanelles and *Vandalia* was already there, so Worden conferred at Smyrna with Turkish authorities, U.S. and European consuls, and Austrian naval commanders. Horace Maynard, the U.S. minister at Constantinople, with whom Worden had maintained frequent communication, also came to Smyrna to confer with the admiral. The breakdown of Ottoman authority in outlying regions had raised significant concern over the safety of American Christians, and the Navy's presence was reassuring.[37]

Trenton's log recorded an incident at Smyrna that triggered a quick reaction with potentially lethal results. *Trenton* was steaming slowly out of Smyrna's harbor on its way to sea at 7:15 p.m. on 5 August 1877 when the crew was "beat to quarters in consequence of a blank cartridge having been fired from the Fort on Sand Jack point. . . . No intimation was given of the firing—our guns were shotted with 180 lb. shell."[38] The crew rushed to battle stations, but at 7:44 the drums beat retreat, "leaving the gun deck battery loaded." *Trenton*'s former chaplain, Rev. Henry H. Clark, revealed more details of this episode during his 1897 eulogy for Worden at the Naval Academy. He was on deck with Worden and his staff as *Trenton* moved out close to dusk. A soldier at the fort made a flag signal for *Trenton* to heave to, based on an order that no vessel should leave or enter the port between sunset and sunrise.

> His [Worden's] decision was instant. . . . He gave no order to put the ship about or to come to anchor. He knew that he was proceeding at great risk. In addition to the danger from the fort the channel was thickly planted with torpedoes. Presently there came a shot across our bows. In distinct, low tones, but with the gravity of battle in them, the Admiral said to the captain, "Beat to quarters, sir." Everyone sprang to his station. There was an instant's silence; then the order came: "Cast loose and provide." Each officer and man . . . cleared the ship for action. A moment more and she was turned full broadside to the fort, her rifled guns frowning in deadly aim. On ploughed the ship, the Admiral's face with its scar of battle set like flint with the determination, at any further demonstration from the fort, to give the order "fire." But the Turkish guns were silent.[39]

Worden knew that the Ottoman authorities were familiar with his ship, and his aggressive response may have been a bit of showboating for the benefit of the midshipmen he had on board. But to Clark, the action demonstrated that "promptness and bravery were not impulses but habits of [Worden's] life." The captain who had gone gunwale to gunwale with the CSS *Virginia* and brought *Montauk* directly under the batteries of Fort McAllister did not hesitate to show fortitude in the face of a Turkish fort.

Except for brief visits to nearby island ports to collect intelligence from local authorities, Worden remained at Smyrna until 25 August. Being close to a combat zone may have been invigorating for the old admiral, but he was ready for relief. Two months earlier he had sent a request to Secretary of the Navy Thompson asking to be relieved of his command, with a suggested termination date of 5 October 1877. After receiving approval, Worden sailed for Villefranche. Cdr. Robert S. Bradford, captain of *Marion*, was left as senior officer in charge at Smyrna, with *Vandalia* and *Alliance* standing by.[40]

Rear Adm. William E. Le Roy relieved Worden as commander in chief of European naval forces on 5 October 1877 at Marseille. Worden's last official acts were submitting a complete set of his general orders and writing a glowing commendation of Master Sidney Augustus Staunton, Naval Academy class of 1871, who had been with Worden from the beginning of their European deployment. Staunton went on to serve as assistant chief of staff of the U.S. fleet at the Battle of Santiago de Cuba in 1898 and retired as a rear admiral in 1912.[41]

Worden and his family left Marseille for Paris, where they were on hand to greet former President Grant and his wife and son when they arrived on 24 October. They were back in New York City by 8 November 1877. Worden's sea service was over. According to the *Navy Register*, he had served a total of twenty-one years and three months at sea.[42]

CHAPTER 14

SERVICE IN WASHINGTON AND RETIREMENT YEARS

By the time he returned from Europe in November 1877, Worden had completed forty-three years of naval service. U.S. Navy retirement was mandated at forty-five years of service or at age sixty-two, of which he was three years shy, but because he had twice received the official thanks of Congress, Worden was allowed to serve beyond the normal retirement date.[1]

A visit his mother in Kent County, Michigan, was among his top priorities. He went there in December and again in 1879 and 1881. Harriet Graham Worden died in 1883 at age ninety. In early 1878 Worden obtained a permit to build a comfortable brick house at 1428 K Street Northwest for Olivia, his daughters, and three live-in servants. Newspapers described it a "fine house" in an "up-town" section of Washington, just three blocks from the White House. The Wordens' immediate neighbors came to include the Swedish ambassador, a Supreme Court justice, an admiral or two, several senators, the Speaker of the House of Representatives, and a Treasury secretary.[2]

Final Duty
On 29 December 1877 Worden was assigned to two Navy boards, one for examining officers for promotion and the other for reviewing those eligible

for retirement. He served on both boards for the next nine years, and for a time was president of both. His office was at the Navy Department, next to the White House. A reporter for the *Troy Weekly Times* said he could be seen there "shuffling through the halls . . . a spare old man." Following the deaths of other senior veterans, Worden—along with David Dixon Porter and Stephen Clegg Rowan—was called one of the "three immortals" of the Navy.[3]

Photo 14.1 Rear Adm. John L. Worden in civilian clothes, photo taken by Levin C. Handy, Washington, DC, 1881 *Mariners' Museum and Park MS0016/02-003#001*

With only light office duty, Worden was available for other work as well. In May 1878 he was appointed to the Naval Academy's Board of Visitors, and in June of that year he presided over the Academy's annual examinations. In January 1881 the House Appropriations Committee designated him to serve on the District of Columbia's proposed Bureau of Charities, charged with advising Congress concerning aid to poor and underemployed residents. It is unknown what effort Worden put into this task, but several years later he donated five dollars to the District's poor relief fund. In February 1882 the Secretary of the Navy appointed Worden to chair a board to study the request from a private company to build railroad tracks across the north end of the Naval Academy campus. Later that year his name was among "the most prominent gentlemen in the city" nominated to the local branch of the Longfellow Memorial Committee. The national committee was raising funds to purchase property in front of Henry Wadsworth Longfellow's house in Cambridge, Massachusetts, and there to erect a monument to the poet, who had died the previous March. Olivia Worden was reported in 1882 to be one of the "lady movers" raising funds for a proposed homeopathic hospital in Washington.[4]

Worden joined Admiral Porter, Admiral Rowan, Adm. John Rodgers, and Adm. Christopher Rodgers in planning the ceremonies for unveiling a statue of Adm. David Glasgow Farragut in Farragut Square. The event took place on 15 April 1881, with President James A. Garfield, Supreme Court justices, and naval celebrities among those in attendance.[5] When a statue of the late Adm. Samuel F. Du Pont was to be dedicated on Du Pont Circle in 1884, Worden again served on the planning committee.[6]

Sued by a Professor

June 1878 brought Worden the unwelcome news that a former Naval Academy professor had filed a lawsuit against him. Back in October 1872, Bernard Maurice, an assistant professor of French, had asked Worden to allow him to resign from the Academy. At first, Worden tried to talk him into staying. But on discovering that Maurice had been accused of "taking grossly improper liberties with the persons of very young girls," Worden forwarded the request to the Secretary of the Navy with a confidential endorsement recommending approval "with as little delay as possible." The Navy Department allowed

Maurice to resign to avoid scandal, but Maurice also had a separate grudge against Worden. He had given French lessons to Worden's daughters, but Worden had ignored his request for compensation.[7]

Maurice renewed his demand for payment in early 1878, soon after Worden returned from Europe. When Worden did not respond, Maurice asked the Navy Department to intervene, but the department declined. In June 1878 Maurice filed two suits against the former Academy superintendent in Anne Arundel County Circuit Court in Annapolis: one sought $201 for compensation for the language lessons; the other asked for $20,000 for defamation of character in Worden's 1872 endorsement of Maurice's resignation request. The court rejected the compensation claim because the statute of limitations had expired. The libel suit was allowed to continue. Recognizing Worden's popularity in Annapolis, Maurice's lawyers asked for a change of venue, and the trial took place in May 1879 in Baltimore's Court of Common Pleas. The court found in Worden's favor, and Maurice appealed both cases to the Maryland Court of Appeals. In June 1880 the Court of Appeals affirmed the lower court's compensation finding, but in the defamation case allowed that Worden's endorsement of Maurice's resignation request was "not absolutely privileged," meaning it was not restricted as confidential or classified. Worden's lawyers appealed the decision in U.S. Circuit Court in Baltimore, and a trial was held in December 1880. Worden testified, as did the young woman whom Maurice had allegedly abused when she was a child. The jury found that Worden's endorsement was absolutely privileged and denied Maurice's appeal. Maurice's lawyers sought a new trial, but the court overruled their motion.

Refusing to give up, in January 1881 Maurice filed a petition with the House of Representatives insisting he had been "unjustly" removed from his Academy professorship. Nothing came of his petition, so Maurice asked the Secretary of the Navy to reinstate him at the Academy. The Navy's judge advocate general advised the Secretary that Maurice had been "dismissed" because of "grave charges." When Maurice learned of this response, he sued the judge advocate general in the Supreme Court of the District of Columbia, asking for $50,000 in damages. The suit pended until January 1890, when it was dismissed by the court. Over the years, *Maurice v. Worden* has been cited in more than thirty-five cases involving privileged government communications—one case as early as 1886 in the New York Court of Appeals and others as recently as 2004 before the Maryland Court of Appeals. The case also has been cited several times before the U.S. Supreme Court.[8]

Involvement in Politics

While Worden was engaged in his naval career, three of his brothers entered public life in Michigan. All were staunch Democrats, as presumably was their father. As a Navy officer, Worden took the neutral approach to politics that his position demanded. On 5 August 1880 he was among the many "eminent men" who called at the Manhattan hotel of James Garfield, who had just secured the Republican Party nomination for president. Garfield reportedly exclaimed, "Why, Admiral Worden, I am really happy to see you!" Worden was no stranger to Garfield. When Garfield was a member of the House of Representatives in 1874, he had asked a favor of Worden. A cadet midshipman who had entered the Academy just two days before wanted leave to spend a few days with his mother before she left for Europe. Worden declined, citing his lack of authority to grant the leave. The day after greeting the Republican Garfield in 1880, Worden offered his congratulations in person to Democratic Party nominee Winfield Scott Hancock at his home on Staten Island.[9]

Worden was on the White House reviewing stand for Garfield's inaugural parade. A week later he was among the officers attending an Army-Navy Night reception at the White House. Worden and other senior naval officers rode in Garfield's special train to Annapolis for the June 1881 Naval Academy commencement. Several days later, Worden met again with Garfield when he visited the White House to introduce William Joseph Bibb as an "old and valued friend, made so through the exigencies of war" when Worden was a prisoner of war in Montgomery, Alabama, in 1861.[10]

The 1884 presidential election of Democrat Grover Cleveland brought another duty for Worden when he was designated one of the fifty men to serve on the General Committee for the forthcoming inauguration, a routine military duty. When Cleveland held his first New Year's Day White House reception, Porter and Worden walked in side-by-side at the head of Navy Department bureau chiefs and Navy officers in line to be greeted by the president.[11]

Appointments for Relatives

Worden was surely pleased in March 1886 when President Cleveland awarded an at-large appointment to the Naval Academy to John William Worden, his brother Frederick William Worden's sixteen-year-old son. Unfortunately, shortly after the lad arrived in Annapolis, before he was even officially admitted, he became ill from overly strenuous exercise and returned home, where he died on 15 June 1886.[12]

Whether or not Worden exerted direct influence on this or other federal appointments for his relatives is open to conjecture. Certainly, his fame would have made their names familiar. His brothers Ananias Graham Worden and Isaac Gilbert Worden held pre–Civil War positions with the Post Office Department in Michigan, and Ananias later in Washington, DC, as well. But those appointments may have been influenced by their elder cousin, John Lorimer Graham, who was postmaster of New York City from 1840 to 1845. On the other hand, within six months of Worden's 1867 reunion with his brother in El Dorado County, California, James Barenloe Worden was appointed as a receiving clerk in the U.S. customs house in San Francisco. He continued there as an assistant storekeeper until two years before he died in 1885. Also in 1885, a Kalamazoo newspaper revealed "it should be mentioned that Admiral Worden . . . is said to be championing the candidacy of his brother Fred, of Grand Rapids" for the position of U.S. marshal for the western district of Michigan.[13] The supposed job title was a misnomer; Frederick Worden became a land claims inspector for the U.S. Department of the Interior, a job he held from 1886 to 1897. In 1886 Isaac Worden was appointed U.S. commercial agent in Wallaceburg, Ontario, Canada, a position he held until he died in 1902.

It was not always jobs that relatives sought. Around 1889 Admiral Worden received a request from his first cousin James Henry Worden to help obtain an increase in his Civil War Navy pension. Worden rightly advised his cousin that the pension law could not be disregarded. However, if James could supply additional "desired evidence" to support his claim, Worden offered to go in person to the Pension Office "to ask their immediate attention to it."[14]

No Grateful Recognition

In December 1881 and January 1882, the Senate and House of Representatives took up Worden's 1874 petition seeking prize money for the damage

Monitor had done to *Merrimack* (i.e., *Virginia*). Worden's petition now had the support of Secretary of the Navy William Hunt, who wrote on 28 January 1882 that although *Monitor* had neither destroyed nor captured *Merrimack*, the damage done by the Union ironclad during their battle had taken the Confederate warship out of the fight. Furthermore, Hunt wrote that *Monitor*'s remaining at Hampton Roads to confront the rebel ironclad should it resume its attacks was an action presumed to have led to *Virginia*'s final destruction on 11 May 1862, for which *Monitor*'s officers and men "deserve grateful recognition by the Government."[15]

The bill had broad support in Congress. Extensive testimony was heard—some in opposition to awarding prize money for performing wartime duties—and the Senate and House naval affairs committees both unanimously approved their bills. The full Senate narrowly passed its version on 24 May 1882, but the bill died in the House. Opposition arose from those who suggested similar monetary rewards be given to the men of *Congress* and *Cumberland*, who had fought *Virginia* at much greater odds than those faced by the men on *Monitor*. A Georgia congressman argued that "honors and emoluments should go to the men who conceived the idea, not of the *Monitor*, but of the iron-clad," and added, "Ought not the honor in fact to go to the men who put the railroad iron on the *Merrimac*?" It was noted that with his $5,000 annual salary, Worden was not indigent, but there were many poor soldiers and sailors who would benefit from such munificence. In the end, a motion to bring the bill to a House vote failed on 8 December: 38 in favor, 102 against. A second motion was approved to lay the bill aside and remove the enacting clause. Worden's effort was at least temporarily dead.[16]

The issue was renewed in May 1884 when the House Committee on Naval Affairs considered a bill that would add $200,000 to an appropriations bill to be distributed to *Monitor*'s crew. After hearing considerable testimony, none of which sustained the claimed destruction of *Virginia*, the committee "report[ed] adversely to the passage of the bill."[17]

Social Life

Little is known about the Worden family's social life until the late 1870s, although some social activities were newsworthy during their time at the Naval Academy (see chapter 12). But now the Wordens were among Washington's elite, and their social activities received frequent mention in newspapers. The November 1879 wedding of Worden's daughter Olivia to Master Perrin Busbee, then serving on the Naval Academy practice ship *Saratoga*, was held at Epiphany Episcopal Church in Washington. It "drew together a brilliant assemblage . . . among those prominent in official life," including Secretary of State William Maxwell Evarts, Rear Adm. John Rodgers, and their families, as well as the daughters of General of the Army William Tecumseh Sherman.[18]

Society pages reported weekly receptions at the home of "Mrs. Admiral Worden." She hosted a "German" dancing party attended by the British minister and Rear Adm. John Rodgers, their wives and daughters, and society women from Washington, Baltimore, and other cities.[19] Daughters Grace and Olivia gave luncheons for their friends at their parents' K Street residence, attended teas and soirees with their mother, and were seen at other high-toned society events with or without their famous father. They were noted as being "particularly elegant" at the 1 January 1882 reception at the White House, President Chester Arthur's first New Year's event. Grace was a guest at a dinner given by Secretary of State Frederick Frelinghuysen and his wife, Matilda, in 1884 for the Washington diplomatic corps. Perhaps there was matchmaking involved in this social whirl, but Grace never married. She made an attractive and eligible guest, and she and her mother remained on the official White House guest list into the Theodore Roosevelt administration.[20]

The Wordens socialized with President Arthur at the 1883 wedding of Alice Blaine, daughter of former Secretary of State James Gillespie Blaine, and were among the "personal friends" and "conspicuous" guests at the White House reception afterward, along with Admiral Porter, Admiral Rodgers, General Sherman, and Gen. George Brinton McClellan and their spouses. Mrs. Worden was among sixteen guests at a breakfast given by Lucy Hale Chandler, wife of Secretary of the Navy William Eaton Chandler, in honor of President Arthur's sister Mary Arthur McElroy. Worden and Rodgers were part of a "distinguished party" that went by boat with Mary McElroy to Mount Vernon in March 1883.[21]

His fame brought Worden many requests for his presence at various events. He was invited in July 1883 to participate in an August ceremony to open the Northern Pacific Railroad Company's main line from Lake Superior to Oregon and Puget Sound. He declined without specifying a reason.

He would have been nearby, because he, his son Daniel, and "a party of New York capitalists" visited Yellowstone National Park in early August. Coincidentally, President Arthur also visited Yellowstone in August and attended the railroad event in St. Paul, Minnesota.[22]

Worden was a founding member of the revived Metropolitan Club. The original club had been established in 1863 by prominent Washingtonians, including John Lorimer Graham, then a Treasury Department clerk, who served as its president in 1864–66. Worden was elected to the club's Board of Governors and was first vice president in 1882. Upon the death of longtime president Adm. C. R. P. Rodgers in 1892, Worden was unanimously elected president. However, as noted in the club's history, "the old sailor was not in good health, and could attend only very few meetings." He resigned the presidency a few weeks later and left the Board of Governors in 1895. His successor as president was his old Naval Academy aide, Commo. George Dewey.[23]

Not all newsworthy events were happy ones. Worden and his family were notably present at numerous funerals for friends, relatives, and dignitaries. Worden served as an honorary pallbearer for Naval Academy Superintendent Commo. Foxhall Parker in 1879, Rear Adm. John Rodgers in 1882, and Gustavus Vasa Fox in 1883.[24]

Worden was evidently out of town or ill because his name was not included among the long list of Navy officers attending the 23 September 1881 Capitol funeral service for assassinated President Garfield. Daniel Toffey Worden, however, was part of a New York Stock Exchange delegation that met the new president, Chester A. Arthur, and attended the funeral. In February 1882 Admiral Worden was one of the first to arrive for a memorial service for Garfield in the House of Representatives chamber and sat directly in front of the clerk's desk.[25]

His most prominent turn as an honorary pallbearer was at former president Grant's funeral in New York City in August 1885. He was in New York again in November that year, not as a pallbearer but to attend the funeral of General McClellan. In retirement, Worden served as an honorary pallbearer for Vice Adm. Stephen C. Rowan in 1890, Adm. David Dixon Porter in 1891, and Rear Adm. C. R. P. Rodgers in 1892. The funeral of Worden's friend Rear Adm. Thornton A. Jenkins "was conducted without military display" in 1893.[26]

Retirement Plans

While they were living in Annapolis in 1869–74 the Wordens considered retiring to Newport, Rhode Island. They purchased a 20,000-square-foot parcel there in 1872 but never developed it and sold it in 1881. Around the same time, Worden's distant cousin Rear Adm. Reed Werden also purchased property in Newport and did build a retirement home there, and the newspapers confused the names of the two men. Their surnames were pronounced the same, but the different spelling was frequently ignored. When Werden died in 1886, the press initially identified him as the "hero of the *Monitor*."[27]

The Wordens' main summer retreat was in rural Quaker Hill, New York. If Worden was at sea, Olivia and the children stayed either with Olivia's sister, Margaret Toffey Craft, in a home still standing next to the Quaker Hill Meeting House, or nearby with cousin Ann Toffey Hayes. Daniel Worden purchased land in Quaker Hill in 1879 in trust for his six-year-old son, John Lorimer Worden, about a quarter mile away from the Craft home. He bought adjacent land in 1881. Admiral Worden named the property "Main Top." Around the time of these purchases, Worden invested in a new 145-room hotel to be built near another Quaker Hill crest. For this he offered the name "Mizzen Top," and it was called that from 1881 until it closed in 1932. The Wordens enjoyed the hospitality of this well-appointed hotel, as did Gen. Lew Wallace from Indiana. Wallace's mother-in-law was a Quaker Hill native and kin to Olivia. Worden and Wallace often strolled together on a rustic shaded path that ran below the hotel "to further their friendship." John Worden may have loved the sea and visiting his family in Michigan, but Olivia, it was said, "was never weaned from Quaker Hill."[28]

Simply a Reminiscence

On 20 December 1886, Congress authorized John Worden's retirement at the highest pay of his grade. He was the most senior rear admiral and eligible for promotion to vice admiral, but after fifty-two years and eleven months of service in the Navy, he was ready to step down. His pension was set at the full rate paid annually for sea duty: $6,000 (worth about $200,000 in 2024).[29]

Worden's final years were marked by tragedy. He lost his daughter-in-law, Annie Wilmot Worden, after a brief illness in 1887, and his brother-in-law Moses Kipp died in 1890. His brother Ananias and his son-in-law Perrin

Busbee committed suicide in 1890 and 1891, respectively. Two of his sisters also passed away: Lucy Harriet in 1893 and Jane Louisa in 1894.[30]

Still involved in national affairs, in March 1889 Worden served on the reception subcommittee for Benjamin Harrison's presidential inauguration. In August 1890 Worden was "the central object of interest" at the New York City embarkation ceremony for the return to Sweden of the remains of John Ericsson, who had died the previous year. Worden had been reluctant to attend and said that he did so "solely due to a long and earnest solicitation" of Secretary of the Navy Benjamin F. Tracy. This might have been either an indication of Worden's disdain for Ericsson or just a desire to remain at Quaker Hill. In 1893 Daniel Worden was a member of the planning committee for the unveiling of a statue of Ericsson at Battery Park in Manhattan, but his father was conspicuously absent.[31]

Worden showed no such disdain for his former enemies. When Hardin Beverly Littlepage, a midshipman on CSS *Virginia* during the Battle of Hampton Roads, applied for a consulship in 1887, Worden, three Southern politicians, and two officers who had been on *Cumberland* and *Congress* during the same battle accompanied Littlepage on his rounds of the State Department. Three years later Worden was a pallbearer for Col. Beverley Kennon, a former U.S. Navy lieutenant who joined the Confederate Navy as an ordnance expert in 1861.[32]

Noted journalist Walter Wellman reported seeing Worden in 1892 at the Army-Navy Club in Washington playing whist with the retired admirals Thomas O. Selfridge and Thornton A. Jenkins. Wellman related a conversation with an unidentified Navy lieutenant who had recently spoken with Worden. The lieutenant said that Worden had told him to

> distinguish yourself in the service of your country if opportunity offers. As for me . . . I am simply a reminiscence. I am living simply to live. My only aim in life is to cultivate longevity. As long as I live, my pay as a retired officer keeps my good wife from want, and we are able to do a little something for others. My health is not good, but I hope to live as long as my wife does for her sake. When she goes I hope to go with her. . . . [Y]ou ought to see how I take care of myself. My sole occupation, I say, is the cultivation of longevity. I study hygiene, dietetics, every law or

rule of health.... My entire time and energies are devoted to taking care of myself—not for myself, understand, but for the $4,500 a year which the government allows me during my lifetime. My good wife needs this as long as she lives and that is what I am living for.[33]

In addition to his clubs, Worden may have become a fan of vaudeville when his niece Oriska Worden came to Washington. Oriska, the adopted daughter of Worden's brother Frederick, had trained in Paris to become an opera singer but ended up a popular entertainer on the vaudeville circuit.[34] In April 1897 she performed at the Lafayette Square Opera House, not far from the Wordens' home, where she stayed. She referred to Worden in a subsequent interview, saying, "Uncle John was one of the kindest and gentlest men I have ever known.... [H]e was always modest as he was brave, and the most loyal man to his country that I have ever met."[35]

In early October 1897 Worden, wife Olivia, and daughter Grace returned to Washington for the winter. He contracted a cold on 13 October; on the sixteenth, Navy doctors discovered pneumonia in his left lung. Rear Adm. John Lorimer Worden died at his K Street home on Monday, 18 October 1897.[36] The Washington *Evening Star* claimed he had been in "very good health" just a few days before, but Oriska disagreed: "For several years before his death he was blind and a great sufferer. He often remarked that he was being spared a long time to endure a great deal. He was a warrior in spirit to the very last."[37]

On the day Worden died, Secretary of the Navy John D. Long wrote that he was the "last survivor of the great naval heroes of our Civil War" and his death was "lamented by the whole country . . . his memory will ever be held in honor." Long directed that on the day after his order was received, all Navy Yards and stations and all ships in commission were to display the flag at half-mast and fire thirteen guns at noon. Worden's death was widely publicized nationally and abroad.[38]

The funeral, held at St. John's Episcopal Church on Lafayette Square with its rector, Rev. Alexander Mackay-Smith, presiding, was attended by President William McKinley and cabinet members, members of the judiciary, government officials, and numerous Navy and Army officers. The honorary pallbearers were Navy Secretary Long, Supreme Court Justice Horace Gray, former U.S. Court of Claims judge John Chandler Bancroft Davis, U.S. Court of Claims judge John Davis, Rear Adm. Samuel Rhoads Franklin, retired Maj. Gen. John Grubb Parke, Commanding General of the U.S. Army Nelson Appleton Miles, and Henry Wise's son-in-law Col. Archibald Hopkins, chief clerk of the U.S. Court of Claims. A guard of twelve bluejackets from

Photo 14.2 Rear Admiral Worden's grave, Pawling Cemetery, Pawling, New York *Courtesy Robert L. Worden*

the Washington Navy Yard under the command of Lt. Reginald F. Nicholson formed the bodyguard.[39]

Worden's remains were conveyed by train to New York City, then to Pawling, New York, for burial in the family plot. On the Sunday after the funeral, Rev. Mackay-Smith gave a moving eulogy in St. John's Church:

> There was a time when his name thrilled the heart of the Nation like the sound of strenuous music, and far beyond our shore, echoing across the Atlantic, the sound of those guns at Hampton Roads, amid whose roar he stood, the central heroic figure, announced to a startled world, that a new epoch in the warfare of Nations has been ushered in. . . . But this unspoiled modest man, remained what he was even to the last, the same quiet, strong, steadfast, simple nature, which one day suddenly found to its surprise "the path of duty was the way to glory."[40]

EPILOGUE

A HERO FOR ALL TIMES

John Lorimer Worden's bravery, valor, kindness, and sophistication gave him a range of skills that set a high standard for his successors. His quickness of mind in challenging situations, and especially his willingness to test an experimental vessel in combat, made him an outstanding commander. Worden made the untried and unseaworthy *Monitor* famous as "the little ship that saved the nation" in a battle that still inspires awe and respect. His career is a testament to the rare command qualities of circumspection, courage, and commitment. These attributes combined to make John Lorimer Worden a true hero for all times.

Worden's legacy lives on in numerous ways. He is memorialized in Herman Melville's 1862 poem "In the Turret," which correctly rhymes his surname with the word "burden." The Soldiers' Monument in Waterbury, Connecticut, dedicated in 1884, has a circular bronze panel showing Worden watching sailors position one of *Monitor*'s guns. Worden's name also appears among the naval heroes and other notable Americans on the front of the Boston Public Library completed in 1895. In 1900 Secretary of War Elihu Root took the unusual step of approving the naming of an Army coastal defense fort and two coastal batteries in honor of three Navy war heroes. Fort Worden, located near Port Townsend, Washington, was commissioned in 1902 and operated until 1953. It was recommissioned in

1957, and the Army, Air Force, and Navy took turns using its facilities. The coast batteries were at Fort Washington, Maryland, named for Commodore Stephen Decatur; and in Savannah Harbor, named in honor of Lt. Thomas M. Brumby, who served on Admiral Dewey's staff at Manila during the Spanish-American War. In 1973 Fort Worden became a state park.[1]

In 1910 the Naval Academy honored its seventh superintendent by renaming its parade ground Worden Field, which is partly located on land he helped acquire in 1873–74. Worden's surname also is on the Memorial Amphitheater, which opened at Arlington National Cemetery in 1920, one of fourteen Navy admirals and fourteen Army generals who served in the period from the American Revolution to the Spanish-American War. A state roadside marker in rural eastern New York, erected in 1949 in Westchester County near where he was born, tells travelers of his exploits on *Monitor*. Worden's 1863 naval bombardment is noted on a historical marker erected in 1957 at the Fort McAllister historical site. From 2002 to 2018 there was an Admiral John L. Worden Camp of the Sons of Union Veterans of the Civil War headquartered in Peekskill, Westchester County, New York, that held biennial graveside commemorations of Worden's death in Pawling, New York.

Of major importance are the exhibits at the USS *Monitor* Center at the Mariners' Museum and Park in Newport News, Virginia. They feature important *Monitor* artifacts, including the turret and the two XI-inch Dahlgren guns on which the names "Ericsson" and "Worden" were inscribed while the ironclad was being repaired at the Washington Navy Yard. The *Monitor* Center also includes engines, pumps, and numerous other artifacts, along with an outdoor full-scale reconstruction of the ironclad. Appropriately, Worden, Samuel Dana Greene, Franklin Buchanan, and Catesby ap Roger Jones are depicted on circular bronze markers at nearby Newport News Point, overlooking the Hampton Roads battle site. The Naval Academy Museum has a special section devoted to the Battle of Hampton Roads that features the Tiffany sword that the New York State Assembly presented to Worden in 1862 and Worden's 1869 portrait by Philipp Gliemann. The library and museum of Abraham Lincoln Memorial University in Harrogate, Tennessee, has the largest collection of his personal papers and various artifacts, including photographs, his speaking trumpet, a bronze plaque, and a lantern from *Monitor*.

Photo 15.1: Bronze bas relief plaque of Rear Adm. John L. Worden, by James Edward Kelly, commissioned by Olivia Worden Busbee in 1892 *Abraham Lincoln Library and Museum, Lincoln Memorial University, Harrogate, TN*

The U.S. Navy has named four ships for John Lorimer Worden. The first USS *Worden* (Torpedo Boat Destroyer No. 16) was laid down in 1899 at Sparrows Point, Maryland, by the Maryland Steel Company; launched in 1901 under the sponsorship of Worden's daughter-in-law Emilie Nielson Worden, second wife of Daniel Toffey Worden; and commissioned in 1902 at the Norfolk Navy Yard. *Worden* I escorted convoys and hunted for German U-boats along the French coast during World War I. It remained in commission until 1919.[2]

The second USS *Worden* (Destroyer No. 288) was laid down in June 1919 at Squantum, Massachusetts, by the Bethlehem Shipbuilding Corporation; launched in October 1919, again under the sponsorship of Emilie Worden; and commissioned in 1920 at the Boston Navy Yard. *Worden* II served in the Atlantic, the Gulf of Mexico, the Mediterranean, and the Pacific and remained in commission until 1930.[3]

The third USS *Worden* (Destroyer DD 352) was laid down at the Puget Sound Navy Yard in 1932; launched in 1934 under the sponsorship of Katrina L. Halligan, the wife of Rear Adm. John Halligan; and commissioned in 1935. *Worden* III shot down a low-flying Japanese bomber during the 7 December 1941 attack on Pearl Harbor and was one of the few ships that got under way—within two hours—and proceeded to the open sea, despite the fear of enemy submarines, dropping depth charges along the way. *Worden* III performed patrol and escort duties off the Hawaiian Islands and beyond, and participated in the Battle of Midway in June 1942 and the attacks on Guadalcanal and Tulagi in August 1942. On 12 January 1943, while *Worden* III was standing guard at Constantine Harbor, Amchitka Island, Alaska, a strong current swept it onto the rocky shore; it broke apart and sank with the loss of fourteen sailors. The name was struck from the Navy list in 1944. *Worden* III was awarded four battle stars for its valorous service.[4]

The fourth USS *Worden* (Guided Missile Frigate DLG 18) was laid down at the Bath Iron Works at Bath, Maine, in 1961; launched in 1962 under the sponsorship of Claudia B. Smedberg, wife of Vice Adm. William R. Smedberg III; and commissioned at Boston's Charlestown Navy Yard in 1963. *Worden* IV was assigned to the Seventh Fleet in the western Pacific and deployed five times to the coast of Vietnam during the Vietnam War, earning nine battle stars. *Worden* IV was redesignated a Guided Missile

Cruiser (CG 18) in 1975 and was decommissioned in 1993.⁵ *Worden IV*'s motto—*id fiat Wordensi* (Let Worden Do It)—aptly described the character of its famous namesake. When given a task, Worden did it.

An obscure reference to a fifth Navy vessel named for Worden was found in 2023 at the National Archives. A notation reading "Worden, Steam Tug, No Records" appears in a list of forty-eight named vessels, thirty-eight unnamed mortar boats, and one large wharf boat that had been under War Department control until 30 September 1862 when they were turned over to the Navy. Further research did not uncover any additional mentions of "Steam Tug Worden." But it is likely that, after the excitement of the 9 March 1862 Battle of Hampton Roads, someone was inspired to name a modest tug after *Monitor*'s captain.⁶

Worden did not seek attention or consider himself a great man or hero, but in so many ways he was one. He fought in some of the Civil War's most dangerous and daring naval combat situations. Each time he did so, his service set new standards of leadership. He pushed the untested capabilities of *Monitor* to the utmost by engaging *Virginia* both in a circular fashion and at close quarters, even seeking to ram the rebel ironclad. He tested *Montauk*'s armor close up under the furious barrage of Fort McAllister's shore guns. His quickness in analyzing a situation and finalizing a viable solution enabled him to save *Montauk* when it struck a torpedo. These actions and many more epitomized his well-practiced skills and determination to achieve his goals. Worden's character, demeanor, and command qualities drew people to him and made them trust him with daring missions, command of experimental warships, and seemingly unsolvable problems. He led by example, and his steadfastness made others willing to follow his commands to achieve success. If Worden could do it, so shall I.

APPENDIX A

CHRONOLOGY

12 March 1818	John Lorimer Worden born in Town of Mount Pleasant, Westchester County, New York, oldest son of Ananias Worden and Harriet Graham Worden
Spring 1827	Family relocates to Town of Fishkill, Dutchess County, New York; around same time, Worden goes to Manhattan to live with his mother's cousins for educational purposes
10 January 1834	Appointed acting midshipman, U.S. Navy
24 June 1834	Boards sloop *Erie* of the Brazil Squadron at Charlestown Navy Yard
1 June 1835	Warranted by President Andrew Jackson as midshipman, retroactive to 10 January 1834
20 September 1837	Ends *Erie* cruise
26 May 1838	Leaves Charlestown Navy Yard in sloop *Cyane*, Mediterranean Squadron
7 September 1839	Leaves *Cyane* at Malta, takes commercial brig *Dove* to Boston
9 December 1839	Enters Naval School at Philadelphia
16 July 1840	Completes Naval School, ranking fourth of twenty-one graduates; promoted to passed midshipman, effective July 20, 1840
2 December 1840	Departs Brooklyn Navy Yard as acting master of storeship *Relief*, Pacific Squadron; deployed along South American coast
6 September 1842	Transfers to sloop of war *Dale* as acting master

APPENDIX A

20 February–6 March 1843	Participates in survey of Monterey Harbor four months after Commo. Thomas Catesby ap Jones seized Monterey's fort
28 October 1843	Completes cruise on *Dale*
9 April 1844	Reports to Naval Observatory, Washington, DC
16 September 1844	Marries Olivia Akin Toffey in Quaker Hill, Dutchess County, New York
25 April 1846	Mexican-American War begins
26 May 1846	Detached from Naval Observatory
13 August 1846	Promoted to master
30 November 1846	Promoted to lieutenant
9 February 1847	Executive officer of supply ship *Southampton*, Pacific Squadron
28 November 1848	Leads rescue mission at San José del Cabo, Baja California, Mexico
20 January 1848	Takes command of prize schooner *Fortuna* at Guaymas, Sonora
2 March 1848	At La Paz, Baja California Sur, commands *Southampton*'s launch with Lt. Henry W. Halleck of the U.S. Army Corps of Engineers on board
10 March 1848	Captures prize schooner *Rosita*
1 April 1848	Leads bluejacket detachment to guard stores at La Paz
4 May 1848	Transfers to frigate *Independence* at La Paz because of illness
10 August 1848	Transfers to sloop storeship *Warren* at La Paz
12 September 1849	Transfers to ship of the line *Ohio* at San Francisco
29 April 1850	Detached from *Ohio* at Charlestown Navy Yard
15 September 1850	Ordered to Naval Observatory, Washington, DC

CHRONOLOGY

1 April 1852	Begins deployment on frigate *Cumberland*, Mediterranean Squadron, at Charlestown Navy Yard
14 February 1855	Transfers to sloop *Levant* at La Spezia, Sardinia
7 May 1855	Detached from *Levant* at Norfolk, Virginia
24 October 1855	Reports to Naval Observatory
16 April 1856	Reports as executive officer, Brooklyn Navy Yard
19 April 1858	U.S. Court of Claims decides in favor of government in *Worden v. United States* (seeking pay commensurate with service as acting lieutenant on *Relief* in 1840–42)
1 July 1858	Reports as first lieutenant of sloop *Savannah*, Home Squadron
19 November 1860	Detached from *Savannah* after cruise to Nicaragua and Mexico
18 January 1861	Requests assignment to New York Naval Rendezvous in Brooklyn
11 April 1861	Delivers verbal secret orders from Gideon Welles to land troops at Fort Pickens, Florida
12 April 1861	Civil War begins with attack on Fort Sumter, South Carolina
13 April 1861	After leaving Pensacola, arrested by Confederate agents, jailed in Montgomery, Alabama
20 November 1861	Released on parole at Hampton Roads, Virginia
16 January 1862	Reports for duty to command Ericsson's Battery (renamed *Monitor*)
30 January 1862	*Monitor* launched at Greenpoint, Brooklyn
25 February 1862	*Monitor* commissioned
5 March 1862	*Monitor* leaves Brooklyn Navy Yard
9 March 1862	*Monitor* engages CSS *Virginia* in a nearly four-hour battle at Hampton Roads; Worden taken to the Washington home of Lt. Henry A. Wise to recover from wounds received during the battle
10 March 1862	President Lincoln goes to Wise home to personally thank Worden for "saving the nation"

13 March 1862	Joint resolution of Congress thanks Worden and *Monitor* officers and crew for their "skill and gallantry"
8 May 1862	Officially detached from *Monitor* and ordered to command of ironclad steamer *New Ironsides*
10 June 1862	Detached from *New Ironsides*
11 July 1862	Second joint resolution of Congress thanks Worden and *Monitor* officers and crew for their "skill and gallantry"
16 July 1862	Promoted to commander
14 August 1862	Ordered to special duty at Brooklyn Navy Yard
10 October 1862	Takes command of ironclad *Montauk*
27 January 1863	*Montauk* leads attack on Fort McAllister, Georgia
1 February 1863	*Montauk* leads second attack on Fort McAllister
3 February 1863	Joint resolution of Congress thanks Worden "for good conduct in the conflict between the *Monitor* and *Merrimac*"; promoted to captain
9–12 February 1863	On hospital ship *Vermont*, Port Royal, South Carolina
27 February 1863	*Montauk* destroys Confederate blockade runner *Rattlesnake* (former CSS *Nashville*, former *Thomas L. Wragg*), supported by consort ships *Dawn*, *Seneca*, and *Wissahickon*
7 April 1863	*Montauk*, with Worden in command, participates in ironclad attack on Charleston, South Carolina
14 April 1863	Detached from *Montauk*
23 April 1863	Returns to special duty at Brooklyn Navy Yard to supervise ironclad construction
1 July 1863	Submits request for prize money for officers and crew of *Montauk* for destruction of *Nashville*
17–22 February 1864	Serves on Grand Reception Committee for the Long Island Sanitary Fair, Brooklyn
8 October 1864	Attends launching of sloop *Idaho* at Greenpoint
19 November 1864	Participates in sea trial of new torpedo boat *Stromboli*

25 February 1865	Inquires how prize money is to be distributed for destruction of *Nashville*
3 May 1865	Appointed to Naval Academy Board of Visitors
31 January 1866	Detached from special duty at Brooklyn to command *Idaho* with son John Lorimer Worden Jr. serving as captain's clerk
23 May 1866	Detached from *Idaho*
16 August 1866	At Brooklyn Navy Yard assumes command of screw steamer *Pensacola*, to be flagship of North Pacific Squadron
6 April 1867	*Pensacola* arrives at San Francisco
8 May 1867	Detached from *Pensacola*
5 January 1868	Sends report to Gideon Welles asking him to "do justice to the gallant and excellent officer [Samuel Dana Greene] as well as to all officers and crew" of *Monitor*
8 January 1868	Along with officers and crews of *Montauk, Dawn, Seneca,* and *Wissahickon,* receives share of prize money for destruction of *Nashville*
23 May 1868	Requests one-year leave of absence on account of health; granted six months
27 May 1868	Promoted to commodore
11 June 1868	Departs for Dresden, Saxony
25 November 1868	Leave extended six months
23 April 1869	Leave extended to twelve months
1 December 1869	Assumes superintendency of Naval Academy
20 November 1872	Promoted to rear admiral
9 October 1873	Presides at inaugural meeting of U.S. Naval Institute; later assigned Member No. 1
23 June 1874	Congress passes "An Act to Prevent Hazing at the Naval Academy"
15 September 1874	Detached from Naval Academy
20 November 1874	Submits petition to Congress to award estimated value of CSS *Virginia* to be distributed among *Monitor* officers and crew

8 January 1875	Boards paddlewheel frigate *Powhatan* at Norfolk, Virginia, with wife and daughters to proceed to Lisbon to take command of the European Squadron
29 January 1875	Boards screw frigate *Franklin* at Lisbon and assumes command of European Squadron
10 June 1875	Transfers flag temporarily to screw sloop *Alaska*
14 September 1876	Transfers flag to screw steamer *Marion*
19 April 1877	Transfers flag to steam frigate *Trenton*
5 October 1877	Detached from command of European Squadron
29 December 1877	Appointed to Navy Examining Board and Navy Retirement Board, Washington, DC
12 December 1881	*Monitor* prize money bill of 1874 renewed in Congress
29 January 1882	Appointed president of Navy Examining Board
30 April 1882	Appointed president of Navy Retirement Board
8 December 1882	House of Representatives bill to award prize money to officers and crew of *Monitor* "laid aside without prejudice"
31 May 1884	House Committee of Naval Affairs reports adversely on a $200,000 bill for relief of officers and crew of *Monitor*
20 December 1886	Congress votes to allow Worden to retire at full sea pay after fifty-two years of service
18 October 1897	Dies of pneumonia at his home in Washington, DC
20 October 1897	Funeral held at St. John's Episcopal Church, Washington, DC; attended by President William McKinley, members of the cabinet and the federal judiciary, high-ranking Navy and Army officers, and others
21 October 1897	Buried in family plot in Pawling Cemetery, Pawling, New York

APPENDIX B

ASSOCIATED U.S. NAVY SHIPS

Alaska
Worden on board: 10–19 June 1875 (temporary flagship of European Squadron)
Namesake: territory acquired from Russia in 1867
Builder: Charlestown Navy Yard, Boston, MA
Launched: 31 October 1868
Commissioned: 8 December 1869
Type: sloop of war
Tonnage: 2,394
Length: 250 feet, 6 inches
Beam: 38 inches
Draft: 16 inches
Propulsion: steam and sails
Complement: 273
Armament: one 11-inch smoothbore, one 60-pounder, two 20-pounder rifles
Fate: decommissioned and sold in 1883

Cumberland
Worden on board: 1 April 1852–14 February 1855 (Mediterranean Squadron)
Namesake: Cumberland River
Builder: William Doughty, Charlestown Navy Yard, Boston, MA
Laid Down: 1824
Launched: 24 May 1842
Commissioned: 9 November 1842
Type: *Raritan*-class frigate
Razeed as sloop of war, Charlestown Navy Yard, Boston, MA, 1857
Tonnage: 1,726

Length: 175 feet
Beam: 45 feet
Draft: 21 feet, 1 inch
Complement as sloop: 400
Complement as razeed: 220
Armament (1861): twenty-two IX-inch Dahlgren shell guns, one X-inch Dahlgren shell gun, one 70-pounder (more likely a 60-pounder Parrott) muzzle-loaded rifle
Fate: sunk by CSS *Virginia* at Hampton Roads, 8 March 1862

Cyane
Worden on board: 7 May 1838–7 September 1839 (Mediterranean Squadron)
Namesake: named in honor of the previous USS (formerly HMS) *Cyane*
Builder: Charlestown Navy Yard, Boston, MA
Launched: 2 December 1837
Commissioned: May 1838
Type: sloop of war
Tonnage: 792
Length: 132 feet, 4 inches
Beam: 26 feet, 3 inches
Draft: 16 feet, 6 inches
Propulsion: sails
Compliment: 200
Armament (1865): fourteen 32-pounders, four 68-pounders, one 12-pounder

Dale
Worden on board: 6 September 1842–23 October 1843 (Pacific Squadron)
Namesake: Commo. Thomas Dale, USN
Builder: Philadelphia Navy Yard
Laid down: 1839
Launched: 8 November 1839
Commissioned: 11 December 1839
Type: sloop of war
Tonnage: 566
Length: 117 feet, 7 inches

Beam: 33 feet, 10 inches
Draft: 15 feet, 8 inches
Propulsion: sails
Complement: 150
Armament (1861): twelve 32-pounders, two 32-pounders, one 12-pounder howitzer
Fate: transferred to Maryland Naval Militia, 1895, renamed *Oriole* 1904, transferred to Coast Guard at Baltimore, 1906, sold 1921

Erie

Worden on board: 24 June 1834–30 September 1837 (Brazil Squadron)
Namesake: Lake Erie
Builder: Thomas Kemp, Baltimore, MD, 1813–14
Launched: 3 November 1813
Commissioned: ca. March 1814
Rebuilt: lengthened, tonnage increased, 1827
Rebuilt: Charlestown Navy Yard, Boston, MA, 1840–43
Type: sloop of war
Tonnage: 509
Length: 117 feet
Beam: 31 feet, 6 inches
Draft: 14 feet, 6 inches
Propulsion: sails
Complement: 140
Armament: two 18-pounders, twenty 32-pounder carronades
Fate: sold 26 November 1850

Franklin

Worden on board: 3 February 1875–14 September 1876 (flagship of European Squadron)
Builder: Portsmouth Navy Yard, Portsmouth, NH
Laid down: May 1854
Launched: 17 September 1864
Commissioned: 3 June 1867
Type: screw frigate
Length: 265 feet
Beam: 53 feet, 8 inches

Draft: 24 feet, 3 inches
Propulsion: sail and steam
Machinery: one screw, two-cylinder horizontal back-acting condensing engine, four boilers
Speed: 10 knots
Complement (1875–76): 621
Armament: thirty-eight IX-inch Dahlgren shell guns, four 100-pounder Parrott rifles, one XI-inch Dahlgren shell gun, one 12-pounder rifled Dahlgren howitzer, one 12-pounder (heavy) Dahlgren howitzer, one 12-pounder (light) Dahlgren howitzer, one Gatling gun
Fate: sold 1915

Idaho
Worden on board: 2 April–26 May 1866 (Home, later Asiatic Squadron)
Namesake: Idaho Territory
Builder: George Steers, Greenpoint, NY
Laid Down: 1863
Launched: 8 October 1864
Commissioned: 2 April 1866
Type: sloop, converted to storeship
Recommissioned: 3 October 1867
Tonnage: 3,241
Length: 298 feet
Beam: 44 feet, 6 inches
Draft: 17 feet
Propulsion: sail and steam, engines removed 1867
Machinery: two screws, two 2-cylinder Dickerson engines, 645 horsepower
Speed: steam 8 knots, sail only after removal of engines 18 knots
Complement: 400
Armament: six 32-pounder shell guns, one 30-pounder Parrott rifle, one 12-pounder howitzer
Fate: dismasted and severely damaged during typhoon off Yokohama, Japan, 1869; hulk sold in 1874

Independence
Worden on board: 4 May–14 July 1848 (Pacific Squadron)
Namesake: freedom, self-government

Builder: Charlestown Navy Yard, Boston, MA
Launched: 22 June 1814
Commissioned: 1814
Tonnage: 2,243
Type: ship of the line
Length: 190 feet, 10 inches
Beam: 54 feet, 7 inches
Draft: 24 feet, 4 inches
Propulsion: sails
Complement: 790
Armament: ninety 32-pounders
Fate: sold 1914, burned 1919 to recover metal fittings

Levant
Worden on board: 15 February 1855–7 May 1855 (Mediterranean Squadron)
Namesake: lands bordering eastern Mediterranean
Builder: Brooklyn Navy Yard, NY
Launched: 28 December 1837
Commissioned: 17 March 1838
Recommissioned: 27 March 1843
Type: sloop of war
Tonnage: 792
Length: 132 feet, 3 inches
Beam: 34 feet, 3 inches
Draft: 16 feet, 6 inches
Propulsion: sails
Complement: 200
Armament: four 24-pounders, thirteen 32-pounder carronades
Fate: lost at sea, 1860

Marion
Worden on board: 14 September 1876–19 April 1877 (flagship of European Squadron)
Namesake: American Revolutionary War hero Francis Marion
Builder: Charlestown Navy Yard, Boston, MA
Launched: 24 April 1839

Commissioned: 1839
Type: sloop of war
Propulsion: sails
Rebuilt as third-rate screw steamer, Portsmouth Navy Yard
Recommissioned 12 January 1876
Tonnage: 1,900
Length: 216 feet
Beam: 37 feet
Draft: 16 feet, 6 inches
Complement: 194
Armament: one XI-inch pivot gun, one 60-pounder Parrott rifle, six IX-inch broadside guns, three 12-pounder light howitzers, one Gatling gun
Fate: transferred to state of California, 1897

Monitor

Worden on board: 13 January–9 March 1862 (North Atlantic Blockading Squadron)
Namesake: monitoring the actions of British and Confederate navies
Builder: John Ericsson, Continental Iron Works, Greenpoint, Brooklyn
Laid down: 25 October 1861
Launched: 30 January 1862
Commissioned: 25 February 1862
Tonnage: 987
Length: 179 feet
Beam: 41 feet, 6 inches
Draft: 10 feet, 6 inches
Propulsion: steam
Machinery: one screw, two Ericsson vibrating-lever engines
Speed: 7 knots
Complement: 49
Armament: two XI-inch Dahlgren shell guns
Armor: turret 8 inches, sides 4.5 inches, deck 2 inches, pilothouse 9 inches
Fate: sunk in storm off Cape Hatteras, NC, 31 December 1862

Montauk

Worden on board: 14 December 1862–14 April 1863 (South Atlantic Blockading Squadron)

Namesake: Native American Montauk tribe
Builder: John Ericsson, Continental Ironworks, Greenpoint, Brooklyn
Launched: 9 October 1862
Commissioned: 14 December 1862
Tonnage: 1,335
Length: 200 feet
Beam: 46 feet
Draft: 11 feet, 6 inches
Propulsion: steam
Machinery: one screw, two-cylinder Ericsson vibrating-lever (trunk) engine, two boilers, 340 horsepower
Speed: 7 knots
Armor: turret 11 inches, side 5 inches, deck 1 inch, pilothouse 8 inches
Armament: one XV-inch Dahlgren gun, one XI-inch Dahlgren gun
Ships captured/destroyed: CSS *Nashville* (*Rattlesnake*)
Fate: sold 14 April 1904

New Ironsides
Worden detailed as commander 8 May–10 June 1862 but there is no record that he was ever on board prior to its commissioning under another captain (South Atlantic Blockading Squadron, later North Atlantic Blockading Squadron)
Namesake: Named in honor of frigate *Constitution* ("Old Ironsides")
Builder: Merrick and Sons, Philadelphia
Laid down: 15 October 1861
Launched: 10 May 1862
Commissioned: 21 August 1862, Philadelphia Navy Yard
Recommissioned: 27 August 1864
Type: three-masted bark-rigged ironclad steamer
Tonnage: 4,120 tons
Length: 232 feet
Beam: 57 feet, 6 inches
Draft: 15 feet, 8 inches
Propulsion: steam and sail
Machinery: one screw, two-cylinder horizontal direct-acting engine by Merrick, four boilers
Speed: 6 knots

Armor: 4.5-inch waterline and gundeck wrought iron belts, 2.5-inch iron bulkhead backed by 12 inches of white oak
Complement: 460
Armament: twelve XI-inch Dahlgren guns, two 150-pounder Parrott rifles
Fate: decommissioned 6 April 1865 at League Island, Philadelphia, destroyed by fire 16 December 1866

Ohio
Worden on board: 12 September 1849–3 May 1850 (Pacific Squadron)
Namesake: state of Ohio
Builder: Brooklyn Navy Yard
Laid down: 1817
Launched: 30 May 1820
Refitted for service: 1838
Commissioned: 1838
Recommissioned: 7 December 1846
Type: ship of the line
Displacement: 2,724 tons
Length: 197 feet
Beam: 53 feet
Draft: 22 feet, 2 inches
Propulsion: sail
Complement: 840
Armament: thirty long 32-pounder guns, thirty-two medium 32-pounder guns, two 32-pounder carronades
Note: at one point during its career, armed with 104 guns
Fate: sold 1883

Pensacola
Worden on board: 6 August 1866–8 May 1867 (North Pacific Squadron)
Namesake: bay and city in Escambia County, Florida
Builder: Warrington Navy Yard, Pensacola, FL
Launched: 15 August 1859
Commissioned: 5 December 1859
Commissioned in full: 16 September 1861
Type: screw steamer
Tonnage: 3,000

Length: 230 feet, 8 inches
Beam: 44 feet, 5 inches
Draft: 18 feet, 7 inches
Propulsion: sails and steam
Complement: 269
Armament: (1866–67) one 100-pounder rifle in pivot, twenty IX-inch shell guns in broadside
Machinery: 1 screw, Isherwood-designed two-cylinder direct-acting engine installed 1864–66

Powhatan

Worden on board: 11–29 January 1875 (Home Squadron)
Namesake: Indian chief, father of Pocahontas
Builder: Gosport Navy Yard, Portsmouth, VA
Launched: 14 February 1850
Commissioned: 2 September 1852
Type: screw steamer
Tonnage: 2,415
Length: 253 feet, 8, inches
Beam: 45 feet
Draft: 18 feet, 6 inches
Propulsion: steam
Complement: 289
Armament: one XI-inch Dahlgren smoothbore, ten IX-inch Dahlgren smoothbores, five 12-pounders
Fate: sold 1886, scrapped 1887

Relief

Worden on board: 1 December 1840–6 September 1842 (Pacific Squadron)
Namesake: aid given in time of need
Builder: Philadelphia Navy Yard
Launched: 14 September 1836
Commissioned: ca. December 1836
Type: storeship
Tonnage: 468
Length: 109 feet
Beam: 30 feet

Depth of hold: 12 feet
Propulsion: sails
Complement: unknown
Armament: four 18-pounders, two 12-pounders
Fate: sold 1883

Savannah

Worden on board: 1 July 1858–20 November 1860 (Home Squadron)
Namesake: Savannah, Georgia
Builder: Brooklyn Navy Yard, NY
Laid down: July 1820
Launched: 5 May 1842
Commissioned: 15 October 1843
Type: frigate
Tonnage: 1,726
Length: 175 feet
Beam: 45 feet
Draft: 24 feet, 4 inches
Propulsion: sails
Complement: 400
Armament (1861): two X-inch shell guns, eight VIII-inch shell guns, fourteen 32-pounder shell guns
Fate: sold 1883

Southampton

Worden on board: 9 February (or earlier) 1847–4 May 1848 (Pacific Squadron)
Namesake: Southampton County, VA
Builder: Mahaffey's Iron Works, Portsmouth, VA
Laid down: October 1841, purchased by Navy 1845, converted to sail
Commissioned: 27 May 1845
Type: initially sidewheel steamer, then sailing storeship
Tonnage: 567
Length: 156 feet
Beam: 27 feet, 10 inches
Draft: 13 feet, 6 inches
Propulsion: sails

Complement: unknown
Armament: two 42-pound carronades
Fate: decommissioned and sold 1855

Trenton
Worden on board: 19 April–5 October 1877 (flagship of European Squadron)
Namesake: capital city of New Jersey
Builder: Brooklyn Navy Yard, NY
Laid down: December 1873
Launched: 1 January 1876
Commissioned: 14 February 1877
Type: steam frigate
Tonnage: 3,900
Length: 253 feet
Beam: 48 feet
Draft: 20 feet, 6 inches at bow
Propulsion: sail and steam
Machinery: one screw, horizontal back-acting three-cylinder compound engine, eight boilers
Speed: 13 knots
Complement: 477
Armament: 9-foot, 5-inch ram affixed to bow, eleven 8-inch rifles, two 20-pounder breech-loading rifles
Fate: wrecked during typhoon at Apia, Samoa, 1889

Vermont
Worden on board: 9–12 February 1863 (South Atlantic Blockading Squadron)
Namesake: state of Vermont
Builder: Charlestown Navy Yard, Boston, MA
Laid down: September 1818
Launched: 15 September 1848
Commissioned: 30 January 1862
Type: sloop (hospital ship)
Tonnage: 2,633
Length: 197 feet, 1 inch

Beam: 53 feet, 6 inches
Draft: 21 feet, 6 inches
Propulsion: sails
Complement: 820
Armament: twenty 8-inch shell guns, sixty-four 32-pounders
Fate: sold 1902

Warren
Worden on board: 10 August 1848–12 September 1849 (Pacific Squadron)
Namesake: Joseph Warren, killed at Battle of Bunker Hill (17 June 1775)
Builder: Charlestown Navy Yard, Boston, MA
Laid down: 1825
Launched: 29 November 1826
Commissioned: 24 May 1827
Recommissioned: 2 September 1831
Type: sloop of war (storeship and receiving ship during Mexican-American War)
Tonnage: 697
Length: 127 feet
Beam: 33 feet, 9 inches
Draft: 15 feet, 9 inches
Propulsion: sail
Armament: twenty 32-pounders
Fate: sold 1863

Sources: Based on information from U.S. Naval History and Heritage Command, *Dictionary of American Naval Fighting Ships*, https://www.history.navy.mil/research/histories/ship-histories/danfs.html (4 October 2023); Log Books, entry 118, RG 24, NARA; and Paul H. Silverstone, *Civil War Navies, 1855–1883* (Annapolis: Naval Institute Press, 2001).

APPENDIX C

MEDICAL CONDITIONS

During his fifty-two-year career and afterward, Rear Adm. John Lorimer Worden suffered a variety of medical conditions. They are listed here in chronological order. Except for two marked with asterisks, the entries are as reported in a summary medical report dated 13 January 1898 from the U.S. Navy Surgeon General, in Olivia Worden's Navy widow's pension file. The dates cover the period of treatment, with the discharge date indicating when Worden was cleared to return to duty. When the report was compiled in 1898, it was noted that the medical journals for some ships and shore stations were "not on file." Research conducted with Navy medical journals at the National Archives in 2024 confirmed that these records are still not on file and presumably not extant. Ship and station medical journals are not extant for the following Worden assignments: *Erie, Cyane, Relief, Dale,* Naval Rendezvous New York, and *Monitor*. Medical journals for *Ohio, Montauk, Pensacola, Franklin,* and *Marion* are available but typically list only enlisted men who consulted a physician during sick call. Definitions are derived from the National Institutes of Health.

- *Southampton*, 28 April–4 May 1848 (discharged to *Independence* for further treatment). Gastric derangement, an obstruction of the gastric outlet, a painful abdominal condition often accompanied by vomiting, a feeling of being overfed, and weight loss.
- Naval Observatory, 2–5 June 1851. Gastro-hepatic: derangement same as above with implications for the liver.
- Naval Observatory, 15–19 January 1852. Catarrhus: a common cold, runny nose, sneezing, low fever, tearing, and nasal congestion with possible implications for the larynx and stomach.

- *Cumberland*, 16–21 June 1852. Parotitis: inflammation of the parotid glands; the most common inflammation of the major salivary glands.
- *Cumberland*, 14–23 October 1853. Orchitis subacute: inflammation of the testicle unilaterally or bilaterally, usually caused by viruses or bacteria.
- *Cumberland*, 15 November–3 December 1853. Orchitis subacute: same as above.
- *Cumberland*, 13–18 December 1853. Orchitis subacute: same as above.
- Naval Observatory, Washington, 1 April 1856. Ulcerated sore throat: inflammation of the mucous membranes of the oropharynx.
- Naval Observatory, Washington, 8 May 1856. Febris intermittens: usually infections localized to urinary tract or biliary ducts or the colon; also infections of a foreign material.
- Naval Observatory, Washington, 4th Quarter 1856. Icterus: jaundice, a yellow discoloration of the body tissue resulting from the accumulation of bilirubin, a metabolic product, a clinical indicator for liver disease.
- Naval Observatory, Washington, 2nd Quarter 1857. Catarrhus: same as above.
- *Savannah*, 22–23 September 1858. Furunculus on right hip: lesions primarily caused by staphylococcus aureus infection of the hair follicles and surrounding skin, found more frequently in persons with immune system disorders.
- *Savannah*, 24 November–2 December 1858. Bilious colic: abdominal pain due to obstruction usually by stones in the cystic duct or common bile duct, typically occurs after eating a large, fatty meal that causes contraction of the gall bladder.
- *Savannah*, 24 November–2 December 1858. Bilious colic: same as above.
- *Savannah*, 22–28 March 1859. Contusio right foot, line of duty while practicing with gun: traumatic injury to foot or ankle.
- *Savannah*, 17–25 April 1859. Contusio right foot: same as above.
- *Savannah*, 3–4 February 1860. Constibatio: symptom or condition characterized by difficult and infrequent bowel movements,

indicative of medical disorders, dietary issues, or structural abnormalities in the gastrointestinal tract.
- *Savannah*, 7–21 February 1860. Nephralgia: kidney pain associated with the nerve supply to the kidneys.
- **Monitor*, 9 March 1862. Severely injured corneal conjunctiva and eyelids; temple and brow also injured.
- **Vermont*, a hospital ship at Port Royal, SC, 9–12 February 1863. Unspecified illness. Deck log records only Worden's arrival, with a servant.
- Naval Dispensary, Washington, 23 April–4 May 1878. Catarrhus acuta: as above, but chronic.
- Naval Dispensary, Washington, 14 December 1878–7 January 1879. Catarrhus: same as above.
- Naval Dispensary, Washington, 1–16 October 1880. Febris intermittens, in line of duty, climatic exposure: same as above.
- Naval Dispensary, Washington, 2–4 March 1881. Malarial cachexia, in line of duty, climatic influences: a wasting disease caused by malaria.
- Naval Dispensary, Washington, 20–22 May 1881. Malarial cachexia, in line of duty, climatic influences: same as above.
- Naval Dispensary, Washington, 29 May–19 June 1882. Colic and malaria, in line of duty from exposure to malarial influences: a rare form of bowel obstruction in adults and an uncommon cause of abdominal pain; and malaria as above.
- Naval Dispensary, Washington, 23–28 January 1890). La grippe, not in line of duty from exposure to malarial influences: influenza.
- Naval Dispensary, Washington, 18 October 1897. Febris pneumonica, in line of duty, long and faithful service and exposure incident thereto: infection affecting one or both lungs caused by bacteria, viruses, or fungi.

Sources: Summary Medical Report in Olivia Worden's Navy Widow's Pension File, Certificate no. 12948, M1279, RG 15, Records of the Department of Veterans Affairs, NARA; *Vermont* log, 8 February 1863, entry 118, Logs of U.S. Naval Ships, RG 24, Records of the Bureau of Naval Personnel, NARA;

Medical Journals of Shore Stations, entry 21, and Medical Journals of Ships, entry 22, RG 52, Records of the Medical Bureau of Surgery, NARA; and National Institutes of Health, National Library of Medicine, https://www.ncbi.nlm.nih.gov/pmc/ (30 March 2024).

ESSAY ON SOURCES

The most important sources used in researching this book were the John Lorimer Worden papers held at three institutions. The largest collection, including Worden's personal reminiscences and correspondence with family, friends, and officials, is at the Abraham Lincoln Memorial University Library in Harrogate, Tennessee. Collections of Worden papers in the library of The Mariners' Museum and Park in Newport News, Virginia, and the Library of Congress in Washington, DC, also provided valuable information and images, as did individual Worden letters found in other institutions.

Official U.S. government records at the National Archives in Washington, DC, were also of critical importance. These included Records of the Veterans Administration (Record Group [RG] 15); Bureau of Ships (RG 19); District Courts of the United States (RG 21); Coast and Geodetic Survey (RG 23); Logs of Naval Ships (RG 24); Bureau of the Census (RG 29); Customs Service (RG 36); Hydrographic Office (RG 37); Naval Records Collection (RG 45, including Appointments, Orders, and Resignations; Officers Letters; Commanders Letters; Captains Letters; Squadron Letters; Miscellaneous Letters Received and Sent by the Secretary of the Navy; and General Letter Books); Bureau of Medicine and Surgery (RG 52); Bureau of Yards and Docks (RG 71); Naval Observatory (RG 78); U.S. Court of Claims (RG 123); Office of the Navy Judge Advocate General (RG 125); Accounting Officers of Department of the Treasury (RG 217); and Government of the District of Columbia (RG 351). Records of the U.S. Naval Academy (RG 405) are located in Special Collections and Archives in the Nimitz Library in Annapolis, MD. Archival materials at the Naval Academy Museum and the U.S. Naval Institute Archives, both in Annapolis, also were of value.

Key legislative and statutory information was obtained from *U.S. Statutes at Large* and journals and reports published by the U.S. Congress available online at the Library of Congress. Published Department of the Navy reports, many of which appear in various volumes of *Official Records of the Union and Confederate Navies in the War of the Rebellion*, were also used.

Diaries, memoirs, and documentary collections provided others' personal observations about Worden. The major ones included Gideon Welles' diary, Samuel Browne's *First Cruise of the Montauk*, Samuel Dana Greene's "In the 'Monitor' Turret," William Keeler's *Aboard the USS Monitor*, William Marvel's *Monitor Chronicles*, and Charlotte Wise's "When I Was a Little Girl."

Digital copies of hard-to-obtain historical articles, books, documents, maps, and photographs were found on Ancestry.com, FamilySearch.org, Fold3.com, HathiTrust.org, Internet Archive, and in Library of Congress online collections. Worden's life story was significantly supplemented with articles from more than seventy contemporaneous U.S. and foreign newspapers found on the websites of America's Historical Newspapers (New York Public Library), Chronicling America (Library of Congress), and Newspaperarchive.com.

The authors consulted numerous secondary sources in the preparation of this book. Important among them were Richard Amero's "The Mexican War in Baja California," Karl Jack Bauer's *Surfboats and Horse Marines*, Robert Browning's *South Atlantic Blockading Squadron during the Civil War*, Donald Canney's *Old Steam Navy*, Thomas Cutler's "Fifteen Founders," Steven Dick's *Sky and Ocean Joined*, Frank Gapp's "The 'Capture' of Monterey in 1842," Robert Johnson's *The Story of United States Naval Forces on Pacific Station*, Virgil Carrington Jones' *Civil War at Sea*, David Long's *Gold Braid and Foreign Relations* and *Biography of Captain John Percival*, Howard Nash's *Naval History of the Civil War*, Rowena Reed's *Combined Operations in the Civil War*, Robert Schneller's *The U.S. Naval Academy's First Black Midshipmen and the Struggle for Racial Equality*, John Schroeder's *Shaping a Maritime Empire*, Paul Silverstone's *Civil War Navies*, James Russell Soley's *Historical Sketch of the United States Naval Academy*, Jack Sweetman and Thomas Cutler's *U.S. Naval Academy: An Illustrated History*, Spencer Tucker's *Civil War Naval Encyclopedia* and *Encyclopedia of the Mexican-American War*, and John Yate's "Insurgents on the Baja Peninsula." *The Big Guns: Civil War Siege, Seacoast, and Naval Cannon* by Edwin Olmstead, Wayne E. Stark, and Spencer C. Tucker was also very useful.

Full bibliographic citations and sources not mentioned here can be found in the endnotes. URLs for internet sources are subject to change, and although all functioned at the time of publication, some of those appearing in the notes may no longer be operable.

ABBREVIATIONS USED IN ENDNOTES

LMU	Abraham Lincoln Memorial University
MSA	Maryland State Archives, Annapolis, MD
NARA	National Archives and Records Administration (all Record Groups were at National Archives in Washington, DC, except RG 23, which is located at the National Archives in College Park, MD
ORN	*Official Records of the Union and Confederate Navies in the War of the Rebellion*
RG	Record Group, NARA
SC&A	Special Collections and Archives, USNA
USNA	U.S. Naval Academy

NOTES

INTRODUCTION

1. Sister Dolores Christi Gartanutti, O.P., "Legacy Unclaimed: The Life of Admiral John Lorimer Worden," History Seminar, St. Francis College, Brooklyn Heights, NY, 26 April 1965; Tim Caldwell, "Admiral John Lorimer Worden's Second Command," master's thesis, Norwich University, Northfield, VT, 12 August 2007, copies of both in author's file.
2. "Summary Medical Report" in Olivia Worden's Navy Widow's Pension File, Certificate no. 12948, M1279, RG 15, Records of the Department of Veterans Affairs, National Archives (NARA).
3. Herman Melville, *Battle-Pieces and Aspects of the War* (New York: Harper and Brothers, 1866); the poem was published in March 1862 and can be seen in full at https://www.gutenberg.org/ebooks/12384.
4. Carl Charlick, *The Metropolitan Club of Washington* (Washington, DC: Metropolitan Club, 1965), 137.

CHAPTER 1. EARLY LIFE

1. Deeds of 10 March 1791, Liber K, folio 342, and 10 April 1794, Liber 75, folio 311, Westchester County Land Records.
2. Helen Graham Carpenter, *The Reverend John Graham of Woodbury, Connecticut and His Descendants* (Chicago: Monastery Hill Press, 1942), 1, 13–14.
3. Carpenter, *Reverend John Graham*, 234–35.
4. John Lorimer Worden to Honorable Secretary of the Navy, 29 January 1834, noting his birth date and place, Letters Received Accepting Appointments, vol. 12, entry 125, Record Group (RG) 45, National Archives and Records Administration (hereafter NARA); William Reynolds, "Road Marker Honors Civil War Hero from Ossining," *Ossining Daily Voice*, https://dailyvoice.com/new-york/ossining/neighbors/road-marker-honors-civil-war-hero-from-ossining/391615/ (24 July 2013).
5. Carpenter, *Reverend John Graham*, 352.
6. Carpenter, *Reverend John Graham*, 240–52; William Cothren, *History of Ancient Woodbury, Connecticut, from the First Indian Deed in 1659 to 1854* (Waterbury: Bronson Brothers, 1854), 2:552.

7. *Columbian* (New York), 16 May 1818; *New York Evening Post*, 25 September 1821; Eugene L. Armbruster, *The Eastern District of Brooklyn* (New York, 1912), 172. A sampling of Kings County, Brooklyn, NY, Grantee/Grantor Indexes shows approximately one hundred purchases and sales of property by James Lorimer Graham and John Lorimer Graham, mostly the latter, between 1835 and 1840, https://www.familysearch.org/search/collection/2078654 (21 April 2022).
8. Carpenter, *Reverend John Graham*, 352, 358–59. Katrina Van Tassel was the mother of Auley Bancker and grandmother of Harriet Graham. Irving's story was part of a collection published in *The Sketch Book of Geoffrey Crayon, Gent.* in 1820. For details on Worden's early education and later reading habits, see Robert L. Worden, "The Early Education of John Lorimer Worden," *Wordens Past* 44, no. 2 (August 2023): 3873–78, http://wordenfamilyassoc.org/John_Lorimer_Worden/JLW/WP_2023_08_Early_Education_of_John_Lorimer_Worden.pdf (15 March 2024).
9. For details on John Hodges Graham's life and naval career, see Robert L. Worden, "'A Partiality for Nautical Pursuits': Why John Lorimer Worden Joined the Navy," *Wordens Past* 39, no. 1 (May 2018): 3446–48, http://wordenfamilyassoc.org/John_Lorimer_Worden/JLW/WP_2013_05_Why_John_Lorimer_Worden_Joined_the_Navy.pdf (15 March 2024).
10. For details on the Chaunceys' naval careers, see Robert L. Worden, "Why John Lorimer Worden Joined the Navy: An Addenda," *Wordens Past* 44, no. 1 (May 2023): 3859–62, http://wordenfamilyassoc.org/John_Lorimer_Worden/JLW/WP_2013_05_Why_John_Lorimer_Worden_Joined_the_Navy_Addenda.pdf (15 March 2024).
11. Woodbury to Worden, 10 January 1834, Appointments, Microcopy T829; Worden to Woodbury, 6 February 1834, Officers Letters, Microcopy M148; Woodbury to Worden, 14 February 1834, Letters Sent, Microcopy M149, all in RG 45, NARA.
12. Woodbury to Worden, 5 May 1834, T829.

CHAPTER 2. BEGINNING A NAVAL CAREER

1. *Erie* log, 22 August 1834, Logs of U.S. Naval Ships, entry 118, RG 24, NARA; David F. Long, *"Mad Jack": The Biography of Captain John Percival, USN, 1779–1862* (Westport, CT: Greenwood Press, 1993), 82, 231.
2. *Erie* log, September 1834–November 1835.
3. Robert L. Worden, "Two Rear Admirals of the U.S. Navy: Reed Werden and John Lorimer Worden," *Wordens Past* 29, no. 4 (February 2009): 2456–64, http://wordenfamilyassoc.org/John_Lorimer_Worden/JLW/WP_2456_Feb_2009_Reed_Werden_and_JLW.pdf (9 March 2024); *Erie* log, August 1834–May 1835.

4. *Erie* log, 19–29 September 1834.
5. *Erie* log, 15 November 1834–14 February 1835; *American and Commercial Daily Advertiser* (Baltimore), 2 January 1835; Percival to Mahlon Dickerson, 12 February 1835, quoted in Long, *Mad Jack*, 107–8; *Liberator* (Boston), 21 March 1835.
6. *Erie* log, 22 February–17 March and 12 August 1835; Long, *Mad Jack*, 109–12, 227.
7. "Record of Service of Rear Admiral John L. Worden," Worden Letterbook, John Lorimer Worden Papers, A80-1364, University Archives and Special Collections, Abraham Lincoln Memorial University, Harrogate, TN; Henry A. Wise journal, vol. 1 (*Erie*), various pages, entry 608, appendix M, File Designation 60, Naval Records Collection, RG 45, NARA; Commission as Midshipman, 1 June 1835, USNA Museum, FICm 010.0003.
8. Worden to Dickerson, 24 December 1837, Officers' Letters, M148; Dickerson to Worden, 30 December 1837, Letters Sent by the Secretary of the Navy, M149; Worden to Dickerson, 29 March 1838, M148; Dickerson to Worden 3 May 1838, Appointments, Orders and Resignations, T829, NARA.
9. Percival to Dickerson, 5 May 1838, Commanders Letters, M147, NARA.
10. *Cyane* log, 26 May–11 June 1838; Wise journal, vol. 2 (*Cyane*), 3 July 1838.
11. *Cyane* log, 5 July 1838; Wise journal, vol. 2 (*Cyane*), 5 July 1838; *Boston Courier*, 30 July 1838.
12. Wise journal, vol. 2 (*Cyane*), 5 July 1838; Wise journal, vol. 8 (Los Gringos); Henry A. Wise (pseud., Harry Gringo), *Tales for the Marines* (Boston: Philips, Samson, 1855), 16, 55–57, 355.
13. For a detailed description of chasing pirates, see Robert L. Worden, "Chasing after 'Dark, Bushy Whiskered Desperadoes,'" *Naval History* 37, no. 4 (August 2023): 54–59.
14. *Cyane* log, 2 September 1838.
15. Long, *Mad Jack*, 127; Department of the Navy, *Navy Regulations, 1814*, https://www.history.navy.mil/research/library/online-reading-room/title-list-alphabetically/n/navy-regulations-1814.html#anchor111158 (11 May 2020).
16. Henry Francis Sturdy, "The Establishment of the Naval School at Annapolis," U.S. Naval Institute *Proceedings* 72, no. 4 (April 1946): 2.
17. Major to Percival, 1 October 1838, quoted in Isaac Hull and Gardner Weld Allen, eds., *Commodore Hull: Papers of Isaac Hull, Commodore, United States Navy* (Boston: Boston Athenaeum, 1929), 167–69.
18. Sturdy, "Establishment," 3.
19. *Cyane* log, 22 October 1838–8 September 1839; Wise journal, vols. 2 and 3, 27 October 1838–9 August 1839; Worden, "Chasing after 'Dark, Bushy Whiskered Desperadoes,'" *Naval History*, 59.

20. Worden, Werden, and Wise to James Kirke Paulding, 1 January 1839, M148; Wise journal, vol. 2, 2 January 1839.
21. Wise journal, vol. 2, 7 February 1839, vol. 3, 2 March and 7 May 1839; *Cyane* log, 1 March–23 May 1839; Percival to Paulding, 2 March 1839, M147.
22. Wise journal, vol. 3, 24 May–15 June 1839; Royal W. Connell and William P. Mack, *Naval Ceremonies, Customs, and Traditions* (Annapolis: Naval Institute Press, 2004), 247.
23. Gene A. Smith, *Thomas ap Catesby Jones: Commodore of Manifest Destiny* (Annapolis: Naval Institute Press, 2000), 103; Charles Oscar Paullin, "Dueling in the Old Navy," U.S. Naval Institute *Proceedings* 35, no. 4 (December 1909): 1158–61, 1194–95.
24. Wise journal, vol. 3, 9 August 1839, vol. 4, 7 September and 27 November 1839; *Boston Courier*, 3 December 1839; Passenger Lists of Vessels Arriving at Boston, M277, NARA; Worden to Paulding, 2 and 12 December 1839, M148.
25. Department of the Navy, *General Regulations for the Navy and Marine Corps of the United States, 1841* (Washington, DC: J. and G. S. Gideon, 1841), articles 35, 379; Edward Shippen, "Some Account of the Origin of the Naval Asylum at Philadelphia," *Pennsylvania Magazine of History and Biography* 7, no. 2 (1883): 138; Charles H. Stockton, *Origin, History, Laws, and Regulations of the United States Naval Asylum, Philadelphia, Pennsylvania* (Washington, DC: Government Printing Office, 1886), 19; Mark C. Hunter, *A Society of Gentlemen: Midshipmen at the U.S. Naval Academy, 1845–1861* (Annapolis: Naval Institute Press, 2010), 10–11; William P. Leeman, *The Long Road to Annapolis: The Founding of the Naval Academy and the Emerging American Republic* (Chapel Hill: University of North Carolina Press, 2010), 196.
26. Paulding to Commo. James Biddle, 19 June 1840, M149; Paulding to Worden, 24 June, 28 July, and 9 October 1840, T829; *Navy Regulations, 1841*; *Globe*, 24 June 1840; Paulding to Worden, July 23, 1840, Worden Letterbook; Worden to Paulding, 18 July and 28 August 1840, M148.
27. *New-York Tribune*, 13 September 1841.
28. *Navy Regulations, 1841*, 63–67.
29. *Boston Morning Post*, 24 April 1841; *Daily Georgian*, 15 July 1841; *Polynesian*, 10 July 1841; *Brooklyn Eagle*, 8 September 1842; *New York Herald*, 17 June 1842; *New York Herald*, 20 September 1842; 27th Congress, 3rd Session, House of Representatives, H.R. No. 422, Ex.Doc. 166, "Taking Possession of Monterey" (hereinafter H.R. 422, Doc. 166); *Worden v. United States*, General Jurisdiction Case File 622, Box 35, entry 1, Records of the United States Court of Claims, RG 123, NARA; *Baltimore Clipper*, 5 December 1840.
30. *Relief* log, 30 May 1842.

31. *Worden v. U.S.*; *Relief* log, 6 September 1842; Spencer C. Tucker, ed., *The Civil War Naval Encyclopedia* (Santa Barbara: ABC-CLIO, 2011), 1:331–32; *Relief* log, 7 September 1842; *Dale* log, 7–14 September 1842.
32. Smith, *Thomas ap Catesby Jones*, 105–6; *Relief* log, 4 July–6 September 1842; Jones to Upshur, 13 September 1842, in H.R. 422, Doc. 166, 68–69; "Webster-Ashburton Treaty, 1842," https://history.state.gov/milestones/1830–1860/webster-treaty (11 December 2020).
33. Frank W. Gapp, "The 'Capture' of Monterey in 1842," *U.S. Naval Institute Proceedings* 105, no. 3 (March 1979): 46–47.
34. David F. Long, *Gold Braid and Foreign Relations: Diplomatic Activities of U.S. Naval Officers, 1798–1883* (Annapolis: Naval Institute Press, 1988), 88–97.
35. *Relief* log, 6 September 1842; *New-York Tribune*, 12 December 1842; *Alexandria Gazette*, 15 December 1842; Jones to Upshur, 11 September 1842; Gene A. Smith, "Thomas ap Catesby Jones and the First Implementation of the Monroe Doctrine," *Southern California Quarterly* 76, no. 2 (Summer 1994): 144.
36. *Dale* log, 8–14 September 1842; Jones to Dornin, 8 September 1842, in H.R. 422, Doc. 166, A No. 1, 73–74; Jones to Armstrong, Stribling, and Dornin, 8 September 1842, 84–86; Long, *Gold Braid and Foreign Relations*, 97; Gapp, "Capture of Monterey," 49.
37. *Dale* log, 11–22 September 1842; Private Journal of Cdr. Thomas A. Dornin, 8 September 1842, vol. 3, entry 608, File Designation 47, RG 45, NARA.
38. *Dale* log, 12–25 September–1 October 1842; Dornin journal, 1 October 1842; *Evening Star* (London), 11 November 1842; *Whig Standard*, 22 December 1843; *St. James Chronicle and General Evening Post* (London), 27 May 1843; *Globe*, 7 June 1843; *Niles' National Register*, 13 May 1843.
39. Dornin journal, 11 September, 21 and 24 October 1842.
40. *Dale* log, 23 October 1842.
41. Dornin journal, 17 November 1842.
42. *Dale* log, 15–29 December 1842.
43. Midn. Alonzo C. Jackson to Alonzo C. Paige, 3 November 1842, quoted in *The Conquest of California: Alonzo C. Jackson's Letter in Detail of the Seizure of Monterey in 1842 and His Letter on the Final Conquest of 1846* (privately printed, 1953), 13; Jones to Upshur, 24 October 1842, in H.R. 422, Doc. 166, 69–73.
44. *Standard* (London), 17 April 1843; Robert Erwin Johnson, *Thence round Cape Horn: The Story of United States Naval Forces on Pacific Station, 1818–1923* (Annapolis: United States Naval Institute, 1963), 64; Gene A. Smith, "The War That Wasn't: Thomas ap Catesby Jones's Seizure of Monterey," *California History* 66, no. 2 (June 1987): 108, 112; Smith, "First Implementation of the Monroe Doctrine," 147–49; Matthew J. Karp, "Slavery and American Sea

Power: The Navalist Impulse in the Antebellum South," *Journal of Southern History* 77, no. 2 (May 2011): 284, 308–9; John H. Schroeder, *Shaping a Maritime Empire: The Commercial and Diplomatic Role of the American Navy, 1829–1861* (Westport, CT: Greenwood Press, 1985), 75–76; Smith, *Commodore of Manifest Destiny*, 107–9.

45. Long, *Gold Braid and Foreign Relations*, 100–101; Smith, *Commodore of Manifest Destiny*, 110–11, 120–21; George M. Brooke Jr., "The Vest Pocket War of Commodore Jones," *Pacific Historical Review* 31, no. 3 (August 1962): 232.

46. *Dale* log, 20 February–6 March 1843; "Harbour of Monterey, Surveyed by the Officers of the U.S.S. *Dale*, 1843," NAID 219246537, File Unit 941-1843, RG 23, Records of the Coast and Geodetic Survey, NARA-College Park. The 1848 map is "West Coast of North America, from the Gulf of Dulce to San Francisco. Spanish and other Authorities. 1848," https://exhibits.stanford.edu/ruderman/catalog/mk508qg0451 (2 March 2024).

47. *Dale* log, 7 March–2 April 1843; Donald K. Yeomans, "Great Comets in History" (April 2007), Jet Propulsion Laboratory, https://ssd.jpl.nasa.gov/?great_comets (30 June 2021).

48. Philo White to Editor, 18 October 1843, *North-Carolina Standard*, 25 October 1843.

49. *Navy Regulations, 1841*, article 205; *Dale* log, 1 April–28 October 1843.

50. *Dale* log, 8 September and 13 November 1842, and logs of other ships on which Worden served, 1834–1877; *Navy Regulations, 1841*, articles 87–90; Connell and Mack, *Naval Ceremonies*, 70–75.

51. *Dale* log, 27 July–28 October 1843; *Globe*, 31 October 1843; Ananias Worden to Mordecai L. Hopkins, 29 July 1888, Mordecai Hopkins Papers, Clarke Historical Library, Central Michigan University, Mount Pleasant, MI.

CHAPTER 3. SCIENCE IS THE KEY

1. Joseph Everett Nourse, *Memoir of the Founding and Progress of the United States Naval Observatory* (Washington, DC: Government Printing Office, 1873), 33; Steven J. Dick, *Sky and Ocean Joined: The U.S. Naval Observatory, 1830–2000* (New York: Cambridge University Press, 2003), 38–44, 47–53.

2. Dick, *Sky and Ocean Joined*, 55–57, 72–73; *Astronomical Observations Made during the Year 1845 at the National Observatory, Washington* (Washington, DC: J. and G. S. Gideon, 1846).

3. Maury to Commodore William M. Crane, Chief, Bureau of Ordnance and Hydrography, 20 October 1845, Letters Sent, vol. 2, entry 42-1, Records of the U.S. Naval Observatory, RG 78, NARA.

4. Naval Record of Commodore John L. Worden (1834–68), Letters Sent, vol. 37, entry 3, Records of the U.S. Naval Academy, RG 405, Special Collections

and Archives (says 7 April); "Record of Service of Rear Admiral John Lorimer Worden" (1834-63), John Lorimer Worden Papers, A80-1364, Library and Museum, Lincoln Memorial University (LMU), Harrogate, TN (says 9 April).
5. Dick, *Sky and Ocean Joined*, 74.
6. Bancroft to Crane, 24 October 1845, Box 2, MSS 52837, Records of the U.S. Naval Observatory, Naval Historical Foundation Collection, Manuscript Division, Library of Congress; Maury to Crane, 25 October 1845, Letters Sent, vol. 2, entry 42-1, RG 78, NARA; Maury to Bancroft, 1 July 1846, quoted in *Astronomical Observations, 1845*, 1.
7. Maury to Crane, 20 October 1845, Letters Sent, entry 42-1, RG 78.
8. Bancroft to Maury, 6 March 1846, Box 2, MSS 52837, Library of Congress.
9. Dick, *Sky and Ocean Joined*, 79, citing *Astronomical Observations, 1845*, appendix 31–32; and Dick, "A History of the American Nautical Almanac Office," *Proceedings: Nautical Almanac Office Sesquicentennial Symposium, U.S. Naval Observatory, March 3–4, 1999*, ed. Alan D. Fiala and Steven J. Dick (Washington, DC: U.S. Naval Observatory, 1999), 11–12, http://adsabs.harvard.edu/full/1999naos.symp . . . 11D (9 November 2019).
10. Maury to Crane, 20 October 1845.
11. Maury to Crane, 20 October 1845; Dick, *Sky and Ocean Joined*, 67, table 2.1, 367, 368, fig. 10.3.
12. *Astronomical Observations, 1845*, 12.
13. *Astronomical Observations, 1845*, 12.
14. *Astronomical Observations, 1845*, xc, 132–52, carrying "W" notations, 133 footnote * reads, "W. Passed Midshipman Worden."
15. Worden Prime Vertical observation notebook, June–August 1845, Box 275, entry 42-18, RG 78, NARA.
16. Worden Prime Vertical observation notebooks, October 1845–April 1846, Box 275, entry 42-18.
17. *Astronomical Observations, 1845*, xc.
18. *Astronomical Observations, 1845*, 12.
19. *Astronomical Observations Made during the Year 1846 at the National Observatory, Washington* (Washington, DC: C. Alexander, 1851), 272–83 carrying "W" notations, and 359; Worden's Meridian Circle observations notebook, September–October 1845, Box 258, entry 42-18, RG 78.
20. Maury to Worden, August 17, 1844, Letters Sent, vol. 1, entry 42-1, RG 78; Maury to Worden, 19 December 1845, Letters Sent, vol. 2, entry 42-1, RG 78.
21. Franklin B. Hough, *The New York Civil List* (Albany, NY: Weed, Parsons, 1858), 222–23.
22. Worden to Olivia Akin Toffy, 19 March 1844, John L. Worden Papers, 1844–1888, MS16.01.03, Mariners' Museum Library, Newport News, VA.

23. Maury to Crane, October 20, 1845; U.S. Department of State, *Register of All Officers and Agents, Civil, Military, and Naval, in the Service of the United States, on the Thirtieth of September 1845* (Washington, DC: J. and G. S. Gideon, 1845), 95.
24. *Daily Union*, 6 January 1846, among others; *Journal of the Senate of the United States of America*, 29th Congress, 1st Session (Washington, DC: Ritchie and Heiss, 1845–46), 6 January 1846, 85, 27 March 1846, 599, 3 March 1847, 275, 20 December 1847, 62, and 5 May 1848, 317; *Journal of the House of Representatives of the United States*, 29th Congress, 1st Session (Washington, DC: Ritchie and Heiss, 1845–46), 7 January 1846, 201, https://memory.loc.gov/ammem/amlaw/lawhome.html.
25. "Record of Service," Worden Papers, LMU; Worden to Bancroft, 26 May 1846, Officers Letters, M148, NARA.

CHAPTER 4. FROM STORESHIP TO WARSHIP

1. John L. Worden, "Record of Service of Rear Admiral John L. Worden," John Lorimer Worden Papers, Lincoln Memorial Library and Museum; Worden to Secretary of Navy George Bancroft, May 26, 1846, Officers Letters, M148, NARA.
2. *Alexandria Gazette*, 7 August 1846 and 18 January 1847; Worden's commission as lieutenant, 17 January 1847, 1912.01.02, USNA Museum, Annapolis.
3. Worden to John Y. Mason, 3 February 1847, Officers Letters, M148, NARA; *Southampton* log, 17–23 February 1847.
4. Myrta Avary, comp. and ed., *A Virginia Girl in the Civil War, 1861–1865; Being a Record of the Actual Experiences of the Wife of a Confederate Officer* (New York: D. Appleton, 1903), 9.
5. *Southampton* log, 20 April 1847.
6. *Southampton* log, 21 April–17 June 1847.
7. Philip St. George Cooke, *The Conquest of New Mexico and California, an Historical and Personal Narrative* (Albuquerque, NM: Horn and Wallace, 1964), 26–48; Dwight L. Clarke, *Stephen Watts Kearny, Soldier of the West* (Norman: University of Oklahoma Press, 1961), 249–53; Karl Jack Bauer, *Surfboats and Horse Marines: U.S. Naval Operations in the Mexican War, 1846–48* (Annapolis: U.S. Naval Institute, 1969), 196–69.
8. Karl Jack Bauer, *The Mexican War, 1846–1848* (New York: Macmillan, 1974), 199, citing Kearny to Stockton, 17 January 1847; Samuel J. Baynard, *A Sketch of the Life of Com. Robert F. Stockton* (New York: Derby and Jackson, 1856), 147–48; Clarke, *Kearny*, 249–53.
9. Bauer, *Mexican War*, 194–96.
10. *Southampton* log, 25–31 August and 7 September 1847.
11. *Southampton* log, 25–31 August and 7 September 1847.

12. *Southampton* log, 31 August 1847.
13. *Southampton* log, 12–19 October 1847.
14. Bauer, *Mexican War*, 344; Richard W. Amero, "The Mexican War in Baja California," *San Diego Historical Society Quarterly* 30, no. 1 (winter 1984), https://sandiegohistory.org/journal/1984/january/war/ (17 May 2020).
15. Amero, "Mexican War"; Peter Gerhard, "Baja California in the Mexican War, 1846–1847," *Pacific Historical Review* 14, no. 4 (December 1945): 413.
16. Francis D. Clark, *The First Regiment of New York Volunteers* (New York: George S. Evans, 1882), 24; Bauer, *Mexican War*, 345, citing "Memorandum of Captain H. W. Halleck concerning His Expedition in Lower California, 1846–1848."
17. Amero, "Mexican War."
18. John Haskell Kemble, ed., "Amphibious Operations of a Cruise in Gulf of California: A Contemporary Account," *American Neptune* 5, no. 2 (April 1945): 122–25; Charles Belknap, ed., "Notes from the Journal of Lieutenant T. A. M. Craven, USN, U.S.S. *Dale*, Pacific Squadron 1846–49," U.S. Naval Institute *Proceedings* 14, no. 1 (January 1888): 304–7, 316; Gerhard, "Baja California," 420; ; Bauer, *Mexican War*, 347, citing Shubrick to Mason, 4 November, 5 November, and 7 December 1847, H. Ex. Doc. 1, 30th Congress, 2d Session, 1058; Bauer, *Surf Boats*, 211–13, 218–19.
19. Halleck, "Memorandum," 14–15, 38–39.
20. *Southampton* log, 11 November 1847.
21. *Southampton* log, 14 November 1847.
22. *Southampton* log, 18 November 1847.
23. *Southampton* log, 17–21 November 1847.
24. *Southampton* log, 25–27 November 1847.
25. Bauer, *Mexican War*, 348.
26. *Southampton* log, 28 November 1847.
27. Spencer C. Tucker, ed., *Encyclopedia of the Mexican-American War: A Political, Social, Military, and Social History* (Santa Barbara, CA: ABC-CLIO, 2013), 1:584; *Southampton* log, 6–21 December 1847.
28. *Southampton* log, 7 January 1848.
29. *Southampton* log, 19–28 January 1848.
30. John D. Yates, "Insurgents on the Baja Peninsula: Henry Halleck's Journal of the War in Lower California, 1847–1848," *California Historical Quarterly* 54, no. 3 (1975): 238–39; *Southampton* log, 2 and 7 March, 1–6 April, and 4 May 1848; Worden "Record of Service."

CHAPTER 5. BETWEEN THE WARS

1. Thomas ap Catesby Jones to John Y. Mason, 29 November 1848 and 9 April 1849, Squadron Letters, M89, NARA; Frank W. Gapp, *The Commodore and*

the Whale: The Lost Victories of Thomas ap Catesby Jones (New York: Vantage Press, 1996), 126.
2. Gapp, Commodore and the Whale, 122–26; Dan O'Neil, "From Forecastle to Mother Lode: The U.S. Navy in the Gold Fields," Southern California Quarterly 71, no. 1 (1989): 69–88.
3. Worden to John Y. Mason, 15 August 1848, Officers Letters, M148.
4. "Summary Medical Report," 15 January 1898, in Olivia Worden's Pension File, Certificate 12948, Navy Widows' Certificates, M127, NARA; "Record of Service of Rear Admiral John L. Worden," Worden Papers, Lincoln Memorial University; Independence log, 4 May–14 July 1848.
5. Warren log, 10 August–29 December 1848; Jones to Mason, 2 September and 19 October 1848, and 9 April 1849, Squadron Letters, M89; O'Neil, "Forecastle," 71–72, 80.
6. Warren log, 26 November 1848.
7. Worden to William Ballard Preston, 23 March 1849, Officers Letters, M148.
8. Warren log, 9 June–26 July 1849; Jones to Pacific Squadron officers, 20 October 1848, Squadron Letters, M89, NARA; Daily Crescent (New Orleans), 11 November 1848; Alta California, 2 August 1849.
9. Warren log, 9 June–26 July 1849; Alta California, 16 August 1849.
10. O'Neil, "Forecastle," 73
11. Warren and Ohio logs, 12 September 1849; Stribling to Jones, 15 August and 19 October 1849, Captains Letters, M125; Ohio log, 15 September–23 October 1849; Alta California, 15 November 1849.
12. Ohio log, 29 October, 23 November, and 13 December 1849.
13. Ohio log, 25 December 1849–4 January 1850; Stribling to Preston, 28 December 1849, Captains Letters, M125.
14. Ohio log, 4 January–28 February 1850; Standard of Freedom (London), 6 April 1850; Boston Post, 9 and 30 April 1850.
15. Ohio log, 28 February–3 May 1850; Republic, 30 April 1850, 3; Boston Post, 30 April 1850.
16. Ohio log, 3 May 1850; Worden to Preston, 5 June and 9 July 1850, and Worden to Secretary of the Navy William H. Graham, 23 August 1850, M148; Worden to Maury, 25 July 1850, Letters Received, Box 7, entry PC 42-7, Records of the U.S. Naval Observatory, RG 78; Republic, 4 September 1850; Maury to Worden, 7 September 1850, Letters Sent, entry PC 42-1, vol. 5, RG 78; "Record of Service."
17. Maury to Commodore Lewis Warrington, Chief, Bureau of Ordnance and Hydrography, 25 July 1851; "List of Officers Assigned and Others Attached to the Natl Oby, at Washington, on 30th Sept 1851," both in Letters Sent, vol. 7, entry 41-1, RG 78.

18. Worden and others to Maury, 27 December 1850; Maury to J. H. Lathrop, 21 January and 22 February 1851, and Maury to Stewart, 8 October 1851, Letters Sent, vol. 6, RG 78; Maury to George Manning, 27 October and 24 November 1852, Box 10, Records of the U.S. Naval Observatory, MSS 52387, Library of Congress; Dick, *Sky and Ocean Joined*, 45 n49; "Summary Medical Report."
19. *Astronomical Observations, Made during the Year 1847 at the National Observatory, Washington*, vol. 3 (Washington, 1853), iv, xxx–xxxi; *Astronomical Observations, Made during the Year 1848 at the National Observatory, Washington*, vol. 4 (Washington, 1856), xxxviii; *Astronomical Observations, Made during the Years 1849 and 1850 at the National Observatory, Washington*, vol. 5 (Washington, 1859), vi, xxvi, and xxix; Dick, *Sky and Ocean Joined*, 78.
20. "Computations of Reductions to Mean Places 1850.0 of Stars Observed with the Prime Vertical, 1848," Box 134, entry 18, RG 78.
21. *Astronomical Observations, Made during the Years 1851 and 1852 at the National Observatory, Washington*, vol. 6 (Washington, 1867), ix and x. Gilliss completed the introduction in 1862. *Astronomical Observations, 1875* (Washington, DC, 1880), vol. 20, appendix I, 6, 7, 73.
22. John Dryden Kazar, "The United States Navy and Scientific Exploration, 1837–1860," PhD diss., University of Massachusetts, Amherst, 1973, 38, 47, 116, https://scholarworks.umass.edu/dissertations_1/1328 (11 March 2024); Report of the Secretary of the Navy, 3 December 1836, 446, and 2 December 1837, 718, https://www.history.navy.mil (11 March 2024); *Daily American Organ*, 26 February and 11 July 1856; Maury to Manning, 27 February and undated but ca. 4 March 1852, Box 12, USNO Papers, MSS 52837, Library of Congress; Robert J. Schneller Jr., *A Quest for Glory: A Biography of Rear Admiral John A. Dahlgren* (Annapolis: Naval Institute Press, 1996), 155.
23. Worden to Graham, 12 March 1852, M148; Wise journal (*Cumberland*), vol. 10, front material.
24. Worden to Graham, 19 April 1852, M148.
25. Stringham to Graham, 25 June 1852, Squadron Letters, M89.
26. Wise journal, 24 May 1852.
27. *Cumberland* log, 12 May–8 June 1852; "Summary Medical Report"; Stringham to Graham, 25 June 1852; Stringham to Dobbin, 10 and 30 September and 7 October 1854, M89.
28. *Cumberland* log, 26 June 1852–4 January 1853, Stringham to Secretary of the Navy John P. Kennedy, 4 December 1852, M89.
29. Stringham to Cdr. George P. Upshur (*Levant*), 10 May 1852, Stringham to Graham, 9 June and 6 August 1852, M89.

30. *Cumberland* log, various dates, 1852–53; Wise journal, 29 May 1853; *Daily National Intelligencer*, 15 July 1853; David F. Long, *Gold Braid and Foreign Relations: Diplomatic Activities of U.S. Naval Officers, 1798–1883* (Annapolis: Naval Institute Press, 1988), 204.
31. *Cumberland* log, 15 June 1853; *New York Times*, 23 July 1853; *Boston Daily Atlas*, 25 July 1853; *Daily Union*, 27 July 1853; Stringham to Dobbin, 29 September 1853, M89.
32. Stringham to Dobbin, 17 May 1854, M89; Alan Dowty, *The Limits of American Isolation: The United States and the Crimean War* (New York: New York University Press, 1971), 125–25, 244, 251; Long, *Gold Braid*, 204–5; Trevor Royle, *Crimea: The Great Crimean War, 1854–1856* (London: Little, Brown, 1999), 84–87; *Cumberland* log, 29 June 1854.
33. Stringham to Dobbin, 22 February 1855, M89; *Levant* log, 14 February–4 May 1855; Worden to Dobbin, 7 August 1855, M148.
34. Dobbin to Maury, September 17, 1855, Matthew Fontaine Maury Papers, MSS 31682, Manuscript Division, Library of Congress.
35. *Worden v. United States*; General Jurisdiction Case File 622, Box 35, entry 1, and General Court Docket, vol. 1: 622, entry 5, Records of the United States Court of Claims, RG 123, NARA.
36. "Record of Service" (Worden); "Summary Medical Report."
37. Worden to Dobbin, 25 March 1856, M148.
38. Dobbin to Worden, 27 March 1856, M149; Worden to Dobbin, 10 and 11 April 1856, M148.
39. *New York Times*, 25 June 1858; Index of Letters Received from New York, January–November 1856, and Worden to De Camp, 14 October 1856, Box 106, entry 5, Records of the Bureau Yards and Docks, RG 71; Worden et al. to Capt. Abraham Bigelow, Commandant, New York Navy Yard, 7 November 1856, Worden to Bigelow, 21 December 1856, De Camp to Smith, 7 March 1857, Box 107, Worden to Kearny, 16 July 1857, Box 108; Worden to various private companies, 28 April 1858, Box 109; Semi-Monthly Abstract, 16–30 April 1857, Box 10, entry 55; Monthly Report of Expenditures, April 1857, Box 5, entry 58; James H. West, *A Short History of the New York Navy Yard* (New York: Navy Yard, 1941), 81.
40. Worden to Dobbin, 16 April 1856, M148; Report of Officers (New York), May 1856, Box 4, entry 27, RG 71.
41. Claude Berube, "The Crucible of Naval Enlightenment," *Naval History* 28, no. 5 (October 2014): 59; John Stobo, "Ships Constructed at the Brooklyn Navy Yard," http://www.columbia.edu/~jrs9/BNY-Ships.html (28 March 2023); Thomas M. Berner, *The Brooklyn Navy Yard* (Charleston, SC: Acadia, 1999), 127.

42. De Camp to Smith, 14 October 1856, Box 106, RG 71; Worden et al. to Kearny, 15 April 1857, Worden et al. to Cdr. Thomas R. Rootes, 24 December 1857, Box 108; Acting Secretary of the Navy Charles W. Welsh to Worden, 16 September 1856, and Secretary of the Navy Isaac Toucey to Worden, 25 July and 16 and September 1857, M149; Worden to Smith, 6 April and 13 May 1857, Box 107; Worden for De Camp, 20 and 29 May 1857, Minutes, Box 6.
43. Kearny to Worden and Graham, 29 March 1858, Letters Received, Box 109, RG 71; *Journal of the Senate of the State of New York at Their Eighty-First Session*, 356; *Journal of the Assembly of the State of New York at Their Eighty-First Session* (Albany: Charles Van Benthuysen, 1858), 931.
44. "Summary Medical Report"; Carpenter, *Reverend John Graham*, 353.
45. Worden to Toucey, 19 June and 1 July 1858, M148.

CHAPTER 6. ON THE EDGE OF WAR

1. Worden to Isaac Toucey, 19 June 1858, Officers Letters, M148, NARA.
2. *New York Times*, 25 June 1858.
3. Worden to Toucey, 1 July 1858, Officers Letters, M148; *New York Times*, 10 July 1858.
4. Paul H. Silverstone, *Civil War Navies, 1855–1883* (Annapolis: Naval Institute Press, 2001), 97.
5. Stephen Dando-Collins, *Tycoon's War: How Cornelius Vanderbilt Invaded a Country to Overthrow America's Most Famous Military Adventurer* (Philadelphia: Da Capo Press, 2008), 504; *Savannah* log, 30 October 1858 and 10 February 1859.
6. *Savannah* log, 25 February 1859–5 February 1860; Worden to Toucey, 19 July 1859, Captains Letters, M125, NARA.
7. Hubert Howe Bancroft, *History of Mexico* (San Francisco: History Company, 1890), 5:777.
8. "Summary Medical Report," in Olivia Worden's pension file, Certificate No. 12948, Navy Widows Pension Applications, M1279, RG 15, Records of the Veterans Administration, NARA.
9. "Record of Service of Rear Admiral John L. Worden," Worden Letterbook, LMU; Isaac Toucey to Worden, 17 January 1861, Letters Sent, M149, NARA.
10. J. E. Kaufmann and H. W. Kaufmann, *Fortress America* (Cambridge: Da Capo Press, 2004), 222–24.
11. Francis B. Renshaw to Editor, *New York Herald*, enclosed in Renshaw to Toucey, 29 January 1861, in *Official Records of the Union and Confederate Navies in the War of the Rebellion* (hereafter ORN), Ser. I, vol. 4 (Washington: Government Printing Office, 1896), 61.

12. Richard S. West Jr., *Mr. Lincoln's Navy* (New York: Longmans, Green, 1957), 12–13; Captain Armstrong's Explanatory Statement, ORN, Ser. I, vol. 4, 48–49.
13. Virgil Carrington Jones, *Civil War at Sea* (New York: Holt, Rinehart and Winston, 1960), 1:56–60.
14. Frank Moore, ed., *The Rebellion Record: A Diary of American Events, with Documents, Narratives, Illustrative Anecdotes, Poetry, etc.* (New York: G. P. Putnam, 1861), 1:42.
15. Jones, *Civil War at Sea*, 59.
16. Olivia Worden to Dear Friend (presumably Mrs. Margaret Marchand), 8 July 1861, enclosed with Jay Cooke to John Sherman, 13 July 1861, Miscellaneous Letters Received by the Secretary of the Navy, M124, NARA.
17. Gideon Welles, *Diary of Gideon Welles, Secretary of the Navy under Lincoln and Johnson* (Boston: Houghton Mifflin, 1911), 1:30–31.
18. *Diary of Gideon Welles*, 1:30–31.
19. Worden, "Sketch of My Trip to Pensacola in 1861," Worden Letterbook, LMU; Olivia Worden to Welles, 2 May 1861, Miscellaneous Letters, M124.
20. Worden, "Sketch"; Worden to LeRoy Pope Walker, Secretary of War, CSA, 16 April 1861, Worden Papers, MS0016/01-001.05#02, Mariners' Museum Library, Newport News, VA.
21. *Memphis Daily Appeal*, 16 April 1861.
22. Olivia Worden to Welles, 2 May 1861.
23. Worden to Welles, 15 April 1861, Worden Papers, MS16.01.05.01, Mariners' Museum Library; telegram and letter of Worden to Mrs. Worden, 15 April 1861, Worden Letterbook, LMU.
24. Olivia Worden to Welles, 2 May 1861.
25. Wise to Olivia Worden, 8 May 1861, Worden Letterbook, LMU.
26. *National Republican*, 5 June 1861.
27. Olivia Worden to Dear Friend, 11 May 1861, John L. Worden Papers, MS0016/01–001.06#01, Mariners' Museum Library, Newport News, VA.
28. Worden, "Sketch."
29. Olivia Worden to My Dear Friend, 8 July 1861, M124.
30. Cooke to Sherman, 13 July 1861, M124.
31. Ten Eyck to Olivia Worden, 19 July 1861, Worden Papers, MS0016/01-001.08#02, Mariners' Museum Library; *National Republican*, 24 July 1861.
32. *New York Times*, 19 April 1861; John V. Quarstein, *Big Bethel: The First Battle* (Charleston: History Press, 2011), 112–14.
33. Joint Resolution, 11 December 1861, ORN, Ser. II, vol. 3 (Washington, DC: Government Printing Office, 1902), 157.
34. Goldsborough to Huger, 10 October 1861, Worden Papers, MS0016/01-001.09#01, Mariners' Museum Library.

35. Goldsborough to Olivia Worden, 8 November 1861, Worden Letterbook, LMU.
36. Parole document, 13 November 1861, Worden Letterbook, LMU.
37. Worden to Welles, 20 November 1861, Officers Letters, M148.
38. "Diary of Abby Jane Leach Landis," *Wordens Past* 19, no. 2 (August 1988): 500.
39. Worden to Welles, 3 December 1861, Officers Letters, M148.

CHAPTER 7. TO PROVE *MONITOR* A SUCCESS

1. John M. Brooke to Mallory, 4 November 1864, ORN, Ser. II, vol. 2, 757.
2. *Mobile Register*, 11 August 1861.
3. Bushnell to Welles, 9 March 1877, Gideon Welles Papers, Henry E. Huntington Library, San Marino, CA.
4. Smith to Worden, 11 January 1862, Worden Letterbook, Worden Papers, LMU.
5. Worden to Smith, 13 January 1862, Worden Letterbook.
6. Welles to Worden, 13 January 1862, Worden Letterbook.
7. Edwin Olmstead, Wayne E. Stark, and Spencer C. Tucker, *The Big Guns: Civil War Siege, Seacoast and Naval Cannon* (Alexandria Bay, NY: Museum Restoration Service, 1997), 75.
8. Dana Wegner, "Ericsson's High Priest: Alban Stimers," *Civil War Times Illustrated* 13, no. 10 (February 1975): 26–34.
9. Worden to Welles, 20 January 1862, Officers Letters, M148, NARA.
10. William Keeler to Anna Keeler, 9 February 1862, in William F. Keeler, *Aboard the USS Monitor: The Letters of Acting Paymaster William Frederick Keeler, U.S. Navy, to His Wife Anna*, ed. Robert W. Daly (Annapolis: Naval Institute Press, 1964), 8.
11. Worden to Welles, 27 January 1862, Officers Letters, M148, NARA.
12. Worden to Welles, 6 February 1862, Officers Letters, M148, NARA.
13. Samuel Lewis (alias Peter Truscott), "Life on the *Monitor*: A Seaman's Story of the Fight with the *Merrimac*; Lively Experiences inside the Famous 'Cheesebox on a Raft,'" in *Camp-Fire Sketches and Battle-Field Echoes of the Rebellion*, comp. William C. King and William Derby (Springfield, MA: W. C. King, 1887), 258.
14. *Monitor* log, 4 March 1862.
15. Welles to Worden, 20 February 1862, ONR, Ser I, vol. 6, 659.
16. Worden to Welles, 27 February 1862, ORN, Ser. I, vol. 6, 670.
17. Keeler to Anna Keeler, 28 February 1862, in Keeler, *Aboard the Monitor*, 18.
18. Worden to Welles, 27 February 1862, Officers Letters, M148, NARA.
19. Paulding to Worden, 4 March 1862, Worden Letterbook, LMU.
20. Worden to Welles, 6 March 1862, Officers Letters, M148.
21. Keeler to Anna Keeler, 6–7 March 1862, in Keeler, *Aboard the Monitor*, 27.

22. S. Dana Greene, "In the 'Monitor' Turret," *Battles and Leaders of the Civil War* (New York: Century, 1894), 1:720.
23. Greene, "In the 'Monitor' Turret," 1:721.
24. Greene as quoted in John Ericsson, "Building of the 'Monitor,'" *Battles and Leaders*, 1:734.
25. Howard K. Beale, ed., *Diary of Gideon Welles, Secretary of the Navy under Lincoln and Johnson* (New York: W. W. Norton, 1960), 1:51–52.
26. Worden to Welles, 5 January 1868, Examining Board Files, Box 56 (S. D. Greene), entry 58, Records of the Judge Advocate General (Navy), RG 125, NARA.
27. Worden to My darling wife, 8 March 1862, Worden Letterbook.
28. Greene to Mother and Father, 14 March 1862, USNAM 1940.028.001, U.S. Naval Academy Museum.
29. Keeler to Anna Keeler, 8 March 1862, in Keeler, *Aboard the Monitor*, 33.
30. Thomas W. Rae, "The Little *Monitor* Saved Our Lives," *American History Illustrated* 1, no. 3 (June 1966): 34.
31. Worden quoted in Keeler to Anna Keeler, 9 March 1862, in Keeler, *Aboard the Monitor*, 33.
32. Irwin Mark Berent, *The Crewmen of the USS Monitor: A Biographical Directory* (Raleigh: North Carolina Department of Cultural Resources, 1985), 103.
33. Worden in Keeler to Keeler, 9 March 1862, in Keeler, *Aboard the Monitor*, 34.
34. Worden in Keeler to Keeler, 9 March 1862, in Keeler, *Aboard the Monitor*, 34.
35. Van Brunt to Welles, 10 March 1862, ORN, Ser. I, vol. 7, 11.
36. John R. Eggleston, "Captain Eggleston's Narrative of the Battle of the *Merrimac*," *Southern Historical Society Papers* 41 (September 1916): 174.
37. Greene, "In the 'Monitor' Turret," 1:723.
38. Greene, "In the 'Monitor' Turret," 1:725.
39. Greene, "In the 'Monitor' Turret," 1:724.
40. Keeler to Keeler, 9 March 1862, in Keeler, *Aboard the Monitor*, 36.
41. Keeler to Keeler, 9 March 1862, in Keeler, *Aboard the Monitor*, 38.
42. Greene, "In the 'Monitor' Turret," 1:727.
43. Keeler to Keeler, 9 March 1862, in Keeler, *Aboard the Monitor*, 38; John V. Quarstein, *The Monitor Boys: The Crew of the Union's First Ironclad* (Charleston: History Press, 2011), 90.
44. Greene to Mother and Father, 14 March 1862.

CHAPTER 8. RECOVERY AND RECOGNITION

1. "Summary Medical Report," copy in Olivia Worden's pension file Certificate No. 12948, RG 15, NARA.
2. "Record of Service of Rear Admiral John L. Worden," Worden Papers, LMU.

3. Charlotte Wise Hopkins, quoted in Mary Lawton, "When I Was a Little Girl," *Good Housekeeping* 97, no. 1 (July 1933): 142.
4. Worden's undated account of his wounding and recovery, Worden Letterbook; "Record of Service," Worden Papers, LMU.
5. Lincoln to Welles, 10 March 1863, in *The Valuable Papers of the Late Hon. Gideon Welles*, Auction Catalog 1342, 24 January 1924, 8, no. 23, Lincoln Financial Foundation Collection, Allen County Public Library, Fort Wayne, IN.
6. Charlotte Wise in Lawton, "When I Was a Little Girl," 142.
7. William Keeler to Anna Keeler, 12 May 1863, in Keeler, *Aboard the Monitor*, 130.
8. *New-York Daily Tribune*, 12 March 1862; *New York Herald*, 15 March 1862.
9. Welles to Worden, 15 March 1862, Worden Letterbook, LMU.
10. Draft letter, Wise to Smith Herman, 29 March 1862, Worden Letterbook, LMU.
11. Draft letter, Wise to Goldsborough, 29 March 1862, Worden Letterbook, LMU.
12. *Cleveland Morning Leader*, 14 April 1862; New York State Assembly Resolution, 23 April 1862, Worden Letterbook, LMU.
13. Ballard to Worden, 16 December 1862, and Worden to Ballard, 20 December 1862, Worden Letterbook, Worden Papers, LMU; *New York Times*, 21 December 1862.
14. *Brooklyn Eagle*, 22 March 1862.
15. *Salem (MA) Register*, 1 May 1862; *American Broadsides and Ephemera*, Series 1, no. 11210, American Antiquarian Society.
16. Keeler to Keeler, 26 March 1962, in Keeler, *Aboard the Monitor*, 56.
17. Marvel, *Monitor Chronicles*, 28.
18. *Monitor* Boys to Worden, 24 April 1862, Worden Letterbook, LMU.
19. *Country Gentleman*, 10 April 1862; Welles to Worden, 8 May 1862, Worden Letterbook and "Record of Service," LMU; "Summary Medical Report."
20. *Sun*, 8 May 1862; *Brooklyn Eagle*, 10 May 1862; *Christian Recorder* (Philadelphia), 17 May 1862; "Diary of Abby Jane Leach Landis," *Wordens Past* 19, no. 2 (August 1988): 500.
21. Worden's account of wounding and recovery, Worden Letterbook, LMU.
22. *Daily Cleveland Herald*, 1 July 1862; Robert L. Worden, "A Grand Fete in Grand Rapids for Lieutenant John Lorimer Worden," *Wordens Past* 29, no. 3 (November 2008): 2435–38, http://wordenfamilyassoc.org/John_Lorimer_Worden/JLW/WP_2435_Nov_2008_Grand_Fete_in_Grand_Rapids.pdf (5 June 2023).
23. *U.S. Statutes at Large* 12 (1862): 622.
24. Welles to Worden, 5 August 1862, Worden Letterbook, LMU.
25. Landis diary.

CHAPTER 9. MEETING *RATTLESNAKE*

1. Paul H. Silverstone, *Civil War Navies, 1855–1883* (Annapolis: Naval Institute Press, 2001), 5.
2. Samuel T. Browne, *First Cruise of the Montauk* (Providence: N. Bangs Williams, 1880), 12.
3. Silverstone, *Civil War Navies*, 5.
4. Olmstead, *Big Guns*, 75.
5. Olmstead, *Big Guns*, 94.
6. Silverstone, *Civil War Navies*, 5.
7. *Brooklyn Eagle*, 9 October 1862; *New York Times*, 3 December 1862.
8. *U.S. Statutes at Large* 12 (1863): 823.
9. Browne, *First Cruise*, 14.
10. *Montauk* log, 14 December 1862, entry 118, RG 24, NARA; Lee to Worden, 29 December 1862, Worden Letterbook, Worden Papers, LMU.
11. Rowena Reed, *Combined Operations in the Civil War* (Annapolis: Naval Institute Press, 1978), 271, 276–78.
12. Browne, *First Cruise*, 16.
13. *Montauk* log, 28 December 1862; Worden, "Notes about *Montauk*" (14 December 1862–4 March 1863), Worden Letterbook, Worden Papers, LMU.
14. Browne, *First Cruise*, 18.
15. Worden to Lee, 5 January 1863, ORN, Ser. I, vol. 8, 361–62.
16. Browne, *First Cruise*, 21.
17. Browne, *First Cruise*, 22–23.
18. Worden to Lee, 5 January 1863, ORN, Ser. I, vol. 8, 361.
19. Du Pont to Welles, 28 January 1863, cited in *Report of the Secretary of the Navy in Relation to Armored Vessels* (Washington, DC: Government Printing Office, 1864), 174.
20. J. E. Kaufmann and H. W. Kaufmann, *Fortress America: The Forts That Defended America, 1600 to the Present* (Cambridge: DeCapo Press, 2004), 271.
21. Browne, *First Cruise*, 38.
22. Silverstone, *Civil War Navies*, 30, 73, 99, 107.
23. Browne, *First Cruise*, 34, 45.
24. Howard P. Nash Jr., *A Naval History of the Civil War* (New York: A. S. Barnes, 1972), 31.
25. Worden to Du Pont, 2 February 1863, ORN, Ser. I, vol. 13, 627.
26. Worden to Du Pont, 2 February 1863.
27. For example, see Keeler to Keeler, 13 February 1862, in Keeler, *Aboard the USS Monitor*, 12.
28. Worden to Du Pont, 2 February 1863, ORN, Ser. I, vol. 13, 628.
29. Worden to Du Pont, 2 February 1863, ORN, Ser. I, vol. 13, 628.

30. Anderson to Capt. George A. Mercer, 2 February 1863, ORN, Ser. I, vol. 13, 628.
31. Browne, *First Cruise*, 43.
32. Worden to Du Pont, 2 February 1863, ORN, Ser. I, vol. 13, 631–32; Stephens to Worden, 27 January and 28 February 1863, ORN, Ser. I, vol. 13, 545 and 700.
33. *Vermont* log, 8 February 1863, entry 118, RG 24, NARA; Cdr. Christopher Raymond Perry Rodgers, *New Ironsides*, Charleston, to Charles Stedman, 16 February 1863, in "The American Civil War: Letters and Diaries," http://solomon.cwld.alexanderstreet.com (24 September 2008).
34. Silverstone, *Civil War Navies*, 160.
35. Du Pont to Welles, 2 March 1863, ORN, Ser. I, vol. 13, 697.
36. Browne, *First Cruise*, 46.
37. Stephens to Worden, 28 February 1863, ORN, Ser. I, vol. 13, 700.
38. Worden to Du Pont, 28 February 1863, ORN, Ser. I, vol. 13, 697.
39. Albert Bigelow Paine, *A Sailor of Fortune: Personal Memoirs of Captain B. S. Osbon* (New York: McClure, Phillips, 1906), 233.
40. Browne, *First Cruise*, 52.
41. Browne, *First Cruise*, 53–54.
42. Browne, *First Cruise*, 53–55.
43. Stephens to Worden, 28 February 1863, ORN, Ser. I, vol. 13, 700.
44. Alvah Hunter, *A Year on a Monitor and the Destruction of Fort Sumter*, edited by Craig L. Symonds (Columbia: University of South Carolina Press, 1987), 32.
45. Stephens to Worden, 28 February 1863, ORN, Ser. I, vol. 13, 702.
46. Worden to Du Pont, 28 February 1863, ORN, Ser. I, vol. 13, 700.
47. Du Pont to Welles, 28 February 1863, ORN, Ser. I, vol. 13, 697.
48. Worden to Du Pont, 28 February 1863, ORN, Ser. I, vol. 13, 697.

CHAPTER 10. INTO THE RING OF FIRE
1. Various writers and recipients, 27 February–2 March 1863, ORN, Ser. 1, vol. 13, 694–710.
2. John D. Hayes, ed., *Samuel Francis Du Pont: A Selection of His Civil War Letters* (Ithaca, NY: Cornell University Press, 1969), 2:387.
3. Reed, *Combined Operations in the Civil War*, 286–88.
4. Gustavus Vasa Fox, *Confidential Correspondence of Gustavus Vasa Fox, Assistant Secretary of the Navy, 1861–1865*, 2 vols., ed. Robert Means Thompson and Richard Wainwright (Freeport, NY: Books for Libraries Press, 1972), 1:195.
5. James Tertius deKay, *Monitor: The Story of the Legendary Civil War Ironclad and the Man Whose Invention Changed the Course of History* (New York: Walker, 1997), 68–79.
6. Fox, *Confidential Correspondence*, 2:126.

7. Reed, *Combined Operations*, 291.
8. Robert M. Browning Jr., *Success Is All That Is Expected: The South Atlantic Blockading Squadron during the Civil War* (Washington, DC: Brassey's, 2002), 155–58.
9. Reed, *Combined Operations*, 289–91.
10. Stimers to Du Pont, 5 March 1863, ORN, Ser. 1, vol. 13, 707–8.
11. Daniel Ammen, *The Old Navy and the New* (Philadelphia: J. B. Lippincott, 1891), 10–23.
12. Browning, *Success Is All That Is Expected*, 171–72; Spencer Tucker, *Blue and Gray Navies: The Civil War Afloat* (Annapolis: Naval Institute Press, 2006), 245.
13. Reed, *Combined Operations*, 291–92.
14. Howard P. Nash Jr., *A Naval History of the Civil War* (New York: A. S. Barnes, 1972), 191; Du Pont, Order of Battle, ORN, Ser. 1, vol. 14, 8–9.
15. U.S. Department of the Navy, Naval History Division, *Civil War Naval Chronology, 1861–1865* (Washington, DC: Government Printing Office, 1971), 3:57–58.
16. Nash, *Naval History*, 191.
17. Rodgers to Du Pont, 8 April 1863, ORN, Ser. 1, vol. 14, 11–13.
18. Worden to Du Pont, 8 April 1863, ORN, Ser. 1, vol. 14, 13–14.
19. Worden to Du Pont, 8 April 1863; *Montauk* log, 7 April 1863.
20. *Naval Chronology*, 3:58–60; Richard S. West Jr., *Mr. Lincoln's Navy* (New York: Longmans, Green, 1957), 234–37.
21. Worden to Du Pont, 8 April 1863.
22. Worden to Du Pont, 8 April 1863.
23. Samuel T. Browne, *The First Cruise of the Montauk* (Providence: N. Bangs Williams, 1880), 34.
24. Worden to Du Pont, 8 April 1863.
25. *Yorkville Enquirer*, 15 April 1863.
26. *New South*, 18 April 1863.
27. Du Pont to Worden, 13 April 1863, Worden Letterbook, LMU.
28. *Montauk* log, 14 April 1863.
29. *Carondelet* log, 19 April 1863; Navy Widows' Certificate 10328 (James Worden), M1279, RG 15, NARA; National Park Service Soldiers and Sailors Database, https://www.nps.gov/civilwar/soldiers-and-sailors-database.htm (7 November 2009).

CHAPTER 11. THE EXPERT

1. *Brooklyn Eagle*, 22 April 1863.
2. Gregory to Worden, 5 May 1863, Worden Letterbook, LMU.

NOTES TO PAGES 137-140   255

3. U.S. Navy Department, *Report of the Secretary of the Navy in Relation to Armored Vessels* (Washington, DC: Government Printing Office, 1864), 131–32.
4. George Parsons Lathrop, *History of the Union League of Philadelphia* (Philadelphia: J. B. Lippincott, 1884), 59; Worden to Watts Sherman, 23 October 1863, American Historical Manuscript Collection, New-York Historical Society; *Brooklyn Eagle*, 11 November 1863 and 23 February 1864.
5. *Brooklyn Eagle*, 11 April 1864.
6. Amanda Akin, *The Lady Nurse of Ward E* (New York: Baker and Taylor, 1909), 212.
7. Gideon Welles, *Diary of Gideon Welles, Secretary of the Navy under Lincoln and Johnson* (Boston: Houghton Mifflin, 1911), 2:7.
8. Paul H. Silverstone, *Civil War Navies: 1855–1883* (Annapolis: Naval Institute Press, 2001), 11.
9. *Brooklyn Eagle*, 22 June 1862.
10. Silverstone, *Civil War Navies*, 9.
11. *New York Times*, 22 August 1864.
12. *New York Times*, 21 November 1864.
13. Silverstone, *Civil War Navies*, 42.
14. Ericsson to Welles, 24 February 1863, John Ericsson Papers, MSS19877, Manuscript Division, Library of Congress.
15. Gregory to Lenthall, 12 May 1864, entry 64, Letters Received from Superintendents outside of Navy Yards, Records of the Bureau of Ships, RG 19, NARA.
16. *Report of the Joint Committee on the Conduct of the War at the Second Session, Thirty-Eighth Congress* (Washington, DC: Government Printing Office, 1865), "Light-Draught Monitors," 5–6.
17. *Brooklyn Eagle*, 21 March 1865; Silverstone, *Civil War Navies*, 11–12.
18. Worden to Lincoln, 1 April 1865, Abraham Lincoln Papers, Series 1, General Correspondence, 1833–1916, Manuscript Division, Library of Congress, https://www.loc.gov/item/mal4154300/ (5 June 2024).
19. Col. James Edmonds Saunders, *Early Settlers of Alabama* (New Orleans: L. Graham and Son, 1899), 439.
20. "Official Intelligence: Regular Navy," *United States Service Magazine* 4, no. 2 (August 1865): 181.
21. William N. Still Jr., ed., *The Confederate Navy: The Ships, Men, and Organization, 1861–65* (Annapolis: Naval Institute Press, 1997), 209; Robert G. Elliot, *Ironclad of the Roanoke: Gilbert Elliott's Albemarle* (Shippensburg, PA: White Mane Books, 1999), 251–55; Silverstone, *Civil War Navies*, 9–10.
22. Worden to Worden, enclosing oath, 5 February 1866, Letters Received from Admirals, Vice Admirals, Rear Admirals and Commandants, vol. 1, entry 58,

RG 45; Returns from Regular Army Infantry Regiments, June 1821–December 1916, M665, RG 94, NARA.
23. *Brooklyn Eagle*, 10 October 1864.
24. Donald L. Canney, *The Old Steam Navy: The Ironclads, 1842–1885* (Annapolis: Naval Institute Press, 1993), 2:124.
25. Donald L. Canney, *The Old Steam Navy: Frigates, Sloops, and Gunboats, 1815–1885* (Annapolis: Naval Institute Press, 1990), 1:139.
26. Canney, *Old Steam Navy*, 1:69, citing Frank M. Bennett, *Steam Navy of the United States* (Pittsburgh: Warren, 1896).
27. Farragut to Fox, 5 March 1862, in *Confidential Correspondence of Gustavus Vasa Fox*, ed. Robert M. Thompson and Richard Wainwright (New York: Naval Historical Society, 1918), 1:304.
28. "Official Intelligence: Regular Navy," *United States Service Magazine* 5, no. 3 (March 1866): 280; *New York Herald*, 13 April 1866.
29. *New York Herald*, 30 April 1866.
30. Frank M. Bennett, *Steam Navy of the United States* (Pittsburgh: Warren, 1896), 526.
31. Canney, *Old Steam Navy*, 1:140.
32. *New York Herald*, 10 June 1866.
33. Canney, *Old Steam Navy*, 1:67–70, 127–29.
34. Worden to Bell, 2 September 1866, Captains Letters, M125, NARA.
35. *Pensacola* log, 16 August 1866; Quarstein, *Monitor Boys*, 87.
36. *Evening Union*, 11 September 1866.
37. Kate Masur, "The Civil War, Reconstruction and the Transformation of African American Life in the 19th Century," 17 November 2015, *Library of Congress Blogs*, https://blogs.loc.gov/kluge/2015/11/the-civil-war-reconstruction-and-the-transformation-of-african-american-life-in-the-19th-century/ (25 March 2024); Robert J. Kaczorowski, "To Begin the Nation Anew: Congress, Citizenship, and Civil Rights after the Civil War," *American Historical Review* 92, no. 1 (1987): 51, 62.
38. *New York Herald*, 14 September 1866.
39. Worden to Welles, 8 November 1866, Captains Letters, M125.
40. Worden to Welles, 24 November 1866, Captains Letters, M125.
41. *Pensacola* log, 9 and 25 November 1866.
42. *Pensacola* log, 4 December 1866.
43. *Pensacola* log, 7 December 1866.
44. Worden to Godon, 9 December 1866, Captains Letters, M125.
45. Worden to Welles, 25 January 1867, Captains Letters, M125.
46. *Pensacola* log, 30 January 1867; "Chincha Islands War," https://www.encyclopedia.com/ (25 April 2023).

47. *Pensacola* log, 25 February–3 March 1867.
48. *San Francisco Bulletin*, 9, 20, and 27 April 1867 and 15 September 1868; *Sacramento Daily Union*, 10 and 11 April 1867; *Daily Alta California*, 7 and 26 April, 11 May 1867; *Flake's Bulletin* (Galveston), 13 June 1867.
49. *Daily Alta California*, 18 May 1867; Passenger Lists of Vessels Arriving at New York, M237, Roll 281, List 565, Records of the Immigration and Naturalization Service, RG 85, NARA; Worden to Townsend, 29 October 1867, Letters Received by the Adjutant General's Office, M619, RG 94, NARA; *Philadelphia Inquirer*, 1 November 1867.
50. Worden to Welles, 5 January 1868, Captains Letters, M125.
51. *New York Evening Post*, 23 April 1868; Records of Proceedings of Naval and Marine Examining Boards, Box 156, entry 58, RG 125, NARA; Naval Record of Commodore John L. Worden, Letters Sent by Superintendent, USNA, vol. 37, entry 3, RG 405, USNA SC&A; *Evening Star*, 6 June 1868.
52. Worden to Welles, 23 May 1868, Worden to Johnson, 23 May 1868, Captains Letters, M125; Welles to Worden, 1 June 1868, General Letter Books, M209, NARA; *Brooklyn Eagle*, 5 May 1868.
53. *Memphis Daily Avalanche*, 12 June 1868; *New York Herald*, 11 June 1868; *Navy Register, 1868*, 39; *Cosmopolitan* (London), 27 June 1868.
54. *Brooklyn Eagle*, 19 August 1869; *Sun*, 27 September 1869; *Deutschland und Österreich: Handbuch für Reisenden* (Coblenz: Karl Baedeker, 1869), 228–44; Oliver Norton Worden, *Some Records of Persons by the Name of Worden* (Lewisburg, PA: Railway Press, 1869), 163.
55. *Daily Alta California*, 26 April 1867; Worden to Lissette Woodworth, 12 January 1870, Box 2, Selim Edwin Woodworth Papers, 1834–1947, Huntington Library, San Marino, CA. The portrait is signed A. Gliemann/69, USNAM 1912.003.002. Carl Clauss, "Gliemann, Philipp Albert," *Allgemeine Deutsche Biographie* 9 (1879), S. 236, online version accessed 10 February 2022, https://www.deutsche-biographie.de/pnd136541399.html#adbcontent; U.S. Naval Academy, *Catalogue of Historic Objects at the United States Naval Academy* (Baltimore: Industrial Printing, 1925), 247.
56. Wise to Welles, 6 February 1869, Captains Letter, M125; Certificates of Dr. Charles D. Maxwell, 10 December 1869, and Dr. Robert Sims, 25 February 1870, in Charlotte Wise's widow's pension file, certificate no. 1818, M1279, Navy Widow's Certificates, RG 15.
57. *New York Herald*, 23 April 1869; *Brooklyn Eagle*, 23 April 1869; *National Republican*, 21 June 1869; *New York Times*, 23 June 1869; Find a Grave, https://www.findagrave.com/memorial/142002066/henry-augustus-wise (9 February 2022).

58. "Summary Medical Report"; *Daily Alta California*, 27 June 1869; *Le Mercure d'Orthez*, 6 November 1869; *San Francisco Bulletin*, 10 December 1869.
59. Robeson to Worden, 26 November 1869, Letterbook, Worden Papers, LMU.

CHAPTER 12. TRAINING THE NAVY'S FUTURE LEADERS

1. Worden served four years, nine months, and twenty-one days. Capt. Francis M. Ramsay (1881–86) served four years, nine months, and twenty-six days.
2. Welles to Blake, 3 May 1865, Letters Received, Box 8, Folder 12, entry 25, RG 405, USNA Special Collections and Archives (hereinafter USNA SC&A); Jack Sweetman, *The U.S. Naval Academy: An Illustrated History*, 2nd rev. ed. by Thomas J. Cutler (Annapolis: Naval Institute Press, 1995), 83.
3. Samuel J. Limneos, "Development of the United States Naval Academy's Unwritten Honor Concept, 1865–1875," McMullen Naval History Symposium, USNA SC&A, 16 August 2021, 11; Sweetman, *Naval Academy*, 84–89; James Russell Soley, *Historical Sketch of the United States Naval Academy* (Washington: Government Printing Office, 1876), 132–33; Robeson to Worden, 26 November 1869, Worden Letterbook, Worden Papers, LMU; Worden to Robeson, 1 December 1869, Letters Sent, vol. 25, entry 9, USNA SC&A.
4. Sweetman, *Naval Academy*, 102.
5. Leland P. Lovette, *School of the Sea: The Annapolis Tradition in American Life* (New York: Frederick A. Stokes, 1941), 97–98.
6. Soley, *Historical Sketch*, 111.
7. Thomas G. Ford, "Thomas G. Ford Manuscript on the History of the United States Naval Academy," unpublished manuscript, 6, NAHC_0005_0021, MS 448, 56, USNA SC&A.
8. George Dewey, *Autobiography of George Dewey, Admiral of the Navy* (New York: Charles Scribner's Sons, 1913), 143.
9. Winfield Scott Schley, *Forty-Five Years under the Flag* (New York: Appleton, 1904), 106–7.
10. Ford, "History," 6.
11. Sweetman, *Naval Academy*, 103–4; Lovette, *School of the Sea*, 97.
12. Ford, "History," 15–21.
13. Ford, "History," 6–7, 22; Soley, *Historical Sketch*, 110–11; Worden to Robeson, 27 October 1873, Letters Sent, vol. 27, entry 9, USNA SC&A.
14. Order 7, 12 January 1871, entry 48, USNA SC&A; Order 155, 25 November 1870, printed copies in John L. Worden Papers, Naval Historical Foundation Collection, MSS 56051, Manuscript Division, Library of Congress; handwritten letterpress copies are in Orders, vols. 2 and 3, entry 48, USNA SC&A.
15. Bradley A. Fiske, *From Midshipman to Rear-Admiral* (New York: Century, 1919), 9–11.

16. *Maryland Republican*, 18 November 1871; *Sun*, 22 November 1871; Order 105, 28 September 1871, Order 117, 6 October 1871, Worden Papers, Library of Congress; Third Class Cadet Midshipmen to Worden, 29 October 1871, Miscellaneous Letters, Box 1, Folder 19, entry 146a, USNA SC&A.
17. Navy Department (14 October 1871), Letters Received, Box 17, Folder 3, entry 25, USNA SC&A; *Evening Star*, 14 October 1871; *New-York Tribune*, 16 October 1871.
18. Park Benjamin, *The United States Naval Academy* (New York: G. P. Putnam's Sons, 1900), 288; *Sun*, 17 October, 21–22 November, and 19 December 1871; Navy Department Order, 16 November 1871, Letters Received, Box 17, Folder 3, entry 25, USNA SC&A.
19. Order 109, 28 September 1872, Orders 132 and 133, both issued 22 October 1872, entry 48, USNA SC&A.
20. Navy Department Order, 31 March 1874, Letters Received, Box 17, entry 25, USNA SC&A; *New York Herald*, 4 April and 5 May 1874; *Maryland Republican*, 12 September 1874; *Port Tobacco Times and Charles County Advertiser*, 3 July 1874.
21. *Journal of the House of Representatives of the United States* (Washington: Government Printing Office, 1873), 4 May 1874, 906; *Sun*, 6 May 1874 and 13 October 1876; *Maryland Republican*, 16 May 1874; *National Republican*, 22 May 1874; *U.S. Statutes at Large* 18 (1874): 203; Ford, "History," 57–58; *18 U.S. Op. Atty. Gen. 292 (U.S.A.G.), 1885 WL 2839, United States Attorney General A. H. Garland* (12 November 1885).
22. Robert J. Schneller Jr., *Breaking the Color Barrier: The U.S. Naval Academy's First Black Midshipmen and the Struggle for Racial Equality* (New York: New York University Press, 2005).
23. Schneller, *Breaking the Color Barrier*, 8–10; *Richmond Dispatch*, 25 September 1872; *Maryland Republican*, 28 September and 5 October 1872.
24. Schneller, *Breaking the Color Barrier*, 15.
25. Worden to Robeson, 3 October 1872, Letters Sent, vol. 27, entry 9, USNA SC&A; Robley D. Evans, *A Sailor's Log: Recollections of Forty Years of Naval Life* (Annapolis: Naval Institute Press, 1993), xiii–xix, 169.
26. Case to Worden, 18 October 1872, Letters and Reports Received, Box 2, Folder 4, entry 75, USNA SC&A.
27. Worden to Robeson, 29 October 1872, Letters Sent, vol. 27, entry 9, USNA SC&A.
28. Navy Department Order, 12 December 1872; *New York Herald*, 15 December 1872; *Daily Dispatch* (Richmond), 16 December 1872; *Sun*, 17 December 1874; *New National Era* (Washington), 19 December 1872; *Maryland Republican*, 21 December 1872.

29. U.S. Naval Registers of Delinquencies, 283 (Conyers), vol. 377, Microfilm Publication M991, USNA SC&A; Schneller, *Breaking the Color Barrier*, 22–23, 30; *Maryland Republican*, 11 November 1873; Robeson to Worden, 8 November 1873, and Robeson to Conyers, 11 November 1873, both in Folder 3, Box 17, entry 25, USNA SC&A.
30. Robeson to Worden, November 8, 1873, Minutes of the Academic Board, vol. 4, entry 205a, USNA SC&A; Schneller, *Breaking the Color Barrier*, 28–32; William B. Gatewood Jr., "Alonzo Clifton McClennan: Black Midshipman from South Carolina, 1873–1874," *South Carolina Historical Magazine* 89, no. 1 (1988): 24.
31. Schneller, *Breaking the Color Barrier*, 32–33; Gatewood, "McClennan," 36–39; Robeson to McClennan, 16 March 1874, Box 17, Folder 3, entry 25, USNA SC&A.
32. Schneller, *Breaking the Color Barrier*, 42, 130–31.
33. *U.S. Statutes at Large*, 15 (1868): 261.
34. Order 56, 8 December 1869, entry 48, USNA SC&A; Ford, "History," 23–24; Sweetman, *Naval Academy*, 102; Robeson to Worden, 18 January 1872, and Worden to Robeson, 19 January 1872, in U.S. Congress, *Miscellaneous Documents of the Senate of the United States*, Misc. Doc. 77 (Washington: Government Printing Office, 1872). Excerpts appear in Charles Lanman, ed., *The Japanese in America* (London: Longmans, Green, Reader, and Dyer, 1872), 68–69; and in Katsuji Kato, "Japanese Students at Annapolis," *Japanese Student* 3, no. 2 (November 1918): 60–61.
35. *Maryland Republican*, 19 and 26 August 1871 and 22 November 1873; Mori Arinori to Acting Secretary of State Charles Hale, 24 September 1872, Box 4, Folder 7, entry 75, USNA SC&A; Worden to Robeson, 30 April 1873, Letters Sent, vol. 27, entry 9, USNA SC&A.
36. J. M. Elliott, "Japanese Students at the United States Naval Academy," U.S. Naval Institute *Proceedings* 73, no. 529 (March 1957): 303–7.
37. "Papers Related to the Removal of Democrats and Appointment of Republicans," Letters Received, Box 9, Folder 9, entry 25, USNA SC&A.
38. *Maryland Republican*, 11 and 18 November 1871.
39. Surgeon General James Croxall Palmer to Robeson, 18 April 1872, Box 16, Folder 12, entry 25, USNA SC&A.
40. Soley, *Historical Sketch*, 119, 121–22; Anne Arundel County Land Records, MSA CE 59-23; *Laws of the State of Maryland, 1867* (Annapolis: Henry A. Lucas, 1867), 571–73 (ch. 297, authorized), 808 (ch. 387, amended); "List of Deeds Showing Additions," General Correspondence, and City of Annapolis Ordinances, 10 March 1874, and 22 April 1874, Box 5, Folder 3, entry 39B, subseries 8c, USNA SC&A; *Maryland Republican*, 11 July 1874;

Anne Arundel County Circuit Court Equity Papers (1874), Case 417, MSA C 70-104; Equity Docket Appearances, July Term, Anne Arundel County Circuit Court, Book 2:11, MSA CE 432-2; Order 44, 20 May 1910, entry 54, USNA SC&A.
41. Robeson to Worden, 21 October 1873, Letters Received, Box 17, Folder 5, entry 25, USNA SC&A *Maryland Republican*, 27 December 1873.
42. *Evening Star*, 17 and 21 February 1874; Worden to Robeson, 10 March 1874, Letters Sent, vol. 27, entry 9, USNA SC&A.
43. Minutes, 9 October 1873, Journal of the United States Naval Institute, 1873–1935, USNI Archives; Thomas J. Cutler, "Fifteen Founders," *Naval History* 37, no. 5 (October 2023): 30–35.
44. Roy C. Smith III, "The First Hundred Years Are," U.S. Naval Institute *Proceedings* 99, no. 10 (October 1973): 56; Minutes, 8 January 1874, USNI Archives; Foxhall A. Parker, "The 'Monitor' and the 'Merrimac,'" U.S. Naval Institute *Proceedings* 1 (1874): 162.
45. Worden to Robeson, 5 January 1874, Letters Sent, entry 9, box 2, USNA SC&A; Richard H. Bradford, *The Virginius Affair* (Boulder: Colorado Associated University Press, 1980), 112–13; Craig L. Symonds, "A Two-Way Street," U.S. Naval Institute *Proceedings* 149, no. 10 (2023): 52–53.
46. Worden to Lissette Woodworth, 12 January 1870, Box 2, Selim Edwin Woodworth Papers, 1834–1947, Huntington Library, San Marino, CA.
47. Owen M. Taylor, *The History of Annapolis* (Baltimore: Turnbull Brothers, 1872), 43–44; *Daily State Journal* (Alexandria), 31 May 1871; James Cheevers email to Robert L. Worden, 15 May 2023; *Maryland Republican*, 3 June 1871.
48. *Sun* and *Evening Star*, both 11 January 1873; Rear Admiral Commission, USNA Museum 1912.001.05; Order 32, 3 March 1873, entry 48, USNA SC&A; Ford, "History," 30–31.
49. Order 82, 25 May 1873, entry 48, USNA SC&A; *National Republican*, 1 June 1874.
50. Worden to Robeson, 5 February 1872, Letters Sent, vol. 26, entry 9, USNA SC&A; *Albany Evening Journal*, 5 February 1872; *Watertown Daily Times*, 7 May 1873; Deed no. 121, 30 July 1872, section 6, lots 12 and 13, Pawling Cemetery, Dutchess County, New York, in author's file, given to him by a direct descendant.
51. *Annapolis Gazette*, 15 July 1873; Cdr. Kidder Randolph Breese to Worden at Mamaroneck, 23 and 25 July 1873, Letters Sent, vol. 37, entry 3, USNA SC&A.
52. Society of the Army of the Tennessee, *Report of the Proceedings of the Society of the Army of the Tennessee, at the Seventh Annual Meeting, Held at Toledo, Ohio, October 15th and 16th, 1873*, 142–43.

53. *Army of the Tennessee*, 158–59.
54. *Annapolis Gazette*, 9 June 1874; *National Republican*, 25 September 1874.
55. Telegram of Eugene Schuyler, U.S. Legation, St. Petersburg, to Worden, 4 July 1874, John L. Worden Papers, MS0016/01-001.31#01, Mariners' Museum Library, Newport News, VA.

CHAPTER 13. COMMANDING THE EUROPEAN SQUADRON

1. *Annapolis Gazette*, 9 June 1874.
2. Prize Case Certificate no. 68958 (I. G. Worden), 25 August 1869, Records of Accounting Officers of the Department of the Treasury, vol. 62, entry 825, RG 217, NARA.
3. Worden "To the Honorable Senate and House of Representatives in Congress Assembled," Broadsides, Leaflets, and Pamphlets from America and Europe, Printed Ephemera Collection; Portfolio 237, Folder 16, Library of Congress Digital ID http://hdl.loc.gov/loc.rbc/rbpe.23701600 (30 August 2022).
4. Worden to Welles, 25 February 1865, Letters Received from Rear Admirals, Commodores, and Captains, vol. 23, entry 54, RG 45; Abstracts of Prize Accounts, *Montauk*, 8 January 1868, vol. 7:297–99, entry 823, RG 217, NARA.
5. *Franklin* log entries for 30 January–3 February 1834, Logs of U.S. Naval Ships, entry 118, RG 24, NARA (hereafter *Franklin* log).
6. *Franklin* log, February 25–April 17, 1875; *Inter Ocean* (Chicago), April 12, 1875.
7. *Philadelphia Inquirer*, 24 April 1875; *Franklin* log, 22 April–1 May 1875.
8. *Franklin* log, 8 June–1 August 1875; Worden to Robeson, 12 and 25 July 1875, M89; Eugene Schuyler, Secretary, U.S. Legation, St. Petersburg, to Secretary of State Hamilton Fish, Washington, 20 July 1875, pp. 1068–69, and C. C. [Christopher Columbus] Andrews, U.S. Legation, Stockholm, to Fish, Washington, 20 July 1875, pp. 1261–62, in 44th Congress, 1st Session, House of Representatives, *Papers Related to the Foreign Relations of the United States, Transmitted to Congress, with the Annual Message of the President, December 6, 1875* (Washington: Government Printing Office, 1875), Ex. Doc. 1, pt. 1, vol. 2, no. 509; *American Register* (London), 7 and 14 August 1875.
9. Worden to Robeson, 18 August 1875, Squadron Letters, M89; *New Orleans Republican*, 11 August 1875; *Chicago Daily Tribune*, 11 August 1875; *San Francisco Evening Bulletin*, 10 August 1875; James A. Field Jr., "A Scheme in Regard to Cyrenaica," *Mississippi Valley Historical Review* 44, no. 3 (December 1957): 445–68.
10. Field, "Scheme," 445.
11. English to Worden, date missing but probably after 20 October 1875, M89.
12. Vidal to Mustapha and Mustapha to Vidal, 5 August 1875, M89.

13. Emile de Testa to Vidal, 25 August 1875; English to Vidal, 25 August 1875; English to Worden, 26 August 1875 and date missing, M89; Field, "Scheme," 460.
14. Worden to Robeson, 20 October 1875; English to Worden, date missing, M89.
15. *Franklin* log, 25 September–4 October 1876; Worden to Robeson, 15 October and 24 December 1875, M89.
16. Worden to Robeson, 15 May and 11 June 1876, M89; *Franklin* log, 4 July 1876.
17. *Daily Argus*, 9 September 1876; *Dallas Daily Herald*, 10 September 1876; *Chicago Daily Tribune*, 10 September 1876; *New York Herald*, 10 September 1876; *National Republican*, 11 September 1876.
18. *Gazzetta Piemontese*, 29 August and 11 September 1876; *Le Figaro*, 9 and 11 September 1876.
19. *Le Figaro*, 13 September 1876.
20. *New York Herald*, 10 September and 29 October 1876; *Philadelphia Inquirer*, 11 September 1876; *National Republican*, 11 September 1876; *Times* (London), 11 September 1876.
21. *Franklin* log, 26 October 1875, 10 July 1876.
22. *Franklin* log, 15 July–1 August 1876.
23. Case 5899 (Stuart), Box 86, and Case 5873 (Almond), Box 85, entry 27A, Records of Proceedings of General Courts Martial, RG 125, NARA.
24. *Times*, 11 September 1876; *New York Times*, 21 October 1876; *Inter Ocean*, 28 October 1876.
25. General Order 17, 1 September 1876, erroneously dated 1875, M89.
26. Worden to Robeson, 30 August 1875, 12 April 1876, and 15 May 1876, M89.
27. Worden to Robeson, 25 October 1876, M89.
28. Worden to Secretary of the Navy Richard W. Thompson, 25 April, 12 May, 7 June, and 18 August 1877, M89.
29. Worden to Robeson, 17 April, 5 July, 16 November, and 15 December 1875, 10 June, 8 July, and 2 October 1876; Worden to Thompson, 29 June 1877, M89.
30. General Order 4, 1 March 1875, and General Order 23, 23 May 1877, M89.
31. General Order 16, 20 August 1876, M89.
32. *National Republican*, 27 July 1876, 5 January 1877, and 14 March 1877.
33. Worden to Secretary of the Navy, 15 March 1877; *Marion* log, 16 March 1877; Worden to Thompson, 17 March 1877, M89.
34. Worden to Thompson, 19 March, 31 March, and 9 April 1877, M89.
35. General Order 7, 15 July 1875, General Order 15, 12 August 1876, General Order 18, 24 November 1876, M89; *Franklin* log, 7 August 1876.

36. Worden to Thompson, 25 April 1877, M89.
37. Maureen P. O'Connor, "The Vision of Soldiers: Britain, France, Germany and the United States Observe the Russo-Turkish War," *War in History* 4, no. 3 (July 1997): 264–95; Francis V. Greene, *The Russian Army and Its Campaign in Turkey in 1877 and 1878* (New York: Appleton, 1879), vii; Worden to Thompson, 12 and 24 May, 3 August 1877, M89.
38. *Trenton* log, 5 October 1877.
39. Rev. Henry H. Clark, "Rear Admiral Worden: Lessons from His Life and Character, a Sermon Preached at the Naval Academy," USNA Museum, FICm.0003.0159, no date, but presumably in October 1897. A note inside dated 10 January 1898 reveals it was printed in *Sailors' Magazine and Seamen's Friend*, of which no copies appear to be extant for vols. 69–70, 1897–98. No reference to the date of this eulogy was found in the USNA Chaplain's Register, 1890–1923, vol. 3, series 1, entry 151i, Office of the Command Chaplain, USNA SC&A.
40. *Trenton* log, 15 May–25 August 1877; enclosures in Worden to Thompson, 3 September 1877, M89.
41. *Trenton* log, 5 October 1877; Worden to Thompson, 5 October 1877, M89.
42. *New York Herald*, 25 October 1877; Worden to Richard W. Thomson, 8 November 1877, Letters Received from Admirals, vol. 21, entry 58, RG 45; *Register of the Commissioned, Warrant Officers, and Volunteer Officers of the Navy of the United States* (Washington, DC: Government Printing Office, 1878), 8–9.

CHAPTER 14. SERVICE IN WASHINGTON AND RETIREMENT YEARS

1. *U.S. Statutes at Large* 13 (1864): 183.
2. *Evening Star*, 19 February 1878; 47th Congress, 2d Session, *Congressional Record* (Washington, DC: Government Printing Office, 1882), House, 8 December 1882, vol. 14, pt. 1, 130; Federal Census, District of Columbia, 1880.
3. *Troy Weekly Times*, 15 November 1883.
4. *Cincinnati Daily Gazette*, 10 May 1878; *Sun*, 11 and 22 June 1878; *Evening Star*, 7 June 1878; *National Republican*, 10 November 1879 and 5 January 1881; *Evening Critic*, 14 November 1882; *Cincinnati Daily Gazette*, 23 February 1882.
5. *Sun*, 5 April 1881; *National Republican*, 26 April 1881.
6. *Evening Star*, 5 December 1884.
7. *Maurice v. Worden*, U.S. Circuit Court, District of Maryland Law Case File No. 197 (22-02891), Records of District Courts of the United States, RG 21, NARA, Philadelphia.
8. *Sun*, 29 December 1880, 10 and 18 January 1881; *Evening Star*, 1 April 1886 and 21 January 1890; Harvard Case Law Access Project, https://cite.case.law/citations/?q=1832511 (9 March 2024).

9. *New York Times*, 6 August 1880; Garfield to Worden, 17 June 1874, Letterbooks and Outgoing Correspondence, vol. 16; Worden to Garfield, 18 June 1874, General Correspondence, vol. 36, James A. Garfield Papers, MSS 291956, Manuscript Division, Library of Congress; *New York Herald*, 6 August 1880.
10. *National Republican*, 5 and 12 March 1881; *Daily Inter Ocean*, 11 June 1881; *Sun*, 16 June 1881.
11. *Evening Star*, 15 and 20 December 1884, 1 January 1886.
12. *New York Herald*, 13 March 1886; *Kalamazoo Gazette*, June 17, 1886.
13. *Kalamazoo Gazette*, 19 June 1885.
14. John L. Worden [Washington, DC] to James H. Worden [Sing Sing, NY], ca. 1889, first page with date missing, private collection of Leone Stangle, Croton-on-Hudson, NY.
15. Hunt to Hon. John R. Thomas, 28 January 1882, in Report No. 1725 of the Committee on Naval Affairs, House of Representatives, 48th Congress, 1st Session, 31 May 1884.
16. *Chicago Tribune*, 15 December 1881; *Evening Star*, 24 May 1882; 47th Congress, 2nd Session, *Congressional Record* (Washington, DC: Government Printing Office, 1882), House, vol. 14, pt. 1, 126–34.
17. "The *Merrimac*; and the *Monitor*—Report of the Committee on Naval Affairs," *Southern Historical Society Papers* 13 (January–December 1885): 90–119.
18. *Evening Critic*, 2 February 1878; *Farmer and Mechanic*, 21 February 1878; *Sun*, 20 November 1879.
19. *Cincinnati Daily Gazette*, 8 May 1879.
20. *Sun*, 3 January 1882; *Times* (Philadelphia), 9 February 1884.
21. *Evening Star*, 6 and 7 February 1883; *New-York Tribune*, 2 March 1883; *Sunday Herald*, 11 March 1883.
22. Worden to Henry Villard, President, NPRR, 23 July 1883, American Historical Manuscript Collection, New-York Historical Society; *Semi-Weekly Miner* (Butte, MT), 8 August 1883.
23. Carl Charlick, *The Metropolitan Club of Washington* (Washington, DC: Metropolitan Club, 1965), 14, 51, 55, 58, 86, 88–89, 135, 290; John A. Baker, *A Brief History of the Metropolitan Club of the City of Washington* (Washington, DC: Press of Byron S. Adams, 1909), 4–5
24. *Sun*, 8 May 1882; *New York Herald*, 9 May 1882; *Evening Critic*, 9 May 1882. *Evening Star*, 31 October 1883.
25. *Evening Star*, 23 September 1881; *National Republican*, 28 February 1882.
26. *Philadelphia Inquirer*, 10 August 1885; *New York Herald*, 3 November 1885; *Evening Star*, 2 April 1890, 17 February 1891, and 11 January 1892.
27. City of Newport Real Property Records, Book 44:441, 27 November 1872, Book 52:21, 28 March 1881; *Morning Oregonian*, 14 July 1886.

28. Helen G. Daniels, *Quaker Hill at the Turn of the Century* (1958; reprint, Pawling: Historical Society of Quaker Hill and Pawling, 1991), 9–10, 13, 30; Amanda Akin Stearns, *Ancient Homes and Early Days of Quaker Hill* (Quaker Hill: Akin Hall Association, 1913), 14.
29. *U.S. Statutes at Large* 24 (1886): 351.
30. *Evening Star*, 2 March 1889; *New York Tribune*, 28 June 1887; *Daily Inter Ocean*, 13 July 1890; *Daily News*, 26 December 1891.
31. *Philadelphia Inquirer*, 24 August 1890; *Brooklyn Eagle*, 24 August 1890; *New York Herald*, 27 March 1893.
32. *Worcester Daily Spy*, February 17, 1887; *Evening Star*, 25 November 1890.
33. *Olean Democrat*, 14 January 1892; *Portland Daily Press*, 12 January 1892.
34. Robert L. Worden, "'My Heart Is There': The Life and Career of Oriska Worden," 4 November 2020, 20 pp., http://wordenfamilyassoc.org/My_Heart_is_There_The_Life_and_Career_of_Oriska_Worden.pdf (15 June 2024).
35. *San Francisco Call*, 7 November 1897.
36. *Evening Star*, 13 October 1897; "Summary Medical Report," in Olivia Worden's Navy Widow's Pension File, Certificate no. 12948, M1279, RG 15, Records of the Department of Veterans Affairs, NARA.
37. *San Francisco Call*, 7 November 1897.
38. Long to Olivia Worden, 18 October 1897, in author's collection; *New-York Tribune*, 20 October 1897.
39. *Evening Star*, 20 October 1897; *New-York Tribune*, 21 October 1897.
40. "A Portion of a Sermon Preached by Dr. Mackay Smith at St. John's Church, Washington, D.C., the Sunday after father's death"; in Robert L. Worden's file, a gift from a direct descendant.

EPILOGUE

1. Timothy Caldwell, "A Brief History of Fort Worden," *Wordens Past* 34, no. 2 (August 2013): 2936–45.
2. "Worden I," https://www.history.navy.mil/research/histories/ship-histories/danfs/w/worden-i.html (17 October 2023).
3. "Worden II," https://www.history.navy.mil/research/histories/ship-histories/danfs/w/worden-ii.html (17 October 2023).
4. "Worden III," https://www.history.navy.mil/research/histories/ship-histories/danfs/w/worden-iii.html (17 October 2023).
5. "Worden IV," https://www.history.navy.mil/research/histories/ship-histories/danfs/w/worden-iv.html (17 October 2023).
6. "Vessel Rolls in Office of the Auditor War Department, to September 30, 1862," one-page typed list found in Index to Prize Cases, 1862–1873, entry 821, RG 217, NARA.

INDEX

Abraham Lincoln Memorial University. *See* Lincoln Memorial University
Academy of Music, Brooklyn, NY, 102, 137
Adams, Henry A., 71
Adelaide (packet sidewheel steamer), 78
Adelaide, Queen, 18
Admiral Wordens Lane, 7
Adriatic (steamer), 66
Africa: West, 13; North, 184–85
Africa Squadron, 35
African Americans: attitudes toward, 145, 161, 163; cadet midshipmen at Naval Academy, 160–61, contraband, 113; sailors and soldiers, 145. *See also* Black enlistments
Akin, Amanda, 137
Alabama, 4, 72, 193
Alabama (bark-rigged screw sloop), 117, 137
Alaska (screw sloop), 176–78, 182
Albemarle (ironclad ram), 140
Alexander III (tsar), 172
Allen, J. Edward, 17
Alliance (*Adams*-class screw gunboat, former *Huron*), 186, 188
Almond, Alfred, 181
Alta California, 23, 26–27, 42–45, 52. *See also* Baja California
America (passenger steamer), 150
Ammen, David, 127
Annapolis, MD, 31, 134, 151, 155, 157–59, 161, 166–67, 169, 172–73, 192–94, 198. *See also* Naval Academy
Anton Lizardo, Battle of (6 March 1860), 6
Arista, José Mariano, 39
Argentina, 12
Arima Kantaro, 165
Armstrong, Charles, 56
Armstrong, James, 24, 70–71
Army, U.S., 41–42; Army of the James Naval Brigade, 134; U.S. Infantry Regiment, 1st, 140, 145

Aroostock War (1838–39), 23
Arrango (transport), 86
Arthur, Chester A., 196
Aspinwall, Panama, 68
Ashley River, SC, 125
Astronomical Observations, 31, 34–35, 57–58, 63
Athens, Greece, 61–62
Atkins, John, 84
Atlanta, GA, 72
Atlantic Ocean, 1, 40, 55, 63
Australia, 16
Austria, 62, 173–74, 187
Austro-Prussian War (1866), 173
Avary, Myrta Lockett. *See* Nellie
Azuma Takahiko, 165

Bahia, Brazil, 56
Bailey, Theodorous, 45
Balkans, 174
Ballard, Horatio, 100
Baltic (passenger steamer), 76
Baltic Sea, 176
Baltimore, MD, 78, 96, 192, 196
Bancker, Auley, 6
Bancroft, George, 33, 42
Barbary Wars (1801–15), 177
Barlett, Washington Allon, 47
Bath Iron Works (Bath, Maine), 206
Baja California, 23, 28, 41–45, 47, 52, 54. *See also* Alta California, Mexico
Beaufort, NC, 107–9, 117
Beauregard, P. G. T., 71, 124–25, 132
Bee, Ephraim J., 56
Beirut, Lebanon, 179
Belnap, William W., 171
Bell, Charles H., 144
Ben De Ford (Army steamer), 133
Benjamin, Judah, 73
Bennett, Frank Marion, 141
Benton (ironclad), 134

- 267 -

Berlin, Germany, 33, 176
Best, Edward, 56
Bibb, George M., 139
Bibb, William Crawford, 139
Bibb, William Joseph, 193
Black enlistments: Army, 113; Navy, 113; midshipmen, 160–61. *See also* African Americans
Blaine, Alice, 196
Blaine, James Gillespie, 196
Blake, George S., 155, 165
Blanton, William L., 22
Bockee, Abraham, 10
Bogue Sound, NC, 109
Bolivia, 22
Boston, MA, 6, 11, 13, 15–16, 20, 53, 55–56, 100
Boston Navy Yard, 206. *See also* Charlestown Navy Yard
Bragg, Braxton, 71–73
Brasher, Thomas, 27, 64
Brazil, 12–14, 41
Brazil Squadron, 12, 41
Briarcliff Manor, NY, 7
Britain, 1, 7, 23, 25–26, 117, 139, 168, 196; intervention (in California), 1, 26, 40; merchant ships, 55; navy, 9, 62, 139, 186; squadron, 23–24, 175
Brooke guns, 89, 93, 99, 125; bolts, 129, 132
Brooklyn (bark-rigged screw sloop), 71
Brooklyn Academy of Music, 102, 137
Brooklyn Navy Yard (*officially known as* New York Navy Yard), 1, 8–9, 21, 35, 64, 66–67, 69, 74, 80–81, 83–85, 103–4, 106–8, 134–35, 138–41, 144, 154, 181
Browne, Samuel T., 105, 107–11, 115, 117–18, 131
Brumby, Thomas M., 204
Buchanan, Franklin, 204
Buenos Aires, Argentina, 13
Buffalo, NY, 56, 100
Buffum, Edward Gould, 46
Bulgaria, 186
Bull Run. *See* Manassas, Battle of First
Busbee, Perrin, 171, 175, 196, 198–99
Bushnell, Cornelius, 80
Buttre, John C., 4

Cabo San Lucas, Baja California, 45
Cahuenga, Treaty of (13 January 1847), 43
Cairo (ironclad), 112
Caldwell, C. H. B., 17

California, 1, 23–27, 40–41, 43–46, 51–52, 54, 67, 143, 147–54, 194. *See also* Alta California, Baja California
California Guard (*also as* New York Legion, New York Volunteers, 1st Regiment), 45, 52, 54
California, Gulf of, 28, 41, 44–45, 47, 49
Californios, 43
Callao, Peru, 22–24, 146–47
Cambridge, MA, 191
Cameron, Simon, 76
Canada, 9, 194
Canandaigua (screw sloop), 128
Canonicus-class monitors, 138
Cape Charles, VA, 86–87
Cape Fear River, NC, 107–8
Cape Hatteras, NC, 108–9, 168
Cape Henlopen Light, DE, 108
Cape Henry, VA, 87
Cape Horn, Chile, 29, 42, 45, 55–56, 143
Caroline (merchant brig), 47
Carondelet (ironclad), 134, 174
Cartagena, Spain, 18
Carter, Samuel P., 176
Carysfort (frigate, Britain), 23–24
Casco-class ironclad monitors, 139–40
Casco-class torpedo boats, 140
Case, Augustus Ludlow, 161, 175
Castle Pinckney, Charleston, SC, 125
Castro, Mauricio, 45
Catskill (ironclad), 127–28, 130, 132
C. H. Delamater Iron Works, NY, 106, 138
C. P. Williams (mortar schooner), 110
Champion (sloop, Britain), 23, 25
Chancellorsville, Battle of (30 April–3 May 1863), 134
Chandler, Lucy Hale, 196
Chandler, William Eaton, 196
Charlestown Navy Yard, Boston, MA, 206, 11–12, 56, 59, 68, 206. *See also* Boston Navy Yard
Charleston, SC, 35, 69, 71, 73, 108–9, 117, 123–26, 128, 131–33, 135–37; batteries: Bee, Glover, Gregg, Wagner, White Point, 125
Chauncey, Charles Wolcott, 10
Chauncey, Isaac, 9
Chauncey, John St. Clair, 10
Chauncey, Wolcott, 9
Chesapeake Bay, 86–87, 167
Chickasaw Bayou Expedition (1862), 112
Chicora (ironclad), 125

Chile, 25, 42
Chimo (monitor), 139
Chincha Islands War (1864–66), 147
Chincoteague Island, VA, 86
Civitavecchia, Italy, 18
Clara (pirate ship), 16
Clark, Ambrose, 147
Clark, Rev. Henry H., 187
Clason, Emily Matilda (*also as* Emily Matilda Graham), 8
Cleveland, Grover, 193–94
Cleveland, OH, 144
Clinton, DeWitt, 8
Coast Survey, U.S., 27, 37, 57, 66–68
Cobb, Edward, 130
Colby, F. W., 17
Colt, Samuel, 141
Columbia (frigate), 41
Columbiad, 110, 114, 125
Confederate States of America, 69, 77; Army, Department of South Carolina, Georgia, and Florida, 125; Department of Norfolk, 77; Navy, 70; James River Squadron, 60, 147; Naval Submarine Battery Service, 112; ships (*see individual ship names*)
Congress (frigate), 43, 47–48, 86–88, 195, 199
Congress, (screw sloop [with European Squadron 1874]), 176–78, 183
Congress, U.S., 17, 30, 37, 39, 58–59, 63–64, 66, 76–77, 79, 99, 102–3, 107, 123, 139, 143, 145, 149–150, 157, 160, 164, 174, 184, 189, 191, 194–95, 198
Connecticut (sidewheeler), 108
Constitution, U.S., amend. XIII–XV, 145
Constantinople, Turkey, 62, 178–79, 183, 186–87
Continental Iron Works, 80, 106, 138
Contoocook-class cruiser, 144
Conyers, James Henry, 161–63
Cooke, Jay, 76
Cooper River, SC, 125
Copenhagen, Denmark, 176
Corfu, Greece, 177
Corinth, Battle of (3–4 October 1862), 134
County Armagh, northern Ireland, 6
Court of Claims, U.S., 64, 201
Courtland, MI, 56
Craft, Margaret Toffey, 198
Crimean War (1853–56), 61, 173
Cuba, 13, 16, 168
Cumberland (frigate, later razed), 35, 40, 59–63, 76–77, 86–87, 89, 199

Currituck (gunboat), 85
Cushing, Caleb, 178
Cushing, William, 140
Cushman, Charles Haddock, 130
Custom House, U.S. (San Francisco), 194
Cyane (sloop), 15–20, 22–24, 26, 47–48, 57, 132

Dacotah (steam gunboat), 81
Daffodil (tug), 81
Dahlgren, John A., 59, 65, 105–6, 137, 147
Dahlgren guns, 81, 105–6, 121, 137, 140, 147, 206
Dale (sloop), 22–29, 50
Dana (schooner), 110
Dardanelles, Turkey, 62, 187
David (torpedo boat), 140
Davidson, Hunter, 89, 112
Davis, Charles Henry, 80
Davis, Jefferson, 74
Davis, John, 112
Davis, John Chandler Bancroft, 112, 201
Davis, Varina, 74
Dawn (screw gunboat), 118, 174
de Brück, Karl Ludwig, 62
De Camp, John, 65
Decatur, Stephen, 204
Delaware Capes, 85–86
Democratic Party, 10, 165–66, 193
"devil's raft," 126
Dewey, George, 157, 197, 204
Dick, Steven, 30
Dickerson, Edward N., 140, 141, 143–4
Dictator (monitor), 138
District of Columbia (DC), 191–92
Dobbin, James Cochran, 63–64
Dornin, Thomas Aloysius, 24–27
Dove (brig), 20
Downes, John, 17, 120, 127
Drayton, Percival, 127, 129, 136
Dresden, Saxony, 151
Drewry's Bluff, Battle of (15 May 1862), 99
Driscoll, John, 89
Dry Tortugas, FL, 71
Du Pont, Samuel Francis, 109–10, 115, 117, 120–4, 126–8, 130–33, 136–37, 175, 191
Dublin (frigate, Britain), 23–24
dueling in U.S. Navy, 19
Durst, Wilhelm, 89, 93
Dutchess County, NY, 7, 10, 36

East Indies Squadron, 66
East River, Brooklyn, NY, 9, 65, 83–84
Edson, Anna Maria, 170–1
Edson, John Tracy, 170
Edward (whaler), 49
Edward VII (king), 186
Edward, Albert, Prince of Wales, 186
El Dorado County, CA, 147, 194
Eld, Henry, Jr., 56
Elizabeth River, VA, 40, 86, 94
Emancipation Proclamation (1 January 1863), 113
English, Earl, 177–8
Ericsson, John, 80–81, 85, 95, 99, 104–5, 123, 126, 138–39, 176, 199, 204
Erie (sloop), 12–16
Esmeraldo (corvette, Chile), 147
Etting, Henry V., 72
European Squadron, 172–74, 176, 181, 183–84
Evans, Robley, 161
Evarts, William Maxwell, 196
Everett, Edward, 74, 100, 152

Fairfax, Donald M., 127
Farragut, David Glasgow, 5, 137, 141, 191
Feeney, Thomas, 84
Fishkill, Town of, Dutchess County, NY, 7, 10, 20, 29, 36
Flag (screw steamer), 76
Florence, Italy, 176
Florida (commerce raider). See *Oreto*
Flye, William P., 57
Foggy Bottom, 31
Forbes, Paul, 140, 143
Ford, Thomas G., 156
Forrest, French, 40
Fort Barrancas (Pensacola, FL), 69–71
Fort Henry (Stewart County, Tennessee), 113
Fort Jefferson (Dry Tortugas, FL), 71
Fort Johnson (Charleston, SC), 125
Fort Macon (Beaufort, NC), 109
Fort McAllister (Genesis Point, GA), 110, 112–16, 118, 121–22, 188, 204, 207
Fort McRee (Pensacola, FL), 69–71
Fort Monroe (Hampton Roads, VA), 71, 77–78, 87, 96, 105, 108
Fort Moultrie (Charleston, SC), 125, 129–30
Fort Pickens (Pensacola, FL), 4, 69–71, 73, 76
Fort Ripley (Charleston, SC), 125

Fort Sumter (Charleston, SC), 71, 76, 124–33
Fort Taylor (Key West, FL), 71
Fort Texas (Brownsville, TX), 39
Fort Worden (Port Townsend, WA), 203–4
Fortuna (prize schooner), 51
Foster, John G., 107, 124
Fox, Gustavus Vasa, 15, 71, 81, 101, 104–5, 122–24, 126, 132, 137, 139, 141, 197
France, 22, 62, 173
Franco-Prussian War (1870–71), 173
Franklin, Samuel Rhoads, 175, 179, 201
Franklin (screw frigate), 175–82, 186
Fredericksburg, Battle of (11–15 December 1862), 134
Frederickson, George, 84
Frelinghuysen, Frederick, 196
Frelinghuysen, Matilda, 196
Frémont, John C., 42

Galápagos Islands, 25
Galena (ironclad), 80, 99, 108
Gallie, John B., 114
Garfield, James A., 191, 193, 197
Garvin, Benjamin F., 84
Gatling gun, 180–81
Geer, George, 101
Genesis Point, GA, 110, 113
Genoa, Italy, 18, 63, 182
George IV (king), 18
Germany, 148, 173–74, 176
Ghent, Belgium, 9
Gibraltar, 16, 60, 175, 183
Gibson, William, 114
Gilliss, James, 30–31, 33, 58–59
Gliemann, Philipp Albert, 151, 204
Godon, Sylvanus W., 146
Goldsborough, Louis Malesherbes, 59, 77, 100–101
Gormson, John, 56
Gosport Navy Yard, Portsmouth, VA (*also as* Norfolk Navy Yard) 40, 77–78, 108
Gracieux, Jack (pseud. for JLW), 16
Graham Avenue, Brooklyn, NY, 8
Graham, Charles Kinnaird, 66, 134, 144
Graham, Curtis Burr, 37
Graham, DeWitt Clinton, 8
Graham, Harriet, 6–7. See also Harriet Worden
Graham, Isaac Gilbert, 6, 133, 194
Graham, James Lorimer, 8, 176
Graham, Rev. John, 6

INDEX 271

Graham, John Andrew, 7
Graham, John Hodges, 9
Graham, John Lorimer (JLG, great-grandson of Rev. JG), 7–8, 194, 197
Graham, John Lorimer, Jr. (son of JLG), 8
Graham, Josephine, 176
Graham, Margaret, 8
Graham, Nathan Burr, 7–8
Graham, Sylvester, 9
Grand Rapids, MI, 103, 194
Grant, Ellen "Nellie," 170
Grant, Mrs. Ulysses S. (Julia), 170, 188
Grant, Ulysses S., 165, 168, 170–71, 188, 197
Gray, Horace, 200
Greece, 18, 61
Green, William, 24,
Greene, Francis Vinton, 186
Greene, Samuel Dana, 3, 82, 101, 149, 157, 168, 174, 176, 186, 204
Greenpoint, NY, 80–81, 83, 106
Gregory, Francis Hoyt, 84, 104, 121, 135, 139, 143
Griswold, John Augustus, 123
Guadalupe Hidalgo, Treaty of (2 February 1848), 52
Guaymas, Sonora, Mexico, 28, 50
Gulf of Mexico. *See* Mexico, Gulf of
Gulf of Panama. *See* Panama, Gulf of

Halleck, Henry Wager, 47, 51
Hamburg, Germany, 176, 183
Hammond, Olivia Steele Worden Busbee, 3. *See also* Worden, Olivia Steele
Hampton Roads, Battle of (8–9 March 1862), 1–2, 58, 60, 99, 107, 144, 147, 152, 157, 168, 174, 199, 204, 207
Hampton Roads, VA, 3, 7, 77, 84–89, 95, 99–100, 104, 107–8, 144, 147, 149, 150, 184, 195, 202, 204. *See also* Hampton Roads, Battle of
Hancock, Winfield Scott, 193
Hannan, Patrick, 89
Hartford (screw sloop), 176–78
Hartford-class (sloops), 69, 141
Harrison, Benjamin, 199
Hartt, Edward, 84
Harvey Birch (merchant ship), 117
Harwood, Andrew Allen, 59
Hastings (sloop, Britain), 18
Hatteras Inlet, NC, 77. *See also* Cape Hatteras, NC
Hayes, Ann Toffey, 198

Hayes, Rutherford B., 184
Hecla (monitor), 48
Herndon, William, 33–35
Herrick, Richard Platt, 37
Heywood, Charles, 47–49, 53
Hilo, HI, 55
Home Squadron, 66–67
Honolulu, HI, 55
Hopkins, Archibald, 201
Housatonic (screw sloop), 128
Hovey, Alvin P., 147
Howard, Samuel, 90, 93, 144
Hubbard, Joseph S., 57–58
Huger, Benjamin, 77
Hull, Isaac, 19
Hunt, William, 195
Hunter, Alvah, 120
Huáscuar (monitor, Peru), 147
Huron (*Unadilla*-class screw gunboat), 128

id fiat Wordensi (Let Worden do it), 23, 207, 223
Idaho (steam-screw sloop/supply ship), 140, 142–43
Independence (frigate), 43, 47–48, 51, 53
Independencia (ram, Peru), 147
Ironclad Board, 79–80
Iroquois (steam sloop), 65
Interior, U.S. Department of the, Pension Office, 194
Irving, Washington, 9
Isabella (merchant brig, Britain), 16
Isherwood, Benjamin Franklin, 139, 141, 144
Island No. 10, TN, 113
Italy, 17, 179–80, 185

Jackson, Andrew, 14
James Alger (sidewheel gunboat), 108–10
James Island, SC, 124–25
James River Squadron, 60, 147
Jamestown (sloop), 68
Japan, 164–65, 206; cadet midshipmen, 164–65
Jarvis, Joseph R., 68–69
Jeffers, William Nichols, 101–2
Jenkins, Thornton A., 197, 199
Jersey City, NJ, 135, 138
Johnson, Andrew, 145, 150
Johnson, Michael, 28
Johnson, Reverdy, 37
Jones, John Paul, 5
Jones, Catesby ap Roger, 58, 89, 204

Jones, Thomas ap Catesby, 22, 52, 54, 58
Juárez, Benito, 68
Juniata (screw sloop), 176–77, 182

Kansas-class gunboats, 146
Katzu Koroku, 164
Kearny, Lawrence, 66
Kearny, Stephen Watts, 43, 45
Keeler, William, 82, 84–85, 88–93, 99, 101, 113
Kennon, Beverley, 199
Kent County, MI, 103, 189
Keokuk (ironclad), 127–28, 130–31
Kiel, Germany, 176
Kilpatrick, Judson, 147
King, Jonas, 62
Knapp, Robert A., 19
Kronstadt, Russia, 176
Kunitomo Jiro, 164–65

La America (corvette, Peru), 147
La Mesa, Battle of (9 January 1847), 43
La Union (corvette, Peru), 147
Lake Champlain, Battle of (11 September 1814), 9
Lancashire, England, 6
Landis, Abby Jane Leach, 102
La Paz, Baja California, 45–47, 49, 51, 54
La Spezia, Sardinia, 176
La Vallette, Elie A. F., 47
Lazzaro, Pericles Hadji, 178
Le Roy, William E., 188
Lee, Samuel Phillips, 107
Leghorn, Italy, 179
Lenthall, John, 139
Levant (sloop), 62–63
Lewes, DE, 108
Lexington (storeship), 45
Liberia, 13
Library of Congress, 3; Worden Papers at, 3
Lincoln Memorial University, 3, 204
Lincoln, Abraham, 86, 107, 123
Lisbon, Portugal, 175, 177, 182–85
Littlepage, Hardin Beverly, 199
Lockwood, Henry Hayes, 166
Lockwood, Samuel, 17
Logue, Daniel, 85. 89, 93, 95–96
London, England, 7–8, 16, 151, 176, 180
Long Island Sanitary Fair, 137
Long, Andrew Kennedy, 54
Long, John D., 200
Longfellow Memorial Committee, 191

Longfellow, Henry Wadsworth, 191
Loreto, Baja California, Mexico, 51
Lorimer, Jean, 8
Lorimer, Margaret (*also as* Margaret Graham), 8
Lorimer, Susannah, 8
Los Angeles, CA, 43
Lovette, Leland, 155
Lower California. *See* Baja California

Machida Keizero, 165
Mackay-Smith, Rev. Alexander, 200–2
Madison Barracks, Sackets Harbor, NY, 171
Madrid, Spain, 178
Magnolia (whaler), 49
Mahopac (monitor), 138
Major, James, 18, 57
Mallory, Stephen Russell, 79, 117, 141
Malta, 20, 183
Manassas, Battle of, First (21 July 1861), 77. *See also* Bull Run
Manassas, Battle of, Second (28–30 August 1862), 134
Manhattan, NY, 4, 7, 9, 36–37, 106, 140, 193, 199
manifest destiny, 27, 39, 52. *See also* Monroe Doctrine
Marchand, John Bonnett, 60, 76
Marchand, Margaret, 75–76
Mare Island Navy Yard, CA, 147–48
Marin, Tomás M., 69
Marion (screw steamer), 180–82, 184, 186, 188
Mariners' Museum and Park, Newport News, VA: *Monitor* artifacts at, 204; USS *Monitor* Center, 204; Worden Papers at, 3
Marquesa Islands, 22
Marseille, France, 18, 188
Marsh, George, 61
Marston, John, 87
Maryland Court of Appeals, 192–93
Maryland Republican Party, 165
Mason, John Y., 44
Mason, Richard, 44
Matsumura, Junzō, 164
Maurice, Bernard, 191–92
Maurice v. Worden, 192
Maury, Matthew Fontaine, 58–59, 63–64, 112; as author, 31, 34; officer in charge, U.S. Depot of Instruments and Charts, 31; superintendent, U.S. Naval Observatory, 31–34; and Worden, 33–35, 57
Maynard, Horace, 178–79, 187

INDEX 273

Mazatlán, Sinaloa, Mexico, 45
McClellan, George Brinton, 196, 198
McClellan, James, 49
McClennan, Alonzo Clifton, 161, 163
McCormick, Cyrus, 141
McCrady, John, 110
McElroy, Mary Arthur, 197
McIntosh v. United States, 64
McKinley, William, 200
McPherson, Norman, 84
Mediterranean Squadron, 10, 16, 18, 59, 61, 63
Mejía, Vicente, 49
Melville, Herman, 3–4, 203
Menorca, Spain, 18, 61
Merrimack (or *Merrimac*), 27, 79–80, 86–91, 94, 100, 103, 107, 142, 157, 168, 195. See also *Virginia*
Messina, Sicily, 18
Metropolitan Club (Washington, DC), 5, 197
Mexican-American War (1846–48), 1, 28, 52, 148, 154
Mexico, 1, 22–23, 44–45, 68; Gulf of, 41, 68, 70, 206; war with United States, 23–24, 26, 37–39, 42, 52. See also California
Miami (sidewheel steamer), 109
Michigan, 15, 29, 53, 63, 149, 193–94
Michigan Infantry Regiment, 13th, 103, 134
Miles, Nelson Appleton, 201
Military Academy, U.S. (West Point, NY), 47, 134, 155, 161
Miller, Jacob Welsh, 37
Miller, Joseph B., 56
Minnesota (frigate), 86–88, 90, 93–94, 140, 142
Miranda, Francisco Palacios, 45
Miramón, Miguel, 68
Mississippi River, 141, 174
Mizzen Top Hotel, Quaker Hill, NY, 198
Mobile Bay, AL, 69
Modoc (monitor), 139
Monitor (ironclad), 1–5, 7, 38, 57, 79, 81, 83–97, 99–103, 105–9, 111, 113, 115, 123, 132, 136–37, 144, 147, 149, 157, 168, 174, 176, 195, 198, 203–4, 207
Monitor Boys, crew members, 102
Monitor fever, 104, 138
Monroe Doctrine (1823), 27. See also manifest destiny
Montevideo, Uruguay, 13, 146
Montauk (ironclad), 1–2, 5, 38, 106–15, 117–22, 126–27, 129–30, 133, 135–36, 174–75, 188, 207

Monterey (capital of Alta California), 22, 26–28, 40, 42–45, 47, 54, 67
Montgomery, AL, 4, 72–74
Montgomery, John B., 45
Morgan Iron Works (Manhattan, NY), 140
Morning Light (blockade ship), 134
Morocco, 18
Morris Island, SC, 125, 127–28
Mount Pleasant, NY, Town of, 6–7, 9
Mount Vesuvius, 18
Murphy (pilot in Georgia), 111, 119
Mustapha, 177–78
Myers, William, 50

Nahant (ironclad), 120, 127, 130
Nanbu Hidemaro, 165
Nantucket (ironclad), 127, 130
Naples, Italy, 18, 62
Napoleon, Louis, 80
Narragansett (whaler), 26
Nashville (brig-rigged passenger steamer), 110, 114, 116–22, 135, 174. See also *Thomas L. Wragg*, *Rattlesnake*
Natchez (sloop), 13
National Archives (Washington, DC), 3, 34, 58, 207
Naubuc (torpedo steamer), 139–40
Nautical Almanac, 33, 59
Naval Academy, U.S. (Annapolis, MD), 2, 31, 59, 66, 145, 151, 153–54, 157–62, 163–66, 170, 172, 181, 186–88, 191–94, 196–97, 204
Naval Asylum (Philadelphia), 167
Naval Lyceum (Brooklyn, NY), 65
Naval Observatory (*known originally as* Depot of Charts and Instruments, Washington, DC), 1, 18, 29–32, 38, 40, 57, 59, 63, 65–67, 154
Naval Rendezvous (New York), 69, 72, 78, 80–81
Naval School (Philadelphia, PA), 18–20
Naval War College (Newport, RI), 157
Navy, Department of: Board of Naval Experts, 141; Bureau of Docks and Yards, 80; Bureau of Ordnance, 74, 96, 106; Bureau of Ordnance and Hydrography, 32–34; Examining Board, 20; Hydrographical Department, 59; judge advocate general, 193; *Regulations for the Navy* (1841), 28; Signal Office, 167
Navy depots: La Spezia, 61; Port Mahón, 61
Nellie (pseud. for Myrta Lockett Avary), 41

Nelson, William, 24
New Ironsides (ironclad), 79, 102, 108–9, 126–27, 130, 140
New Jersey, 37, 76, 135, 138
New York City, 8, 36, 45, 57, 66, 80, 85, 137, 150, 188, 194, 197, 199, 202. *See also* Manhattan
New York Heavy Artillery Regiment, 13th, 134
New York Infantry Regiment, 13th, 134
New York Navy Yard, 1. *See also* Brooklyn Navy Yard
New York State, 65, Assembly, 36, 100, 204; Chamber of Commerce, 99
New York Stock Exchange, 197
Newport, RI, 155, 165, 198
Newport News, VA, 3, 204
Newton, Isaac, Jr., 83
Niagara (steam frigate), 65
Niagara Falls, NY, 137
Niagara River, 9
Nicaragua, 68
Nice, France, 175, 179–80, 183–84
Nicholas, John, 21–22
Nicholson, Reginald F., 202
Nipsic (gunboat), 146
Norfolk, VA, 40–41, 66, 77, 80, 94, 97, 174–75; Navy Yard, 206. *See also* Gosport Navy Yard (Norfolk)
North Atlantic Blockading Squadron, 77, 101, 107
North Carolina (receiving ship), 83
North Pacific Squadron, 143

Oahu, HI, 25–26
Ogeechee River, GA, 110, 174; Big Ogeechee River, 110–11, 114–15, 117, 122; Little Ogeechee River, 114
Ohio (receiving ship), 55–56, 76
Old Inlet, Cape Fear River, NC, 107
Ontario (sloop), 10
Oregon, 196
Oreto (commerce raider [*Florida*]), 117–18
Osbon, Bradley, 118
Oscar II (king) 176
Ossabaw Sound, GA, 110, 120
Ottoman Empire, 62, 174, 177–79. *See also* Turkey

Pacific Ocean, 1, 22, 31, 39, 42, 58, 146–48
Pacific Squadron, 20, 22–24, 27, 38, 40–44, 52–53, 55, 148

Palermo, Sicily, 18
Palmer, James Croxall, 166
Palmetto State (ironclad), 125
Palo Alto, Battle of (8 May 1846), 39
Palos Prietos, Mexico, 47
Panama, 23, 68, 149; *Dale* at, 24–26; Gulf of, 24; Isthmus of, 24
Parke, John Grubb, 201
Parker, Foxhall Alexander, Jr., 167–68, 197
Paris, France, 20, 153, 188, 200
Parrott gun, 122, 147
Parrott, John, 23
Passaic (monitor), 108, 127, 129, 136
Passaic-class monitors, 105–6, 109, 115, 120–22, 132
Patapsco (monitor), 127–28, 130
Paulding, Hiram, 74, 80–81, 84–85
Pawling, Town of, Dutchess County, NY, 36, 171, 202, 204
Peekskill, NY, 204
Pemberton, John C., 125
Pensacola, FL, 4, 10, 69–73. *See also* Warrington Navy Yard
Pensacola Pass, 71
Pensacola (steam sloop), 5, 69, 141, 143–47, 149
Percival, John "Mad Jack," 12–20, 127, 136
Perseus constellation, 34–35
Peru, 22, 25, 146–47
Peterhof Palace. *See* Russia
Peters, Rev. Samuel, 8
Petrel (privateer), 76
Philadelphia, PA, 20, 76, 77, 102, 149, 167; Navy Yard, 29
Picket Boat No. 1, 140
Pickett, James, 24
Piedmont-Sardinia, Kingdom of, 173
Pierce, Franklin, 63
Pineda Muñoz, Manuel, 45
Pinkney, Bishop William, 164
Piraeus, Greece, 19, 62
pirates, 13–14, 16, 168
Pistor-and-Martin prime vertical transit, 33
Polk, James K., 39–40, 44
Polk, Josiah F., 64
Pompeii, Italy, 18
Port Mahón, Menorca, 18
Port Royal Sound, SC, 109–10, 125–26; Naval Station at, 126
Porter, David Dixon, 71, 133, 155, 190, 197
Portsmouth, VA, 40, 177. *See also* Gosport Navy Yard

Portsmouth (sloop), 42–43, 45, 48
Portugal, 16, 18, 184–85
Post Office Department, U.S. 194
Potsdam, Germany, 176
Powhatan (steam frigate), 71, 147, 175
prisoners of war, 75–76; exchanges, 77; Worden (JLW) as, 75
Puget Sound, WA, 196; Navy Yard, 206
Puritan (monitor), 138

Quaker Hill, Town of Pawling, Dutchess County, NY, 36–37, 137; Main Top, 198; Mizzen Top Hotel, 198; Quaker Meeting House, 198; Worden (JLW) at, 36–37, 40, 56, 63, 69, 72, 78, 102–3, 198–99

Rae, Thomas, 88
Rains, Gabriel, 112
Ramsey, Ashton, 3
Rattlesnake (privateer, former *Nashville*, former *Thomas L. Wragg*), 116–17
Reconstruction, 140, 144–45, 161
Reindeer (transport), 86
Relief (storeship), 20–22, 37, 63–64
Renshaw, James, 13–14
Republican Party, 80, 193
Resaca de la Palma, CA, 39
revolutions of 1848, 173
Rhind, Alexander C., 127, 176
Rhode Island (sidewheel steamer), 108
Richmond, VA, 72, 77, 88, 138, 161
Rio de Janeiro, Brazil, 13, 22, 41–42, 56, 146
Rio Grande, 39
Rio San Gabriel, Battle of (8 January 1847), 43
Ripley, Roswell S., 125, 132
Roanoke (screw frigate), 87, 89
Robelledo, J. Williams, 147
Robert Gilfillan (merchant ship), 117
Robeson, George M., 153, 159, 161–63, 165, 167, 170–71, 184
Robie, Edward D., 141
Rodgers, Christopher Raymond Perry (C. R. P.), 127, 191, 197
Rodgers, George M., 127
Rodgers, George Washington, 130
Rodgers, John, 126, 191, 196–97
Rodman shell gun, 105
Rodman, Thomas Jackson, 105
Rome, Italy, 18, 151
Ronckendorff, William, 60
Roosevelt, Theodore, 196

Root, Elihu, 203
Rosita (merchant schooner), 51
Rowan, Stephen Clegg, 190–91, 197
Royle, Trevor, 62
Ruggles, Henry, 66
Russia, 62; admiral, 137, 176; army, 186; grand duke, 176; ironclads, 176; navy, 176; Peterhof Palace, 172; St. Petersburg, 176, 186; tsar, 172, 176
Russo-Swedish naval review, 176
Russo-Turkish War (1877–78), 182–83, 186
Ryan, William, 16

Sabine (frigate), 71–73, 83
Sachem (gunboat), 85
Sackets Harbor, NY, 171
Sacramento, CA, 53
Salonica, Turkey, 178
San Francisco, 26, 42, 44, 47, 55, 147, 149, 151, 194
San Juan del Norte, Nicaragua, 68
San José del Cabo, Baja California, 45, 47–49, 51
Sandwich Islands, 24–26. *See also* Hawaii
Sandy Hook, NJ, 84–85, 108
Santa Fe, NM, 43
Santa Rosa Island, FL, 70
Santee (practice ship), 163
Santiago de Cuba, Battle of (3 July 1898), 188
Saratoga (sloop), 9, 68–69, 196
Sardinia, Kingdom of, 60, 172
Sataro Ise, 164
Savannah (sloop), 66–69, 72
Savannah, GA, 110, 117, 204
Savannah and Florida Railroad, 110, 121
Schley, Winfield Scott, 157
Schneller, Robert, 163
Scorpion (torpedo boat), 48
Scott, Winfield, 70–71
Scarborough Corners, Westchester County, NY, 7
Sedgwick, Theodore, 66
Selfridge, Thomas O., Jr., 101, 199
Seminole (gunboat), 69
Seneca (gunboat), 110, 114, 118, 174
Seth Low (tug), 85–86
Seward, William H., 123
Shark (schooner), 22–24
Sharp, William Southall, 77
Sherman, John, 76
Sherman, William Tecumseh, 171, 196

Shiloh, Battle of (6–7 April 1862), 103, 134
Shubrick, William Branford, 43–44, 47–49, 51
Sicily, 18, 61, 184
Sinaloa, Mexico, 48
Sing Sing, Westchester County, NY, 36
Skinner, Charles W., 40
Sleepy Hollow, Westchester County, NY, 9
Slemmer, Adam Jacoby, 70–71
Sloat, John Drake, 42
Smith, Joseph, 4, 64, 80–81
Smyrna, Greece, 19, 179, 186–88
Society of the Army of the Tennessee, 171
Soldiers and Sailors Convention (1866), 144
Soley, James Russell, 156
Soley, John C., 180
Sonora, Mexico, 44, 50
Sons of Union Veterans of the Civil War, Admiral John L. Worden Camp, 204
South Atlantic Blockading Squadron, 109, 126, 137
South Pacific Squadron, 147
Southampton (storeship), 38
Southampton, England, 117, 176
Southport, CT, 56–57
Spain, 18–19, 61, 147, 168, 178, 181
Spanish: naval arsenal at Cartagena, 18; squadron at Valparaíso, 147
Sparta, Westchester County, NY, 7
Spicer, William Francis, 63
Spuyten Duyvil (torpedo boat), 138
Squib (torpedo boat), 140
St. Lawrence (frigate), 76, 86
St. Lawrence River, 7
St. Louis (sloop), 23, 62
St. Paul, MN, 71
St. Petersburg. *See* Russia
Staten Island, NY, 193
Stanton, Edwin M., 86–87
Staunton, Sidney Augustus, 188
Star of the West (transport), 71
Steers, Henry, 140–41
Stephens, Thomas A., 115, 117, 120, 122
Sterrett, Isaac, 22
Stevens, Henry K., 49
Stevenson, Jonathan D., 45
Steward, Henry H., 141
Stewart, Arthur, 57
Stimers, Alban, 82, 84–85, 126, 136, 139
Stockton, Robert Field, 42–43
Stodder, Louis N., 83
Storer, George Washington, 41
Strait of Magellan, Chile, 146

Stribling, Cornelius Kinchiloe, 24, 55–56
Stringham, Silas Horton, 59, 61–62, 72, 74, 128
Stromboli (torpedo boat), 138
Stuart, Charles, 180
Sullivan's Island, SC, 125–26, 128
Supply (storeship), 69–70
Supreme Court, U.S., 189, 191–93, 201
Swartoutville, NY, 7
Sweden, 176, 199; king of, 176; navy, 176; Stockholm, 176
Syria, 185–86

Tabasco, Mexico, 40
Tales for the Marines, 16
Tangier, Morocco, 18, 175
Tatnall, Edward F., 17
Taylor, Zachary, 39
Telles, Rafael, 47
Ten Eyck, John Conover, 76
Tenerife, Canary Islands, 16
Terrett, Colville, 58
Terry, Edward, 167–68
Texas, 23, 39, 134; Republic of, 22; revolution (1836–37), 23
Thomas L. Wragg (blockade runner), 117. *See also Nashville, Rattlesnake*
Thompson, Richard W., 184, 188
Thornton, Robert D., 40
Tiffany and Company, 100, 204
Toffey, Betsey Hollaway, 36
Toffey, Daniel, 36–37, 83, 91, 93
Toffey, Olivia Akin, 36. *See also* Worden, Olivia T.
torpedoes, 110–13, 122, 125, 129, 131, 137, 187
Toucey, Isaac, 71
Townsend, Edward Davis, 149
Tracy, Benjamin F., 199
Treasury, U.S. Department of the, 175, 197
Trenton (steam frigate), 182, 185–87
Trent's Reach, Battle of (24 January 1865), 138
Trieste, 183
Tripoli, 176–78, 185
Truscott, Peter, 83
Tucker, John Randolph (*also as* J. Randolph), 60, 147
Tunis, 185
Turkey, 61–62, 178, 181–82, 185. *See also* Ottoman Empire
Turner, Charles C., 59

Tuscarora (steam-screw sloop), 117
Tweed, William M. "Boss Tweed," 181
Tyler, John, administration, 27

Unadilla (gunboat), 128, 136
Union Department of Virginia, 77
Union ships. *See individual vessel names*
United States (frigate), 22–24
United States, Capitol, 197; Centennial (1876), 179; Circuit Court, Baltimore, 192
United States Naval Institute (Annapolis, MD), 2, 167–68
United States Sanitary Commission, 101
Upper California. *See* Alta California
Uruguay, 12

Valparaíso, Chile, 42, 147
Van Brunt, Gershon Jacques Henry, 88, 90
Van Buren, Martin, 9, 63
Van Tassel, Katrina, 9
Vandalia (steam sloop), 183–84, 186–88
Veracruz, Mexico, 10, 22, 68–69
Vermont (receiving ship), 109
Vesuvius (bomb gun [mortar] vessel, Britain), 48
Vicksburg, MS, 133–34, 171
Vidal, Michel, 177
Vigo, Spain, 181
Villefranche-sur-Mer (Villefranche), France, 63, 175–76, 178–79, 181, 184–86, 188
Virginia, 3, 79, 86–95, 97, 99, 101, 108, 115, 132, 149, 168, 174, 188, 195, 199, 207. *See also Merrimack* (or *Merrimac*)
Virginia State Navy, 78
Virginius (paddlewheel steamer), 168
Vogdes, Israel, 71

Wabash (screw frigate), 109, 133
Walker, William, 68
Wallace, Lew, 103, 198
Wanaloset (cruiser), 144
War of 1812 (1812–15), 9, 65
Warren (storeship), 43, 53–55
Warrington Navy Yard (Pensacola, FL), 10, 68, 70–71, 141
Washington, DC, 3, 29–30, 74, 194
Washington Navy Yard, 141, 149, 152, 202, 204
Webber, John J. N., 83
Webster-Ashburton Treaty (9 August 1842), 23

Weehawken (ironclad), 126–29, 132
Welles, Gideon, 4, 71–74, 78–80, 82–84, 87, 97, 99, 102–4, 107–9, 117, 120, 123–24, 126, 135, 137–38, 145–46, 149–50, 155
Wellman, Walter, 199
Wells, George, 16
Werden, Peter. *See* Worden, Peter
Werden, Reed, 12, 15–20, 198
West Gulf Blockading Squadron, 134
West Indies, 23, 137
West Point, NY, 105, 155, 161. *See also* Military Academy, U.S.
Westchester County, NY, 6–7, 36, 204
Whig Party, 36–37
Whilden (transport), 86–87
White Point Battery, SC, 125
Wilkes, Charles, 137
Williams, John M., 28–29
Williams, Peter, 90, 93
Wilmington, NC, 107
Wilmot, Anna Augusta. *See* Worden, Anna Augusta Wilmot
Winslow, John Flack, 123
Wise, Charlotte (daughter of HAW), 97, 151
Wise, Charlotte Brooks Everett (wife of HAW), 74, 151
Wise, Edward, 151
Wise, Henry Alexander, 41
Wise, Henry Augustus (HAW), as midshipman, 12, 17–20; as lieutenant, 53, 74, 96; journals, 14–16, 18, 60; as "Harry Gringo," 16; at Ordnance Bureau, 138; at Battle of Hampton Roads, 97, 152; accompanies Lincoln to visit JLW, 97; on *Erie*, 15; on *Cyane*, 15–16; on *Cumberland*, 59–60; resigns from Navy, 150; dies in Italy, 152
Wise, Katherine, 151
Wissahickon (gunboat), 110, 117–18, 128, 174
Wood, John Taylor, 93, 99
Woodbury, Levi 10
Woodhouse, Anthony, 49
Woodworth, Frederick Augustus, 151
Woodworth, Lissette Marie Flohr, 151, 169
Woodworth, Selim E. (SEW), 148, 151
Woodworth, Selim E., Jr. (son of SEW), 151
Woodworth, William McMichael, 151
Wool, John Ellis, 77
Worden Field, Annapolis, MD, 166, 204
Worden name (*originally spelled* Werden), 4
Worden Street, San Francisco, 148

Worden v. United States, 64
Worden, Ananias (father of JLW), 7
Worden, Ananias Graham (brother of JLW), 194, 198
Worden, Anna Augusta Wilmot, 171
Worden, Daniel Toffey (DTW), 198–99
Worden, Emilie Nielson, 206
Worden, Eugene Bucharnois, 103
Worden, Frederick William, 103, 194
Worden, George, 6
Worden, Grace, 59, 151, 170, 175, 196, 200
Worden, Harriet Graham (mother of JLW), 6–7, 171, 189
Worden, Harriet (daughter of DTW), 171
Worden, Isaac Gilbert, 174, 194
Worden, James Barenloe, 147, 194
Worden, James Henry, 134, 194
Worden, Jane Louisa, 199
Worden, John Lorimer (JLW), birth, 7; marriage, 36–37; death, 5, 200, 202; as "Jack Gracieux," 16; on *America*, 150; on *Cyane*, 15–20; on *Dale*, 22; on *Erie*, 12–14; on *Franklin*, 174–82; on *Independence*, 51–53; on *Marion*, 181–82; on *Monitor*, 1, 2, 5, 80–96; on *Montauk*, 1, 2, 5, 106–33; on *Ohio*, 55–56; on *Pensacola*, 141–49; on *Relief*, 20–22, 37, 63; on *Savannah*, 66–69; on *Southampton*, 38–51; on *Trenton*, 182–87; on *Warren*, 53–55; on Naval Academy Board of Visitors, 155; on Navy Examining Board, 189–90; on Navy Retirement Board, 189–90; assigned to *New Ironsides*, 102; at Brooklyn Navy Yard, 1, 35, 64, 66; at Naval Academy, 65, 153–72; at Naval Observatory, 1, 18 30, 38, 40, 57, 59, 63, 66–67, 154; at Naval School, 18; at Naval Rendezvous (New York), 69, 72, 78, 80–81; at Quaker Hill, 37, 40, 56, 63, 69, 72, 78, 102–3, 198; at Pensacola, 72–73; at Fort Pickens, 4, 73; at Hampton Roads, 2–3, 58, 77, 84–86, 95, 108; at Fort McAllister, 110–16, 118; at Charleston, SC, 126–28; at White House, 193, 196; in Dresden, 151; in Mexico, 1, 26, 42–43, 47–51, 68–69; in Nicaragua, 68; in Washington, DC, 1, 29–38, 57–58, 63–64, 96–102, 135, 137, 149, 153, 160, 189–201; as prisoner of war, 3–4, 73–78; political involvement, 193–94; retirement, 198–200; report on Battle of Hampton Roads (5 January 1868), 149; nicknamed "Jack," 10, 16, 97; with Home Squadron, 66–69; with Pacific Squadron, 20–29, 41–55; with Mediterranean Squadron, 15–20, 59–63; with European Squadron, 173–88; sues United States, 64; lawsuits against, 166, 191–93; petitions Congress, 63–64, 174–75, 194–95; prize money, 149, 174–75, 194–95; with Matthew Fontaine Maury, 31–34, 57–58, 63; visited by Lincoln, 97; thanks of Congress, 103, 107, 189; memorialized by Herman Melville, 3; Worden Field, 166, 204; ships named for, *see* Worden; United States Naval Institute, 167–68; Admiral John L. Worden Camp, Sons of Union Veterans of the Civil War, 204
Worden, John Lorimer, Jr. (son of JLW), 37, 134, 140, 149, 170
Worden, John Lorimer (son of DTW), 171, 198
Worden, John William, 194
Worden, Lucy Harriet, 199
Worden, Olivia Steele, "Lilly," 171, 175
Worden, Olivia T., 72, 74, 76, 103, 151, 175, 191, 196. *See also* Toffey, Olivia Akin
Worden, Oriska, 200
Worden, Peter (Werden), 6
Worden, William, 134
Worden (Torpedo Boat Destroyer No. 16), 206
Worden (Destroyer No. 288), 206
Worden (Destroyer DD 352), 206
Worden (Guided Missile Frigate DLG/CG 18), 206–7
Worden (steam tug), 207
Wyandotte (steam gunboat), 69–73

Yates, John D., 133
Yellowstone National Park, 197
Yerba Buena, CA, 42, 44, 47. *See also* San Francisco
Yokohama, Japan, 143
Yorktown (gunboat), 22, 35

Zeno Secor and Company, 138
Zouave (screw tug), 86

ABOUT THE AUTHORS

John V. Quarstein served as the director of the Virginia War Museum until he retired in 2008 after thirty years of service. He is director emeritus of the USS *Monitor* Center at The Mariners' Museum and Park. Quarstein is the author of nineteen books and numerous articles, exhibits, essays, and documentaries.

Robert L. Worden retired from the Library of Congress in 2007 after thirty-eight years of federal service, during which he authored and edited more than one hundred Asia-related historical and current-affairs studies and books for government agencies. A collateral descendant of John Lorimer Worden, he has written extensively about the admiral's career.

The Naval Institute Press is the book-publishing arm of the U.S. Naval Institute, a private, nonprofit, membership society for sea service professionals and others who share an interest in naval and maritime affairs. Established in 1873 at the U.S. Naval Academy in Annapolis, Maryland, where its offices remain today, the Naval Institute has members worldwide.

Members of the Naval Institute support the education programs of the society and receive the influential monthly magazine *Proceedings* or the colorful bimonthly magazine *Naval History* and discounts on fine nautical prints and on ship and aircraft photos. They also have access to the transcripts of the Institute's Oral History Program and get discounted admission to any of the Institute-sponsored seminars offered around the country.

The Naval Institute's book-publishing program, begun in 1898 with basic guides to naval practices, has broadened its scope to include books of more general interest. Now the Naval Institute Press publishes about seventy titles each year, ranging from how-to books on boating and navigation to battle histories, biographies, ship and aircraft guides, and novels. Institute members receive significant discounts on the Press' more than eight hundred books in print.

Full-time students are eligible for special half-price membership rates. Life memberships are also available.

For more information about Naval Institute Press books that are currently available, visit www.usni.org/press/books. To learn about joining the U.S. Naval Institute, please write to:

Member Services
U.S. Naval Institute
291 Wood Road
Annapolis, MD 21402-5034
Telephone: (800) 233-8764
Fax: (410) 571-1703
Web address: www.usni.org

www.ingramcontent.com/pod-product-compliance
Lightning Source LLC
Jackson TN
JSHW022031080425
82244JS00001B/1